with a gnawing gnat,

Usborne
Illustrated
ENGLISH
SPELLING
Dictionary

and, for the very first time in an English Spelling Dictionary ...

a vaulting vampire

... three dwarves in a scarf!

Caroline Young

Designed by
Stephanie Jones

Illustrated by
Alex Latimer

Contents

About this dictionary

This dictionary shows you how to spell 24,000 English words. It also gives you tips and hints on how to spell words, along with information about their history and how they are used. There are explanations of the rules and patterns that govern spelling, too.

How to look up a word

The words are listed in **alphabetical order**, with a **chapter for each letter**. To find how to spell 'colander', for instance, go to the 'c' chapter.

These **two words tell you which words you'll find on that page**. Page 36 has words from 'coin' to 'commencement', so 'colander' will be on this page.

If you're **not sure how a word begins**, say the first part aloud: 'col-', for 'colander'. This may help you find which page you need to search in.

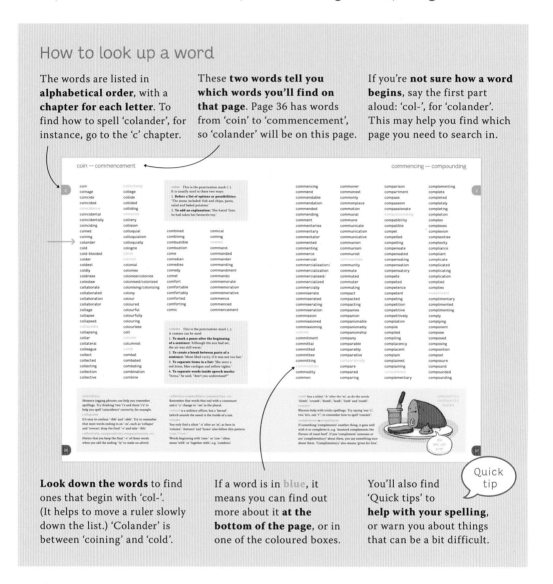

Look down the words to find ones that begin with 'col-'. (It helps to move a ruler slowly down the list.) 'Colander' is between 'coining' and 'cold'.

If a word is in blue, it means you can find out more about it **at the bottom of the page**, or in one of the coloured boxes.

You'll also find 'Quick tips' to **help with your spelling**, or warn you about things that can be a bit difficult.

Quick tip

~~Trickey~~ ~~Trichey~~ Tricky words

One of the hard things about English spelling is that **many words are not spelt as they sound**. Letters can make different sounds and be in different combinations. For example, the 'g' sound can be spelt 'g' in 'gate', 'gg' in 'egg', 'gh' in 'ghost', and 'gu' in 'guest'.

This can make it difficult to find the word you need. At the **end of each chapter**, you'll find some **words that are especially tricky to spell**. Learn them if you can, as the more you practise, the sooner you'll be able to spell them correctly.

Grammar – some words you need to know

English is a rich and complicated language and, like other languages, it is governed by a set of rules called 'grammar'. To help you get the most from this dictionary, here are some basic grammatical terms you may come across, and what they mean.

Adjective

An adjective **describes a thing or a person**, telling you more about it, e.g. 'He is a *hairy* dog.' The 'comparative form' is '*hairier*', and the 'superlative form' (meaning 'the most hairy') is '*hairiest*'. Most adjectives follow this pattern, but some, such as '*obscure*', become '*more obscure*'/'*most obscure*'.

hairy... hairier... hairiest

Adverb

An adverb **tells you more about a verb**, or how something is being done: 'She loved him *passionately*.' Many adverbs end in '-ly', but lots, such as '*fast*', don't.

Conjunction

A conjunction is **a word that links other words together**. For example, 'Mr Jones loves cake, *but* Mrs Jones loves cheese.' Conjunctions are sometimes also called 'connectives', as they 'connect' parts of a sentence together. You'll find a list of common conjunctions on page 214.

Consonant

A consonant is any one of the 21 letters in the alphabet that is **not one of the five vowels**: 'a', 'e', 'i', 'o' or 'u'. Several spelling rules relate to where vowels or consonants are found in a word.

Noun

A noun is **a thing, or an object (including a person)**. Nouns can be singular (just one of them, e.g. '*hat*'), or plural (more than one, e.g. '*hats*').

Pronoun

A pronoun is used in a sentence **instead of naming a person or thing**, and includes the words 'he', 'she', 'it', 'them', 'you' and 'we', e.g. '*She* lives in that house.' There are several different kinds of pronoun, but they all do a similar job in a sentence. You'll find a longer list of pronouns on page 214.

Preposition

A preposition **tells you more about other elements of a sentence**, such as a noun, e.g. 'The car was *beside* the van.' There are hundreds of prepositions and phrases that use prepositions in English. You'll find a list of the most common ones on page 215.

Syllable

A syllable is **one of the sounds in a word**. The words 'pen' and 'dig' only have one syllable, but 'dictionary' has four: '*dic-tion-a-ry*'. Sounding out the syllables of a word can help you spell it.

Verb

A verb is an 'action word', **an active, 'doing' word**, such as 'dance', 'eat' and 'run'. Verbs change tense according to when that action takes place. The three main tenses are: the present ('I *love* you' – now, in the present); the past ('I *loved* you' – in the past, not now), and the future ('I *will love* you' – at some point in the future, not now).

Vowel

A vowel is one of the **five letters 'a', 'e', 'i', 'o' and 'u'**. Many spelling rules apply to words with certain types, or combinations, of vowels. 'Y' can also behave like a vowel in English, sounding like an 'ee' in 'heavy', for instance.

General spelling rules

Many words follow spelling rules and, in general, if you follow the rules and guidelines on these pages, it will help you to spell accurately. There are words that are exceptions and so don't follow these rules, but, over time, you will get to know them individually.

Rules that almost always apply

1. The letter 'q' is always followed by a 'u': '*queen*'; '*quaint*'.

2. The letters 'j' and 'v' are always followed by a vowel (or a 'y'): '*jar*'; '*live*'; '*vying*'.

3. English words don't start with two consonants.

4. The letters 'h', 'j', 'k', 'q', 'v', 'w', 'x' and 'y' are never doubled in an English word.

Rules that usually apply

Soft or hard sound?

The letters 'c' and 'g' usually make a soft sound if they come before an 'i', 'e' or 'y' (as in '*circus*', '*gem*' and '*cycle*'), but are hard if they come before an 'a', 'o' or 'u' (as in '*cat*', '*got*', and '*gun*'). Exceptions include '*girl*' and '*give*'.

The 'magic', silent '-e'

Adding '-e' to a one-syllable word ending with one vowel and one consonant, such as '*mat*', makes the vowel sound long, as in '*mate*'. You don't say the 'e' so it's called a silent '-e'.

Is it '-ise' or '-ize'?

In most words ending in the '-ise' sound, **it's correct to use '-ise' or '-ize'**. For the following words, and words linked to them, you can only use '-ise', however:

> *advertise; advise; chastise; comprise; compromise; despise; devise; disguise; excise; exercise; franchise; improvise; prise; revise; supervise; surprise; televise*

In the words '*capsize*' and '*prize*', and words related to them, you can only use '-ize'. In general, whether you use '-ise' or '-ize', remember to be consistent.

It's 'i' before 'e'... usually

When the letters 'e' and 'i' are together in a word, they often cause spellers problems. The spelling guideline to bear in mind is **'i' comes before 'e', except after 'c', when the letters make an 'ee' sound**. Some exceptions to this guideline include:

> *caffeine; heinous; seize; species; protein; weird*

In these words, 'e' and 'i' don't make an 'ee' sound so the guideline doesn't apply:

> *ancient; counterfeit; deficient; efficient; either; financier; foreign; forfeit; heifer; height; heir; kaleidoscope; leisure; neigh; neighbour; neither; rein; scientist; seismologist; sleigh; sleight; society; sufficient; surfeit; their*

Most words just add '-s' to change from singular (one single thing) to plural (more than one thing) but some follow other rules:

Words ending in '-f'

Many words that end in an '-f' just add an '-s' in the plural:

belief → *beliefs*	chief → *chiefs*
brief → *briefs*	roof → *roofs*
chef → *chefs*	waif → *waifs*

Some change to '-ves', including:

calf → *calves*	loaf → *loaves*
elf → *elves*	self → *selves*
half → *halves*	shelf → *shelves*
knife → *knives*	thief → *thieves*
leaf → *leaves*	wife → *wives*
life → *lives*	wolf → *wolves*

A few words ending in an '-f' can correctly be spelt with either an '-s' or '-ves':

dwarfs/dwarves
hoofs/hooves
scarfs/scarves

three dwarves in a scarf

Words ending in '-o'

Many words that end in an '-o' add an '-s' to become plural, but some add '-es', including:

cargoes; dominoes; echoes; heroes; mosquitoes; potatoes; tomatoes

There are a few words you will see spelt with an '-s' or '-es', including:

flamingos/flamingoes
mementos/mementoes
zeros/zeroes

It is becoming more common to spell the plural of more words ending with an '-o' with an '-s', so check the word in a dictionary if you are unsure.

Words ending in '-y'

Words that end in a consonant and a '-y' change to '-ies' in the plural, so 'ferry' becomes *'ferries'*. Words ending in a vowel and '-y' add an '-s': 'boy → *boys*'.

Words ending in hissing sounds

Words ending in '-ch', '-tch', '-s', '-ss', '-tz', '-x' and '-z' add '-es' in the plural: 'witch → *witches*'. An exception to this is 'ox → *oxen*'. If the hissing sound is followed by a silent '-e', you just add '-s' to make a plural: 'cheese → *cheeses*'.

Words ending in '-eau'

Words ending in '-eau', a French spelling pattern, can add an '-s' or an '-x' (the French plural), and be correct: *'bureaus/ bureaux'*; *'chateaus/chateaux'*.

Words from Latin and Greek

Many English words come from Latin or Greek and, as a general rule, they just add an '-s' in the plural. A few still follow Latin or Greek plural spelling patterns: 'radius' becomes *'radii'*; 'curriculum → *curricula*'; 'phenomenon → *phenomena*' and 'criterion → *criteria*'.

Irregular plurals

Words that don't follow a pattern in their plurals are called 'irregular plurals'. Here are the most common:

aircraft → *aircraft*	man → *men*
child → *children*	mouse → *mice*
deer → *deer*	person → *people*
fish → *fish*	sheep → *sheep*
foot → *feet*	species → *species*
goose → *geese*	tooth → *teeth*
louse → *lice*	woman → *women*

Plural nouns

A few nouns only have a plural form, so you never see them in the singular. They are called plural nouns. Examples include *'scissors'* and *'trousers'*.

Lots of words in English contain letters you can't hear. These silent letters can cause spellers real problems. Here are the main ones you'll come across, and where you'll find them:

b: after an 'm', as in *'comb'*, or before a 't', as in *'debt'*.

e: thousands of words have a silent '-e', such as *'cage'* and *'date'*. A silent '-e' (sometimes called a magic '-e') on the end of a word can make the vowel sound long: 'rip' becomes *'ripe'*, for instance.

g: usually before an 'n', as in *'gnat'* and *'sign'*.

gh: at the end of a word, as in *'weigh'*, or before a 't', as in *'daughter'*.

h: at the beginning of a word, as in *'heir'* and *'hour'*, after an 'r', as in *'rhubarb'*, or after a 'w', as in *'while'*.

k: before an 'n', as in *'knee'* and *'knife'*.

l: in words such as *'calm'*, *'half'* and *'talk'*.

n: after an 'm', as in *'autumn'* and *'hymn'*.

p: before an 'n', 's' or 't': *'pneumonia'*; *'psychic'*; *'pterosaur'*.

s: in *'island'*, *'isle'* and *'aisle'*.

t: usually after an 's', as in *'castle'* and *'whistle'*. Watch out for it in *'fetch'*, too.

w: before an 'r', as in *'wrong'* and *'write'*, or before an 'h', as in *'who'* and *'whole'*.

a psychic pterosaur

This gnat likes to gnaw.

If you can't find the word beginning with an 'n' sound here, check the 'gn-', 'kn-' and 'pn-' pages.

Silent letters can make it tricky to look up a word: If you need to look up 'gnaw', you won't find it on the 'n' pages, as it begins with a silent 'g-'. Where these confusions might occur, you'll find ideas for where to look in these coloured strips at the top of each page.

~~Spell chequers~~ Spellcheckers

You may wonder why you need a dictionary when computers have spellcheckers. **Spellcheckers** are useful for pointing out simple slips, but **won't find every mistake**. They may not flag up errors in: 'Yule bee wear? Ova their?' which is made up of real words, but makes no sense. It should read: 'You'll be where? Over there?'

A spellchecker may also point out 'mistakes' that are not mistakes, or give the American English spelling of a word. Some words can be spelt in two ways, such as 'mediaeval/medieval', so this book gives you alternative spellings, both of which are correct. **If you are unsure, always check a spelling in a dictionary**, just in case.

Throughout this dictionary, there are tips like these, which will help you with your spelling. Practice can really help you to become a more confident speller, so try some of these techniques on a regular basis.

1. Look at a tricky word, say it aloud, cover it up, write it down and check your spelling.
Keep repeating this until you feel confident in spelling that word. You may have to do it many times.

2. Make up a saying using the letters in a word, or the parts of that word you find tricky.
These sayings, called mnemonics, can help you remember the letters in a word, in the right order. For example, for 'heir', think '**h**e **e**vidently **is r**ich'.

3. Keep a notebook of words you find difficult to spell, such as those with silent letters.
Add to your list when you meet a new word you struggle with, and read the words through regularly.

4. Try to think of words in groups, or families.
Words often follow a pattern, so keep a look-out for ones that behave like other, similar, words.

5. Break a long word down into its individual sounds.
This can help you spell each part of it, such as '*re-mem-ber*' and '*hu-mil-i-ate*'.

6. Think of an image to remind you of a spelling.
It can help to imagine a picture when you think of a word, to help you spell it. For example, '*a limo with a mouse in*' may remind you of the word 'limousine'.

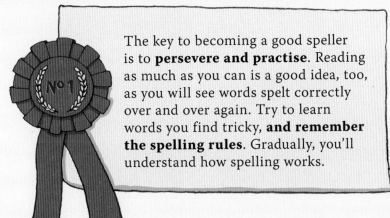

The key to becoming a good speller is to **persevere and practise**. Reading as much as you can is a good idea, too, as you will see words spelt correctly over and over again. Try to learn words you find tricky, **and remember the spelling rules**. Gradually, you'll understand how spelling works.

accessorise *or* **accessorize?**
Either of these spellings is correct for most words, but a few can only ever have a 'z' and others can only have an 's'. You'll find a full list of these words on page 4.

aardvark	abduction	abolishes	absconded
aback	abet	abolishing	absconding
abacus	abetted	abolition	abseil
abacuses	abetting	abominable	abseiled
abandon	abhor	abominably	abseiling
abandoned	abhorred	abort	absence
abandoning	abhorrent	aborted	absent
abandonment	abhorring	aborting	absentee
abate	abide	abortion	absenteeism
abated	abided	abortive	absent-minded
abatement	abiding	abound	absent-mindedly
abating	abilities	abounded	absolute
abattoir	ability	abounding	absolutely
abbey	abject	about	absolution
abbot	ablaze	above	absolutism
abbreviate	able	abrasion	absolve
abbreviated	able-bodied	abrasive	absolved
abbreviating	abler	abrasively	absolving
abbreviation	ablest	abreast	absorb
abdicate	ably	abridge	absorbed
abdicated	abnormal	abridged	absorbent
abdicating	abnormalities	abridging	absorbing
abdication	abnormality	abroad	absorption
abdomen	abnormally	abrupt	abstain
abdominal	aboard	abruptly	abstained
abduct	abode	abscess	abstaining
abducted	abolish	abscesses	abstention
abducting	abolished	abscond	abstinence

abacuses; abscesses; abysses, accesses
Notice that words that end with a hissing sound, such as an '-s', '-ss', '-sh' or '-ch', add '-es' in the plural. (Most words in English just add an '-s'.)

abating; abbreviating; abdicating, etc.
If you add an ending that starts with a vowel to a word ending in a silent '-e', you usually drop the 'e'.

abbey
'Abbey' just adds an '-s' in the plural as it has a vowel before the '-y'. (Many words which end in a '-y' change to '-ies' in the plural.)

abet → abetted; abhor → abhorred
Remember to double the final consonant when adding '-ed' to these words (and any word that ends with one vowel and a consonant, if you stress the end of the word).

abilities; abnormalities; absurdities, etc.
Notice that words which have a consonant before the final '-y' change to '-ies' in the plural.

able-bodied; absent-minded
These compound words (made up of two words) are joined with a hyphen (-), but some are not, so you may need to check their spelling in this dictionary.

abstract
abstraction
absurd
absurdities
absurdity
absurdly
abundance
abundant
abundantly
abuse
abused
abuser
abusing
abusive
abysmal
abysmally
abyss
abysses
academic
academically
academies
academy
accelerate
accelerated
accelerating
acceleration
accelerator
accent
accented
accentuate
accentuated
accentuating
accept
acceptability
acceptable

acceptance
accepted
accepting
access
accessed
accesses
accessibility
accessible
accessing
accessories
accessorise/
accessorize
accessorised/
accessorized
accessorising/
accessorizing
accessory
accident
accidental
accidentally
acclaim
acclaimed
acclaiming
acclimatisation/
acclimatization
acclimatise/
acclimatize
acclimatised/
acclimatized
acclimatising/
acclimatizing
accolade
accommodate
accommodated
accommodating

accommodation
accompanied
accompanies
accompaniment
accompaniments
accompanist
accompany
accompanying
accomplice
accomplish
accomplished
accomplishes
accomplishing
accomplishment
accord
accordance
accordingly
accordion
accordionist
accost
accosted
accosting
account
accountable
accountant
accounted
accounting
accrue
accrued
accruing
accumulate
accumulated
accumulating
accumulation
accumulative

accuracy
accurate
accurately
accusatory
accuse
accused
accuser
accusing
accusingly
accustomed
ace
ache
achieve
achieved
achievement
achiever
achieving
aching
achy
acid
acidic
acidity
acknowledge
acknowledgement
acknowledging
acne
acorn
acoustic
acquaint
acquaintance
acquainted
acquainting
acquire
acquired
acquiring

absorb → absorption; abstain → abstention
Look carefully at how the verbs 'absorb' and 'abstain' change when you make them into nouns.
abysmal; abyss
The letter 'y' sounds like an 'i' in these words.
accept means 'take something you are offered'. Try not to confuse it with 'except', meaning 'apart from'.
achievement; acknowledgement
If you add an ending that starts with a consonant to a word ending with '-e', you sometimes keep the 'e'.
achy is not spelt 'achey', as the 'e' is dropped.

Quick tip

An odd or funny image can help you to remember a tricky spelling. You could imagine the double 'c' and double 'm' in accommodation as 'cups of coffee' (cc) and 'marmalade muffins' (mm) for example.

acquit
acquittal
acquitted
acquitting
acrid
acrimonious
acrimony
acrobat
acrobatic
acronym
across
acrylic
act
acted
acting
action
activate
activated
activating
activation
active
activist
activities
activity
actor
actress
actual
actually
acupuncture
acupuncturist
acute
acutely
adamant
adapt
adaptable

adaptation
adapted
adapter/adaptor
add
added
adder
addict
addicted
addiction
adding
addition
additional
additionally
additive
address
addressed
addressee
addresses
addressing
adept
adequacies
adequacy
adequate
adequately
adhere
adhered
adherent
adhesion
adhesive
adjacent
adjectival
adjective
adjoin
adjoined
adjoining

> **adjective**
> A word that is used **to describe something or someone**: 'She wore a *beautiful* hat.'
> 'He is a *smelly* dog.' 'I love *red* shoes.'

adjourn
adjourned
adjourning
adjournment
adjudicate
adjudicated
adjudication
adjudicator
adjust
adjusted
adjusting
administer
administered
administering
administrate
administrated
administrating
administration
administrator
admirable
admiral
admiration
admire
admired
admirer
admiring
admiringly
admissible
admission
admit

admittance
admitted
admittedly
admitting
admonish
admonished
admonishes
admonishing
admonishment
adolescence
adolescent
adopt
adopted
adopting
adoption
adorable
adorably
adoration
adore
adored
adoring
adorn
adorned
adornment
adrift
adult
adulterate
adulterated
adulterating
adulterer

acquit; acquittal, etc.
Don't forget the 'c' after the 'a' in these words and that 'q' is always followed by 'u'.

acronym
An acronym is **formed from the first letters of words in a phrase**. For instance, the word 'radar' (used to detect things) is from the letters of '**ra**dio **d**etecting **a**nd **r**anging.'

acquittal; admittance
Remember to double the '-t' when you add endings that begin with vowels ('-al' and '-ance') to 'acquit' and 'admit'.

actor; adjudicator, etc.
Words ending in '-or' often mean 'a person who does something': an 'actor' acts.

an ageing (or aging) actor

To be or not to be...

adulterous
adultery
adulthood
advance
advanced
advancement
advancing
advantage
advantageous
advent
adventure
adventurer
adventurous
adverb
adverbial
adversarial
adversaries
adversary
advertise
advertised
advertisement
advertiser
advertising
advice
advisable
advisably
advise
advised
adviser
advising
advisory
advocate
advocated
advocating
aerial

aerobatic
aerobic
aeroplane
aerosol
aesthetic
aesthetically
afar
affable
affair
affect
affectation
affected
affectedly
affecting
affection
affectionately
affinities
affinity
affirm
affirmation
affirmative
affirmed
affix
affixed
affixes
affixing
afflict
afflicted
afflicting
affliction
affluence
affluent
afford
afforded
affording

afield
afloat
afraid
afresh
after
afternoon
afterthought
afterwards
again
against
age
aged
ageing/aging
ageism/agism
ageist/agist
agencies
agency
agenda
agent
aggravate
aggravated
aggravating
aggravation
aggregate
aggression
aggressive
aggressively
aghast

agile
agilely
agility
agitate
agitated
agitating
agitation
agitator
ago
agonies
agonise/agonize
agonised/agonized
agonising/agonizing
agony
agoraphobia
agoraphobic
agree
agreeable
agreed
agreeing
agreement
agricultural
agriculture
aground
ahead
aid
aided
aiding

adverb
A word that **describes a verb** and tells you how, when, where, how often or how much something is done: 'She danced *beautifully.*' 'He drove *fast.*' Many adverbs end with '-ly', but some don't.

adolescence
Words ending in '-scence' often mean 'a state of being', and are scientific words.
advertise; advertisement; advertising, etc.
'Advertise' always ends in '-ise' (not '-ize'). There's a list of other words that always end in '-ise' on page 4.
advice *vs* advise
This is spelt with a 'c' when it's a noun ('I gave her some advice'), but with 's' when it is a verb ('I advised her not to go').
affect means 'to influence'. Don't mix it up with 'effect'.

aerial; aerobatic; aerobic, etc.
Words that begin with 'aer-' are usually to do with the air, or flying. They come from a Greek word 'aer', which means 'air'.
ageing/aging; ageism/agism; ageist/agist
You can keep the final '-e' of 'age' when you add an ending, or drop it – both are correct.
aghast
It's easy to misspell this word. Try looking at it, covering it up, writing it and then saying it aloud to help you learn it.

ail
ailed
ailing
ailment
aim
aimed
aiming
air
airborne
air-conditioning
aircraft
aircraft carrier
aired
airfield
air force
airier
airiest
airily
airing
airline
airmail
airport
air raid
airsick
airsickness
airspace
airtight
airway
airy
aisle
ajar
alacrity
alarm
alarmed
alarming

alarmingly
alas
albatross
albatrosses
albino
album
alcohol
alcoholic
alcoholism
alcopop
alcove
ale
alert
alerted
alerting
algae
alias
aliases
alibi
alien
alienate
alienated
alienating
align
aligned
aligning
alignment
alike
alive
all
allay
allayed
allaying
allegation
allege

alliteration
This means
**putting words
with the same
consonant
sounds
together**.

Round and round the rugged
rock the ragged rascal ran.

alleged
allegedly
allegiance
alleging
allegorical
allergic
allergies
allergy
alley
alliance
allied
allies
alligator
alliteration
allocate
allocated
allocating
allocation
allot
allotment
allotted
allotting
allow
allowance
allowed
allowing
alloy

allude
alluded
alluding
allure
allured
alluring
ally
allying
almighty
almond
almost
alms
alone
along
alongside
aloof
aloud
alphabet
alphabetical
alphabetically
already
alright
also
altar
alter
alteration
altercation

---

ail *vs* ale
If you 'ail', you become ill, but it sounds the same
as 'ale', which is beer, usually darkish in colour.

air-conditioning; aircraft; air force
Compound words (made up of two words) can stay
separate ('air force'), form a new word ('aircraft'),
or be joined with a hyphen ('air-conditioning').

aisle
An 'aisle' is a passageway in a church or theatre.
It's easily confused with 'isle' which is a small
island. Look out for the silent 's' in both words.

albatrosses; aliases
Remember that words ending with a hissing sound,
such as '-ss', '-s' or '-ch', add '-es' in the plural.

algae are tiny plants. This word is always used
in the plural, and it follows a Latin plural spelling
pattern, as many scientific words do.

alibi (pronounced 'al-ee-bye') is a Latin word
that means 'elsewhere'. It's used to describe where
people say they were when a crime was committed:
'His alibi was that he was at home.' Only words
from other languages end in an '-a', '-i' or '-u'.

altered	ambushed	amplest	anarchy
altering	ambushes	amplification	anatomical
alternate	ambushing	amplified	anatomy
alternated	amend	amplifier	ancestor
alternately	amended	amplifies	ancestral
alternating	amending	amplify	ancestry
alternative	amendment	amplifying	anchor
alternatively	amenities	amply	anchorage
although	amenity	amputate	anchored
altitude	amethyst	amputated	anchoring
altogether	amiable	amputating	anchovies
aluminium	amiably	amputation	anchovy
always	amicable	amputee	ancient
am	amicably	amuse	anecdotal
amateur	amid	amused	anecdote
amaze	amidst	amusing	angel
amazed	amiss	anachronism	angelic
amazement	ammunition	anachronistic	anger
amazing	amnesties	anaesthetic	angle
amazingly	amnesty	anaesthetised/	angler
ambassador	amok	anaesthetized	angling
amber	among	anaesthetising/	angora
ambience	amongst	anaesthetizing	angrier
ambient	amoral	anaesthetist	angriest
ambiguity	amorous	anagram	angry
ambiguous	amorously	analogies	anguish
ambition	amorousness	analogous	anguished
ambitious	amount	analogy	angular
ambivalence	amounted	analyse	animal
ambivalent	amounting	analysed	animated
amble	amphibian	analyses	animatedly
ambled	amphibious	analysing	animation
ambling	amphitheatre	analysis	animosity
ambulance	ample	analytical	ankle
ambush	ampler	anarchist	annex

align
If there is a silent 'g' in a word, it will usually be before an 'n': 'align', 'malign', 'sign'.

'all-' vs 'al-'
You may see 'all' and a hyphen (-) in front of another word, such as 'all-inclusive'. When 'all' is joined to the word, it drops an 'l': 'almighty', 'altogether'.

ally → allies
'Ally' has a consonant before the '-y', so you add '-ies' to make the plural, 'allies'. 'Alley', for example, has a vowel before the '-y', so you just add an '-s': 'alleys'.

allowed vs aloud
'Allowed' means 'permitted'. 'Aloud' means 'out loud'.
allude means 'refer to'. 'Elude' means 'avoid being seen'. Try not to muddle them up.
alms are gifts of money given to the poor. 'Arms' can mean 'weapons', or 'limbs with hands on them'.

altar vs alter
An 'altar' is a special table in a place of worship. It sounds like 'alter', which means 'to change'.
amoral means 'having no moral standards', but 'immoral' means 'disregarding moral standards'.

annexation
annexed
annexes
annexing
annihilate
annihilated
annihilating
annihilation
anniversaries
anniversary
announce
announced
announcement
announcer
announcing
annoy
annoyance
annoyed
annoying
annoyingly
annual
annually
annul
annulled
annulment
anoint
anointed
anointing
anomalies
anomaly
anonymity
anonymous
anonymously
anorak
anorexia

anorexic
another
answer
answerable
answered
answering
answerphone
ant
antagonise/
antagonize
antagonised/
antagonized
antagonising/
antagonizing
antagonist
antagonistic
anteater
antecedent
antelope
antenatal
antenna
antennae
anthem
anthologies
anthology
anthropological
anthropologist
anthropology
antibiotic
antibodies
antibody
anticipate
anticipated
anticipating
anticipation

anticlimax
anticlimaxes
anticlockwise
anticyclone
antidote
antipathetic
antipathy
antiperspirant
antiquated
antique
antiquities
antiquity
antiseptic
antisocial
antitheses
antithesis
antler
anvil
anxieties
anxiety
anxious
anxiously
anybody
anyhow
anyone
anything
anyway
anywhere
apart
apartheid
apartment
apathetic
apathy
ape
apex

apexes
aphid
aphrodisiac
apiece
aplomb
apocalypse
apocalyptic
apocryphal
apologetic
apologetically
apologies
apologise/apologize
apologised/
apologized
apologising/
apologizing
apology
apostle
apostrophe
appal
appalled
appalling
appallingly
apparatus
apparent
apparently
apparition
appeal
appealed
appealing
appear
appearance
appeared
appearing
appease

apostrophe
This is the mark (') that you use in writing:
1. To show the owner of something: 'The *girl's* voice.' If there is more than one owner, it comes after the final '-s': 'The *boys'* behaviour.'
2. To show that a letter or letters are missing: '*I'm* back' (for 'I am back'); or if a word has been shortened: 'He *won't*' (for 'He will not').
3. To mean someone's home or workplace: 'I was at *Amy's*. She is at the *doctor's*.'

I'm at Dad's and Mum's at the hairdresser's. My key's in Ben's bag and I can't get in...

appeased	appointing	approaching	arch
appeasement	appointment	appropriate	archaeological
appeasing	appraisal	appropriately	archaeologist
appendices	appraise	approval	archaeology
appendix	appraised	approve	archaic
appetiser/appetizer	appraising	approved	archbishop
appetising/	appreciable	approving	arched
appetizing	appreciate	approximate	archer
appetite	appreciated	approximately	archery
applaud	appreciating	approximation	arches
applauded	appreciation	apricot	arching
applauding	appreciative	apron	archipelago
applause	appreciatively	apt	architect
apple	apprehend	aptitude	architectural
appliance	apprehended	aptly	architecture
applicable	apprehending	aquarium	archive
applicant	apprehension	aquatic	ardent
application	apprehensive	aqueduct	ardently
applicator	apprehensively	arbiter	ardour
applied	apprentice	arbitrary	arduous
applies	apprenticeship	arbitrate	are
apply	approach	arbitrated	area
applying	approachable	arbitration	arena
appoint	approached	arc	arguable
appointed	approaches	arcade	arguably

appeasement; appeasing
Notice that you keep the final '-e' of 'appease' when you add an ending that starts with a consonant ('-ment'), but drop it if it begins with a vowel ('-ing').

appendix → appendices
This is one of the few words where '-x' becomes '-ces' in the plural. 'Vortex' and 'index' can do the same.

apply → appliance/applicable, etc.
When you add to a word ending in a consonant and '-y', you usually change the 'y' to 'i' (except for very short words: 'wry/wryly', or if adding '-ing': 'applying').

arc means 'a curved line'. An 'ark', which sounds just the same, means 'a huge boat'.

An **archipelago** is a group of small islands. It's originally an Italian word.

are is a part of the verb 'to be', but it sounds a lot like 'our', which means 'belonging to us', and a bit like 'hour', which is 60 minutes.

We are putting on our play in the lunch hour.

argue	arranged	ascending	assembly
argued	arrangement	ascent	assent
arguing	arranging	ascribe	assert
argument	array	ascribed	asserted
argumentative	arrears	ascribing	asserting
arid	arrest	ash	assertive
arise	arrested	ashamed	assertively
arisen	arresting	ashen	asses
arising	arrival	ashes	assess
aristocracy	arrive	ashore	assessed
aristocrat	arrived	aside	assesses
aristocratic	arriving	ask	assessing
arithmetic	arrogance	asked	assessor
arithmetical	arrogant	asking	asset
ark	arrow	asleep	assign
arm	arson	asparagus	assigned
armadillo	art	aspect	assignment
armament	artefact	asphalt	assist
armchair	artful	aspiration	assistance
armful	artfully	aspire	assistant
armies	artichoke	aspired	assisted
armistice	article	aspiring	assisting
armour	articulate	ass	associate
armoured	articulated	assailant	association
armoury	articulating	assassin	assonance
armpit	artificial	assassinate	assorted
army	artificially	assassinated	assortment
aroma	artillery	assassination	assume
aromatic	artist	assault	assumed
arose	artistic	assaulted	assuming
around	artistry	assaulting	assumption
arouse	ascend	assemble	assurance
aroused	ascendancy	assembled	assure
arousing	ascendant	assemblies	assured
arrange	ascended	assembling	assuring

an ark sailing under the arc of a rainbow

arguing; argument; argumentative, etc.
Note that 'argue' drops its final '-e' when an ending is added. English words don't tend to end in a '-u', so you nearly always find another letter after one: 'argue'.

ark means 'a huge boat', but 'arc', which sounds just the same, means 'a curved line'.

ascent *vs* **assent**
An 'ascent' is a climb upwards. 'Assent' means 'to agree'.

assault
The 'au' in 'assault' is one of the more unusual ways in which the 'o' sound is spelt in English words.

asterisk

This is the mark (*), used **to draw a reader's attention to the bottom of a page**. It's from the Ancient Greek word 'asterikos', or 'little star'.

asterisk	atlases	attendant	auditing
asteroid	atmosphere	attended	audition
astonish	atmospheric	attending	auditorium
astonished	atom	attention	augment
astonishes	atomic	attentive	augmentation
astonishing	atone	attic	augmented
astonishingly	atoned	attire	augmenting
astonishment	atonement	attired	aunt
astound	atoning	attiring	aura
astounded	atrocious	attitude	aural
astounding	atrocities	attorney	auspices
astray	atrocity	attract	auspicious
astride	attach	attracted	austere
astringent	attached	attracting	austerity
astrologer	attaches	attraction	authentic
astrological	attaching	attractive	authorise/authorize
astrology	attachment	attractively	authorised/
astronaut	attack	attractiveness	authorized
astronomer	attacked	attune	authorising/
astronomical	attacking	attuned	authorizing
astronomy	attain	attuning	authoritative
astute	attainable	aubergine	authorities
asylum	attained	auburn	authority
asymmetrical	attaining	auction	autism
ate	attainment	auctioned	autistic
atheism	attempt	auctioneer	autobiographical
atheist	attempted	auctioning	autobiographies
athlete	attempting	audacious	autobiography
athletic	attend	audacity	autograph
atlas	attendance	audible	automate
		audibly	automated
		audience	automatic
		audio-visual	automation
		audit	automobile
		audited	autumn

'astro-'

Words beginning with 'astro-' are usually to do with the stars or space. They are based on the Greek word for 'star', which is 'astron'. The word 'astronaut' actually means 'star sailor'.

audio-visual stems from the Latin verbs 'audire', meaning 'to hear', and 'videre', 'to see'.

auditorium is a Latin word, which means 'a place where things are heard'. An 'auditorium' is a large hall or theatre where concerts and plays are performed. You may sometimes see the plural spelt 'auditoria'.

aura means 'atmosphere that surrounds someone'. In Latin, 'aura' means 'breeze' or 'wind'.

aural means 'to do with hearing and ears', but 'oral' means 'to do with mouths': 'Oral hygiene is very important.' Make sure you use the right one.

autobiography; automatic, etc.

Words that begin with 'auto-' usually mean something to do with 'doing it yourself', or 'on its own'. An 'autobiography' is written by someone about themselves, and something that is 'automatic' does whatever it does by itself, without help.

autumnal	averting	avowed	awe
auxiliary	aviaries	await	awed
availability	aviary	awaited	awesome
available	aviation	awaiting	awful
avalanche	aviator	awake	awfully
avarice	avid	awaken	awkward
avenue	avocado	award	awning
average	avoid	awarded	awoke
averse	avoidable	awarding	awoken
aversion	avoidance	aware	awry
avert	avoided	awareness	axe
averted	avoiding	away	azure

An avalanche is a huge fall of snow. It is originally a French word. The ending is pronounced 'sh'.

aviary; aviation; aviator, etc.
Words beginning 'avia-', such as 'aviation' and 'aviator', are usually to do with flight, as they stem from the Latin word for 'bird', 'avis'.

awful; awfully
When 'full' is added to a word to make it mean 'full of', it only has one 'l': 'awful'. When you add '-ly' to a word to make it into an adverb, then it has a double 'l': 'She drove awfully well.'

 Quick tip

Mnemonics

A mnemonic (pronounced 'ne-mon-ik') is **a saying that helps you remember something,** such as the letters in a tricky word. For example, to remember the letters in 'aghast' (shocked), you could think of:

'a ghost haunts a scary tower'

If using mnemonics helps your spelling, it doesn't matter how silly they sound.

Some tricky words to spell that start with an 'a'

Here are some words beginning with 'a' that are particularly tricky to spell. See how many of them you can get right. There are some tips to help you on page 7.

absence	aesthetic	appal
abstinence	aghast	apparatus
accelerate	altogether	appearance
accident	aluminium	arbitrary
accompany	amateur	archaeologist
accumulate	anaesthetic	architect
acknowledge	analysis	atheist
acquaint	anonymous	atrocious
acronym	answer	awkward
advertisement	anxious	awry

Bb

a balaclava

balaclava; balsa; banana
'Balaclava' is a Russian word for a kind of hat. **Words that end in '-a', '-i' or '-u' always come from other languages.** They include 'banana' and 'balsa'.

babble	backlog	baggy	ballad
babbled	backpack	bagpipes	ballast
babbling	backpacker	bail	balled
babies	backside	bailed	ballerina
baboon	backstage	bailiff	ballet
baby	backstroke	bait	balloon
babyish	back-up	baize	balloonist
baby-sat	backward	bake	ballot
baby-sit	backwards	baked	ballroom
baby-sitter	bacon	baker	balm
baby-sitting	bad	bakeries	balmier
bachelor	badge	bakery	balmiest
back	badger	baking	balmy
backbone	badgered	balaclava	balsa
backdate	badgering	balance	bamboo
backdated	badly	balanced	ban
backdating	badminton	balancing	banal
backed	badness	balconies	banana
backfire	baffle	balcony	band
backfired	baffled	bald	bandage
backfiring	baffling	balder	bandaged
background	bag	baldest	bandit
backhand	bagel	baldly	bang
backhanded	baggage	baldness	banged
backhander	bagged	bale	banger
backing	baggier	baled	bangle
backlash	baggiest	baling	banish
backlashes	bagging	ball	banished

babbling; backdating; backfiring, etc.
If you add an ending that starts with a vowel to a word that ends with '-e', you usually drop the '-e'.

backlashes
Words that end with a 'sh', or another hissing sound, such as '-tch' ('witch'), '-ss' ('hiss'), '-x' ('box') or '-z' ('buzz'), nearly always take '-es' in the plural.

badness; baldness
The ending '-ness' means 'a state of being'. It doesn't change the spelling of words it is added to, unless they end with a '-y': 'beastly → beastliness'.

bail *vs* **bale**
The noun 'bail' means 'money paid to free someone from jail until their trial starts'. A 'bale' is a tied-up bundle of hay, paper or straw.

ballet *vs* **ballot**
Take care not to confuse 'ballet', which is originally a French word for a style of of dance, and 'ballot', which is part of an election.

balmy means 'warm': 'The evening was balmy.' 'Barmy' is a slang word for 'crazy': 'My dog is completely barmy.'

banishing
banishment
banister/bannister
banjo
banjoes/banjos
bank
banked
banker
banking
banknote
bankrupt
bankruptcies
bankruptcy
banned
banner
banning
banquet
banqueting
banter
bantered
bantering
bap
baptise/baptize
baptised/baptized
baptising/baptizing
baptism
baptismal
bar
barb
barbarian
barbaric
barbarism
barbarity
barbarous
barbecue/barbeque

barbed
barber
bard
bare
bareback
bared
barefaced
barefoot
barely
barer
barest
bargain
bargained
bargaining
barge
barged
barging
baring
bark
barked
barking
barley
barmy
barn
barnacle
barnyard
barometer
baron
baroness
baronesses
baronial
barracks
barrage
barred
barrel

barren
barricade
barricaded
barricading
barrier
barring
barrister
barrow
bartender
barter
bartered
bartering
base
baseball
based
basement
bash
bashed
bashes
bashing
basic
basically
basin
basing
basis
bask
basked
basking
bass
bassoon
bat
batch
batches
bath
bathe

bathed
bathing
bathroom
baton
batsman
batsmen
battalion
batted
batten
battened
battening
batter
battered
batteries
battering
battery
batting
battle
battlefield
battlements
battleship
bawl
bawled
bawling
bay
bayonet
bazaar
be
beach
beaches
beacon
bead
beady
beak
beaker

bard *vs* **barred**
A 'bard' is a poet, but the word 'barred' means 'prohibited' or 'not allowed'.

bare *vs* **bear**
'Bare' means 'without clothes', but a 'bear' is a large mammal. To 'bear' something is to carry or endure it.

bareback; barefaced; barefoot
Some compound words are joined with a hyphen (-), some stay separate words, and some, like these, form one word.

a bare bear

barmy is a slang word for 'crazy', but 'balmy' means 'warm': 'The wind was balmy.'

baron *vs* **barren**
A 'baron' is a nobleman, but 'barren' can mean 'unable to have children' or 'poor growing land'.

barracks; battlements
'Barracks' (the buildings soldiers live in) and 'battlements' (fortifications) are always plural.

base *vs* **bass**
The 'base' of something is its lowest point, or bottom. 'Bass' is a musical term for low, deep notes.

beam	beefburger	behaviour	bench
beamed	beefier	behead	benches
beaming	beefiest	beheaded	bend
bean	beefy	beheading	bending
bear	beehive	behind	beneath
bearable	been	behold	beneficial
beard	beer	beholder	benefit
bearing	beetle	beige	benefited
beast	beetroot	being	benefiting
beastliness	befall	belch	benefits
beastly	befallen	belched	benevolence
beat	before	belches	benevolent
beaten	beforehand	belching	benevolently
beating	befriend	belief	benign
beautiful	befriended	believable	bent
beautifully	befriending	believe	bequeath
beauty	beg	believed	bequeathed
beaver	began	believer	bequest
became	beggar	believing	bereaved
because	begged	bellies	bereavement
beckon	begging	bellow	bereft
beckoned	begin	bellowed	berries
beckoning	beginner	bellowing	berry
become	beginning	bellows	berth
becoming	begrudge	belly	berthed
bed	begrudged	belong	berthing
bedclothes	begrudging	belonged	beseech
bedding	beguile	belonging	beseeched
bedecked	beguiled	beloved	beseeches
bedraggled	beguiling	below	beseeching
bedridden	begun	belt	beserk
bedroom	behalf	belted	beside
bee	behave	belting	best
beech	behaved	bemused	bestow
beef	behaving	bemusing	bestowed

bazaar

This word is based on a word for 'market', pronounced 'ba-zar', and comes from the ancient kingdom of Persia (now called Iran).

beach *vs* **beech**

'Beach' can mean 'the seashore', or 'to be washed ashore' or 'stranded'. A 'beech' is a type of tree.

bean *vs* **been**

A 'bean' is a kind of seed that people plant, grow and eat. It sounds like 'been', which is part of the verb 'to be': 'I've been to London.'

bellow *vs* **below**

To 'bellow' means 'to shout'. 'Below' means 'underneath'.

A **berth** is a bed in a ship, or where it is tied up in a harbour. 'Birth' means 'the event of being born'.

beserk

Viking warriors called 'beserkers' went 'beserk' (mad) before battles to terrify their foes.

a beserker going beserk

bestowing	bigger	biscuit	blackmailed
bet	biggest	bisect	blackmailer
betray	bigot	bisected	blackmailing
betrayal	bigoted	bisecting	blackness
betrayed	bigotry	bisexual	blackout
betrayer	bike	bishop	blacksmith
betraying	biker	bison	bladder
betroth	bikini	bit	blade
betrothal	bilingual	bitch	blame
betrothed	bilingualism	bitches	blamed
better	bill	bite	blameless
betting	billiards	biting	blaming
between	bind	bitten	bland
beverage	binding	bitter	blander
beware	binge	bitterest	blandest
bewilder	binged	bizarre	blank
bewildered	bingeing	blab	blanker
bewildering	bingo	blabbed	blankest
bewilderment	binoculars	blabbing	blanket
beyond	biochemistry	black	blankly
bias	biodegradable	blackberries	blare
biased	biodiversity	blackberry	blared
bib	biographer	blackbird	blaring
bibliographies	biographical	blackboard	blaspheme
bibliography	biographies	blackcurrant	blasphemed
bicentenaries	biography	blacken	blasphemous
bicentenary	biological	blackened	blasphemy
bicycle	biologist	blackening	blast
bid	biology	blacker	blasted
bidden	bionic	blackest	blasting
bidding	biplane	blackhead	blast-off
bidet	bird	blacklist	blatant
biennial	birth	blacklisted	blatantly
biennially	birthday	blacklisting	blaze
big	birthmark	blackmail	blazed

bicentenary; bicycle; biennial; bilingual, etc.
Words beginning with 'bi-' usually have something to do with 'two', as they are based on the Latin word for 'two', 'bis'.

bingeing
Notice that you keep the silent '-e' at the end of 'binge' when you add an ending that starts with a vowel. Almost all words ending with '-ce' and '-ge' follow this pattern: 'outrageous'; 'changeable'.

birth means 'the event of being born', but a 'berth' is a bed onboard a ship, or where it is tied up in a dock.

bite
To 'bite' means 'break something off with your teeth', but a 'byte' is used to measure how much data a computer stores. See page 204 for computing words.

blameless
If you add '-less' to a word, it doesn't mean 'less', but 'without any'. 'Blameless' means 'without any blame'.

blasphemy
There are four ways of spelling the 'f' sound in English: 'ph' ('blasphemy'); 'f' ('frog'); 'ff' ('bluff') and 'gh' ('cough'). Try to use the right one.

blazer	blinked	bloodstain	bluff
blazing	blinking	bloodstained	bluffed
bleach	bliss	bloodstream	bluffing
bleached	blissful	bloodthirstiness	blunder
bleaches	blissfully	bloodthirsty	blundered
bleaching	blister	bloody	blundering
bleak	blistered	bloom	blur
bleaker	blistering	bloomed	blurred
bleakly	blitz	blooming	blurring
bleary	blitzed	blossom	blurt
bleat	blitzes	blossomed	blurted
bleated	blitzing	blossoming	blurting
bleating	blizzard	blot	blush
bled	bloat	blotch	blushed
bleed	bloated	blotched	blushes
bleeding	bloating	blotches	blushing
bleep	blob	blotching	bluster
bleeped	blobby	blotted	blustered
bleeping	block	blotting	blustering
blemish	blockade	blouse	boar
blemished	blockaded	blouses	board
blemishes	blockading	blow	boarded
blend	blocked	blowing	boarder
blended	blocking	blown	boarding
blender	blond	blubber	boast
blending	blonde	blubbered	boasted
bless	blonder	blubbering	boasting
blessed/blest	blondest	bludgeon	boat
blessing	blood	bludgeoned	bob
blew	bloodhound	bludgeoning	bobbed
blind	bloodier	blue	bobbin
blinded	bloodiest	bluebell	bobbing
blinding	bloodless	blueprint	bodice
bling	bloodshed	bluer	bodies
blink	bloodshot	bluest	bodily

blew vs blue

'Blew' is the past tense of the verb 'to blow' ('The wind blew fiercely yesterday'), but 'blue' is a colour.

blissful

Remember that when '-ful' is added to a word to mean 'full of', it only has one 'l': 'blissful'. When you add '-ly' to make an adverb, it has a double 'l': 'I slept blissfully.'

blond/blonde

To describe a boy or a man with pale yellow hair, use 'blond', and for a girl or a woman, use 'blonde'.

blood; bloom

The letters 'oo' can make an 'uh' sound, in 'blood', or an 'oo' sound, as in 'bloom'.

blot → blotted; blur → blurred; bob → bobbed

These words of one syllable that end in a short vowel and a consonant double their final consonant before an ending that starts with a vowel is added.

A boar is a wild pig, but a 'bore' is an uninteresting person. 'Bore' can also be the past tense of 'to bear': 'She bore six children.' 'Board' (a flat piece of wood) is also easy to confuse with 'bored' (uninterested).

body	bone	bordered	bottling
bodyguard	bonfire	bordering	bottom
bog	bonier	borderline	bottomless
boggier	boniest	bore	bough
boggiest	bonnet	bored	bought
boggy	bonus	boredom	boulder
bogus	bonuses	boring	bounce
boil	bony	born	bounced
boiled	boo	borne	bouncier
boiler	booed	borrow	bounciest
boiling	booing	borrowed	bouncing
boisterous	book	borrower	bouncy
boisterously	booked	borrowing	bound
bold	booking	bosom	boundaries
bolder	book-keeping	boss	boundary
boldest	booklet	bossed	bounded
boldly	bookmaker	bosses	bounding
bollard	bookmark	bossier	bountiful
bolster	bookworm	bossiest	bountifully
bolstered	boom	bossiness	bounty
bolstering	boomed	bossing	bouquet
bolt	boomerang	bossy	bourgeois
bolted	booming	botanical	bourgeoisie
bolting	boon	botanist	bout
bomb	boost	botany	boutique
bombard	boosted	botch	bow
bombarded	booster	botches	bowed
bombarding	boosting	botching	bowing
bombed	boot	both	bowl
bomber	booted	bother	bowled
bombing	booth	bothered	bowling
bombshell	booty	bothering	box
bond	booze	bottle	boxed
bonded	boozy	bottled	boxer
bonding	border	bottleneck	boxes

bolder *vs* **boulder**
To be 'bolder' is to be 'more brave' or 'more courageous'. A 'boulder' is a large rock.
bomb
A silent '-b' is usually found after an 'm', as here, and in 'climb', 'comb', 'dumb', 'lamb' and 'numb'.
bonus is the Latin word for 'good'.
bore means 'an uninteresting person', and is also the past tense of 'to bear' ('He bore me up.'). A 'boar' is a wild pig. Take care with 'board' (a flat piece of wood) and 'bored' (uninterested), too.

born *vs* **borne**
The word 'born' means 'come into the world, as a baby'. 'Borne' means 'endured' or 'tolerated', and is also part of the verb 'to bear': 'It could not be borne.'
bough *vs* **bow**
A 'bough' is a branch. To 'bow' (rhyming with 'cow'), means 'bend over'. 'Bow' (rhyming with 'low') can be a weapon or a way of tying a ribbon (for example).
boy
A 'boy' is a male child, but a 'buoy' is a floating ball or marker that shows where something is under water.

boxing
boy
boycott
boyfriend
boyhood
boyish
bra
brace
braced
bracelet
bracing
bracket
brag
bragged
bragging
braid
braided
braiding
brain
brainier
brainiest
brainstorm
brainstormed
brainstorming
brainwash
brainwashed
brainwashes
brainwashing
brainwave
brainy
brake
braked
braking
bramble
bran

branch
branched
branches
branching
brand
branded
brandies
branding
brandish
brandished
brandishes
brandishing
brandy
brash
brasher
brashest
brass
brat
bravado
brave
braved
bravely
braver
bravery
bravest
braving
brawl
brawled
brawling
brawn
brawny
bray
brayed
braying
brazen

brazenly
breach
breached
breaches
breaching
bread
breadline
breadth
breadwinner
break
breakable
breakage
breakaway
breakdown
breaker
breakfast
breaking
breakneck
breakthrough
breakwater
breast
breaststroke
breathalyse
breathalysed
breathalysing
breathe
breathed
breathing
breathless
breathlessly
breathlessness
breathtaking
breathtakingly
bred
breed

breeding
breeze
breezed
breezing
breezy
brew
brewed
brewer
breweries
brewery
brewing
briar
bribe
bribed
bribery
bribing
bric-a-brac
brick
bricklayer
bricklaying
bridal
bride
bridegroom
bridesmaid
bridge
bridged
bridging
bridle
brief
briefcase
briefer
briefest
briefly
brigade
bright

brainstorm; brainwash
Compounds can have different meanings from the two words they contain. To 'brainstorm' means 'to pool ideas', and 'brainwash' means 'to make someone believe something unquestioningly', for instance.

brake vs break
A 'brake' is the part of a vehicle that makes it stop. To 'break' means 'to destroy or damage something'.

bread vs bred
'Bread' is a kind of food, but 'bred' is part of the verb 'to breed', which means 'mate, and produce young'.

breathalyse
You can use either 's' or 'z' in many words, but in British English, you spell this word with an 's'. The spelling 'breathalyze' is used in America.

bric-a-brac
This means 'small household things of little value', and comes from an Old French phrase, 'à bric et à brac', meaning 'in no particular order, at random'.

bridal vs bridle
The word 'bridal' means 'to do with brides', but a 'bridle' is a harness put around a horse's head.

brighten	broadly	browsing	budget
brightened	broad-minded	bruise	budgetary
brightening	broccoli	bruised	budgeted
brighter	brochure	bruising	budgeting
brightest	brogue	brunette	budgie
brightly	broke	brunt	budging
brightness	broken	brush	buff
brilliance	brollies	brushed	buffalo
brilliant	brolly	brushes	buffer
brilliantly	bronze	brushing	buffet
brim	brooch	brusque	buffeted
brimstone	brooches	brusquely	buffeting
brine	brood	brutal	bug
bring	brooded	brutality	bugged
brink	brooding	brutally	buggies
briny	broody	brute	bugging
brisk	brook	bubble	buggy
brisker	broom	bubbled	bugle
briskest	broth	bubbling	bugler
briskly	brother	bubbly	build
briskness	brotherhood	buck	builder
bristle	brother-in-law	bucked	building
bristly	brotherly	bucket	built
brittle	brothers-in-law	bucking	bulb
brittleness	brought	buckle	bulbous
broach	brow	buckled	bulge
broached	browbeat	buckling	bulged
broaching	browbeaten	bud	bulging
broad	browbeating	budded	bulk
broadcast	brown	buddies	bulkier
broadcaster	browner	budding	bulkiest
broadcasting	brownest	buddy	bulky
broaden	browse	budge	bull
broader	browsed	budged	bulldog
broadest	browser	budgerigar	bulldozer

broach _vs_ brooch

To 'broach' something is to mention it: 'Mr Darcy broached the subject of marriage.' A 'brooch' is a piece of jewellery, pinned to someone's clothes.

brolly

People shorten words in every language, and you may hear or read 'brolly' instead of 'umbrella'. 'Umbrella' comes from the Latin word for 'shadow', 'umbra'.

browsing; bubbling; buckling; budging, etc.

Words that end in a silent '-e' usually drop it when you add an ending that starts with a vowel, such as '-ing'.

brunette

This is an Old French word for 'a dark-brown-haired woman', and it means just the same in English.

brusque

Whenever you see a 'q' in a word, you can be sure that a 'u' will come after it.

buffet

This can mean 'knocked about', when it's pronounced 'buff-et': 'She was buffeted by wind.' 'Buffet', when pronounced 'boofay', is a French word for a selection of food laid out on a table: 'The buffet was impressive.'

bullet	bunker	burned/burnt	bustling
bulletin	bunting	burning	bust-up
bulletproof	buoy	burp	busty
bullfight	buoyancy	burped	busy
bullfighter	buoyant	burping	but
bullied	burble	burrow	butcher
bullies	burbled	bursaries	butchery
bullion	burbling	bursary	butt
bullock	burden	burst	butter
bully	burdened	bursting	buttercup
bullying	burdening	bury	buttered
bump	burdensome	burying	butterflies
bumped	bureau	bus	butterfly
bumper	bureaucracies	buses	buttering
bumpier	bureaucracy	bush	buttery
bumpiest	bureaucrat	bushes	buttock
bumping	bureaucratic	bushier	button
bumpy	bureaus/bureaux	bushiest	buttoned
bun	burgeon	bushy	buttonhole
bunch	burgeoned	busier	buttoning
bunched	burgeoning	busiest	buy
bunches	burger	busily	buyer
bundle	burglar	business	buying
bundled	burglaries	businesses	buzz
bundling	burglary	businesslike	buzzard
bung	burgle	businessman	buzzed
bungalow	burgled	businesswoman	buzzes
bunged	burgling	busked	buzzing
bunging	burial	busker	by
bungle	buried	busking	bygone
bungled	buries	bust	bypass
bungler	burlier	busted	bypasses
bungling	burliest	busting	by-product
bunk	burly	bustle	bystander
bunk-bed	burn	bustled	byte

buoy

A 'buoy' is a floating ball or marker in water, but a 'boy' is a male child.

bureaus/bureaux

As 'bureau' is French for 'office' or 'department', both '-x' or '-s' are correct plurals, so you can use either.

A boy clinging to a buoy.

but *vs* **butt**

The word 'but' is a conjunction in English: 'He sings, but not well.' To 'butt' means 'to ram or push something'. A 'butt' is slang for a bottom.

buy *vs* **by**

To 'buy' means 'to pay for something with money'. 'By' is a preposition, a word that connects words to each other in some way: 'She lives by the sea.'

byte

A 'byte' measures how much data a computer stores. To 'bite' means 'break with your teeth'.

Quick
tip

Five spelling steps

The key to spelling difficult words is to practise them lots of times.
Try following these five quick steps with words you find tricky:

1. **Look** at the word carefully.
2. **Say** it out loud to yourself.
3. **Cover** it up with your hand.
4. **Write** it down.
5. **Check** whether you've spelt it correctly.

If you still make some slips, repeat these five steps again. The more you practise
reading, saying, and writing a word down, the easier it will get to spell it.

Some tricky words to spell that start with a 'b'

Here are some words beginning with 'b' that are particularly tricky to spell. Have a go,
and see how many you can get right. There are some more tips to help you on page 7.

bachelor	beneficial	bruise
baggage	benefiting	budget
balloon	boundary	bulletin
baptism	bouquet	buoyancy
battalion	breach	buoyant
beautiful	breadth	bureaucracy
because	breathe	bureaucratic
beggar	broccoli	burglar
beginner	brochure	business

Silly sayings and images or pictures can remind
you how words are spelt. Try this for 'because':

'**b**ig **e**lephants **c**an't **a**lways **u**se **s**mall **e**xits'

Cc

one calf, two calves

C

calves
Most words that end in '-f' add an '-s' in the plural. Some, like 'calf', take the ending '-ves'. You'll find a list of which word does what on page 5 of this dictionary.

cab	cake	calorie	cancerous
cabaret	caked	calves	candid
cabbage	caking	came	candidacy
cabin	calamities	cameo	candidate
cabinet	calamitous	camera	candidly
cable	calamity	cameraman	candied
cackle	calculate	camomile	candle
cackled	calculated	camouflage	candlelight
cackling	calculating	camouflaged	candlelit
cacophony	calculation	camouflaging	candlestick
cacti	calculator	camp	candour
cactus	calendar	campaign	candyfloss
cadence	calf	campaigned	cane
cadet	calibre	campaigner	caned
cadge	call	campaigning	canine
cadged	called	camped	caning
cadging	caller	camper	cannabis
café	calligraphy	camping	canned
cafeteria	calling	campus	cannibal
caffeinated	callous	campuses	cannibalism
caffeine	callously	can	cannon
cage	callousness	canal	canoe
caged	callus	canaries	canoeing
cagey	calm	canary	canopies
cagoule	calmed	cancel	canopy
cajole	calming	cancelled	cantankerous
cajoled	calmly	cancelling	cantankerousness
cajoling	calmness	cancer	canteen

cacti
This is a Latin spelling pattern for the plural of words ending in '-us'. It's fine to write 'cactuses', however.

cadence
Take care with your spelling when you see the endings '-ence' and '-ance', as they sound the same.

caffeine is an exception to the guideline: 'i' before 'e' except after 'c', where those letters make an 'ee' sound.

callous vs callus
To be 'callous' is to be unfeeling. A 'callus' is an area of hard skin, often on the feet or elbows.

camouflage; campaign; cantankerous
With tricky spellings, try covering them up, writing them down and then checking your spelling. Do this several times, until you feel confident spelling them.

campuses
Remember that most words that end with '-s', '-ch', '-z' or '-ss' take '-es' when they become plural.

caned; canned
The word 'caned' means 'beaten with a stick', but 'canned' means 'put into a can'. The extra 'n' makes a big difference to both sound and meaning.

C

canter	captain	carelessly	cart
cantered	captained	carelessness	cartoon
cantering	captaining	carer	cartoonist
canvas	caption	caress	cartridge
canvases	captioned	caressed	cartwheel
canvass	captivate	caresses	carve
canvasser	captivated	caressing	carved
canvasses	captivating	caretaker	carver
canvassing	captive	caretaking	carving
canyon	captivity	cargo	cascade
cap	captor	cargoes	cascaded
capabilities	capture	caricature	cascading
capability	captured	caring	case
capable	capturing	carnage	cash
capacities	car	carnal	cashed
capacity	caramel	carnation	cashes
cape	carat	carnival	cashier
caped	caravan	carnivore	cashing
caper	carbohydrate	carnivorous	cashmere
capered	carbon	carob	cashpoint
capering	carbonated	carol	casino
capital	carcase/	carousel	cask
capitalism	carcass	carp	casket
capitalist	carcasses	carpenter	casserole
capitulate	card	carpet	cassette
capitulated	cardboard	carpeted	cast
capitulating	cardigan	carpeting	castanets
capped	cardinal	carriage	castaway
capping	care	carriageway	casting
cappuccino	cared	carried	castle
capricious	career	carries	casual
capsize	careered	carrion	casually
capsized	careering	carrot	casualness
capsizing	carefree	carry	casualties
capsule	careless	carrying	casualty

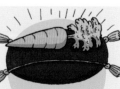

canvas *vs* canvass
'Canvas' is strong cloth, often used for paintings or sails. To 'canvass' is to ask people to support a cause, or candidate: 'He canvassed for Bill Smith.'

cappuccino
This is the Italian name for a coffee topped with milky froth, in which 'cc' makes a 'ch' sound.

captor; censor
Words that end in '-or' usually mean 'the person who does something': a 'captor' captures, a 'censor' censors. (See note on facing page for the meaning.)

carat *vs* carrot
A 'carat' is a unit for measuring gold, but a 'carrot' is a long root vegetable.

caught
A silent 'gh' is often found at the end of a word, before a '-t', as it is here, and in 'weight', and 'light'.

cede means 'to let someone else win': 'He ceded the point.' A 'seed' is the part of a flower or tree that grows into a new one. Try not to mix them up.

a 24 carat carrot

If you are looking for words that begin with an 's' sound, look at the 's' pages as well.

cat — chairwomen

C

cat	caught	ceded	central
catalogue	cauldron	ceding	centrally
catalogued	cauliflower	ceiling	centre
cataloguing	causal	celebrate	centred
catalyst	cause	celebrated	centring
catapult	caused	celebrating	centuries
catapulted	causeway	celebration	centurion
catapulting	caustic	celebratory	century
catastrophe	caution	celebrities	ceramic
catastrophic	cautionary	celebrity	cereal
catch	cautious	celery	cerebral
catches	cautiously	cell	ceremonial
catchier	cavalier	cellar	ceremonially
catchiest	cavalries	cellist	ceremonies
catching	cavalry	cello	ceremony
catchy	cave	cellophane	certain
categorical	caved	cellphone	certainly
categorically	caveman	cellular	certainties
categories	cavemen	cement	certainty
categorise/	cavern	cemented	certificate
categorize	cavernous	cementing	certificated
categorised/	caving	cemeteries	certification
categorized	cavities	cemetery	certified
categorising/	cavity	cenotaph	certifies
categorizing	cavort	censor	certify
category	cavorted	censored	certifying
cater	cavorting	censoring	chain
catered	cease	cent	chained
catering	ceased	centaur	chaining
caterpillar	ceasefire	centenaries	chair
cathedral	ceaseless	centenary	chairman
catkin	ceaselessly	centigrade	chairmen
catseye	ceasing	centilitre	chairperson
cattle	cedar	centimetre	chairwoman
catwalk	cede	centipede	chairwomen

ceiling follows the guideline: 'i' before 'e' except after 'c', when the letters make an 'ee' sound. Try not to confuse it with 'sealing', which means 'closing'.

cell can mean 'the room a prisoner is kept in', or 'a microscopic part of an animal or plant'. To 'sell' means 'to exchange something for money'.

A cellar is the basement of a building. A 'seller' is a person who is selling something.

censor means 'to remove parts of a book, film or letter in case they are secret, or rude'. A 'sensor' is an instrument that senses movement, light or sound.

A cent is a small coin. 'Scent' is a smell, or perfume. 'Sent' is the past of the verb 'to send'.

centenary; centigrade; centilitre, etc.
Words that start with 'cent-' often have something to do with 100, as the Latin word 'centum' means '100'.

cereal is grain, such as oats, wheat or barley. A 'serial' is a story told in parts.

chairmen; chairwomen
To make words ending with '-man' or '-woman' plural, you change the main noun to '-men' or '-women', as in 'groundsmen' and 'chairwomen'.

chalet	chaotic	charred	check
chalice	chaotically	charring	checked
chalk	chap	chart	checking
chalked	chapel	charted	checkmate
chalkier	chapter	charter	checkup
chalkiest	char	chartered	cheek
chalking	character	chartering	cheekier
chalky	characterise/	charting	cheekiest
challenge	characterize	chase	cheekily
challenged	characterised/	chased	cheeky
challenger	characterized	chasing	cheer
challenging	characterising/	chasm	cheered
chamber	characterizing	chat	cheerful
chameleon	characteristic	chateau	cheerfully
champagne	characteristically	chateaux	cheerfulness
champion	characterless	chatted	cheering
championed	charcoal	chatter	cheery
championing	charge	chattered	cheese
championship	chargeable	chattering	cheesecake
chance	charged	chattier	cheesy
chanced	charging	chattiest	cheetah
chancellor	chariot	chatting	chef
chancing	charioteer	chatty	chemical
change	charisma	chauffeur	chemically
changeable	charismatic	chauvinism	chemist
changed	charismatically	chauvinist	chemistry
changeover	charitable	chauvinistic	cheque
changing	charitably	cheap	chequered
channel	charities	cheaper	cherish
channelled	charity	cheapest	cherished
channelling	charm	cheaply	cherishing
chant	charmed	cheat	cherries
chanted	charmer	cheated	cherry
chanting	charming	cheater	chess
chaos	charmingly	cheating	chest

changeable; changeover; chargeable
Here, you keep the silent '-e' when you add an ending that begins with 'a-' or 'o-', to keep the 'g' sound soft.

channelled; chiselled
When you add an ending that starts with a vowel to words that end in a vowel and a single '-l', such as 'channel' and 'chisel', you double the 'l'.

charred; chatted; chopped
Remember to double the final consonant when you add '-ed' to a one-syllable word (such as 'char' or 'chat') that has a short vowel and a consonant.

cheater vs cheetah
A 'cheat' or 'cheater' is someone who cheats, but a 'cheetah' is a big cat, that can run extremely fast. It's easy to mix these two words up.

a cheating cheetah

START

Remember to check the 's' pages as well if you are looking for a word that begins with an 's' sound.

chestnut — circumnavigated

C

chestnut	china	chopstick	chug
chew	chink	choral	chugged
chewed	chintz	chord	chugging
chewing	chip	chore	chum
chewy	chipmunk	choreographed	chunk
chic	chipped	choreographer	chunkier
chick	chipping	choreography	chunkiest
chicken	chirp	chortle	chunky
chickenpox	chirped	chortled	church
chief	chirping	chortling	churches
chieftain	chisel	chorus	churchyard
child	chiselled	chorused	churn
childbirth	chiselling	choruses	churned
childhood	chivalrous	chorusing	churning
childish	chivalry	chose	chute
childishly	chive	chosen	chutney
childishness	chock-a-block	christen	cider
childless	chocolate	christened	cigar
childlike	choice	christening	cigarette
childminder	choir	chrome	cinder
children	choke	chronic	cinema
chill	choked	chronicle	cinnamon
chilled	choking	chronicled	cipher
chilli	choose	chronicling	circle
chillier	choosier	chronological	circled
chillies	choosiest	chrysanthemum	circling
chilliest	choosing	chubbier	circuit
chilling	choosy	chubbiest	circular
chilly	chop	chubby	circulate
chime	chopped	chuck	circulated
chimed	chopper	chucked	circulating
chiming	choppier	chucking	circulation
chimney	choppiest	chuckle	circumference
chimpanzee	chopping	chuckled	circumnavigate
chin	choppy	chuckling	circumnavigated

check *vs* **cheque**
A 'check' is a safeguard, to ensure things are working well. Writing a 'cheque' is a way of paying someone.

cheerful; cheerfully
The adjective ending '-ful' means 'full of', but notice that it only has one 'l': 'cheerful'. The adverb ending, '-fully', has two: 'cheerfully'.

chic (say 'sheek') is a French word for 'stylish'.

chilli *vs* **chilly**
A 'chilli' is a spicy pepper, but 'chilly' means 'rather cold': 'It was a chilly day.'

chord means 'a combination of musical notes'. A 'cord' is a length of string or thin rope.

chronicle; chronological
Many words beginning with 'chron-' are to do with the idea of 'time', and come from the Greek word for 'time', 'khronos'.

chute means 'a slide-like tunnel', as used by builders to move rubble, for instance. To 'shoot' is to fire a gun.

circuit has a silent 'u', which is easy to miss. You'll find it in 'biscuit' and 'built' as well.

C

circumnavigation
circumspect
circumstance
circumstantial
circumvent
circumvented
circumventing
circus
circuses
cities
citizen
citizenship
citric
citrus
city
civic
civil
civilian
civility
civilization
civilized
civilly
clad
claim
claimant
claimed
claiming
clam
clamber
clambered
clambering
clammier
clammiest
clammy
clamorous

clamour
clamoured
clamouring
clamp
clamped
clamping
clan
clandestine
clang
clanged
clanging
clank
clanked
clanking
clap
clapped
clapping
claret
clarification
clarified
clarifies
clarify
clarifying
clarinet
clarinettist
clarity
clash
clashed
clashing
clasp
clasped
clasping
class
classes
classic

classical
classier
classiest
classification
classified
classifies
classify
classifying
classroom
classy
clatter
clattered
clattering
clause
claustrophobia
claustrophobic
claw
clawed
clawing
clay
clean
cleaned
cleaner
cleanest
cleaning
cleanliness
cleanse
cleansed
cleansing
clear
clearance
cleared
clearer
clearest
clearing

clearly
cleavage
cleave
cleaver
cleft
clementine
clench
clenched
clenches
clenching
clergy
clergyman
clergymen
clergywoman
clergywomen
clerical
clerk
clever
cleverer
cleverest
cleverly
cliché
click
clicked
clicking
client
clientele
cliff
clifftop
climate
climatic
climax
climaxes
climb
climbed

---

circumnavigation; circumspect, etc.
Words starting with 'circ-' often mean 'around'.
They are based on the Latin for 'around', 'circum'.

clamorous
Notice this spelling pattern: 'clamour' drops the 'u'
when you add an ending that starts with a vowel, '-ous'.
The words 'glamour' and 'humour' follow this pattern
too: 'glamorous'; 'humorous'.

classroom; clergyman; clifftop; cloakroom, etc.
Breaking compounds down into their separate words
can help you to spell them, e.g. 'cloak' and 'room'.

claustrophobia
Words ending with '-phobia' are to do with a fear
of something, and come from the Greek word for
'fear', 'phobos'. 'Claustrophobia' is a fear of enclosed
spaces, for example.

cliché; clientele
A few French words used in English keep their accents:
'cliché' (an over-used phrase) does, but 'clientele'
(a group of clients, spelt 'clientèle' in French) does not.

climaxes
Words ending in '-x' usually take '-es' in the plural.

climber	close-up	clumping	coating
climbing	closure	clumsier	co-author
cling	clot	clumsiest	coax
clingfilm	cloth	clumsy	coaxed
clinging	clothe	clung	coaxing
clinic	clothed	cluster	cobbler
clinical	clothes	clustered	cobra
clink	clothing	clustering	cobweb
clinked	clotted	clutch	cocaine
clinking	clotting	clutched	cock
clip	cloud	clutches	cockatoo
clipboard	clouded	clutching	cockerel
clipped	cloudier	clutter	cockier
clipper	cloudiest	cluttered	cockiest
clipping	clouding	cluttering	cockpit
clique	cloudless	coach	cockroach
cloak	cloudy	coached	cockroaches
cloakroom	clout	coaching	cocktail
clock	clouted	coal	cocky
clockwise	clouting	coalesce	cocoa
clockwork	clove	coalescence	coconut
clog	clover	coalescing	cocoon
clogged	clown	coalition	cod
clogging	clowned	coarse	code
cloister	clowning	coarsely	coded
clone	cloying	coarseness	coding
cloned	club	coarser	coffee
cloning	clubbed	coarsest	coffin
close	clubbing	coast	cog
closed	cluck	coastal	coherence
closely	clucked	coastguard	coherent
closeness	clucking	coasting	cohesion
closer	clue	coastline	coil
closest	clump	coat	coiled
closet	clumped	coated	coiling

cloth; clothes
The 'o' sound is short in 'cloth', and rhymes with 'moth'. Notice that when a silent '-e' is added, the 'o' becomes the longer 'o' sound it makes in 'clothes'.

coarse means 'rough' or 'unrefined', but 'course' can mean 'a route': 'The ship's course was set for Spain', or 'a programme of study or treatment'.

co-author
'Co-' before a word means 'with someone else'. A 'co-author' writes with another writer, and a 'co-worker' works with another worker, for instance.

cocky is an informal word for 'cheeky': 'He was a cocky boy.' Most languages have words like these.

cocoa; coconut
'Cocoa' comes from 'cacao' (the name for the cacao beans which produce cocoa in the South American language, Nahautl). 'Coconut' (a nut with a hairy shell) sounds similar, but has no 'a' in the middle.

coherence; coherent
You'll usually find the '-ence' ending ('coherence') on the end of a noun, and '-ent' on the end of an adjective: 'She was a coherent speaker.'

C

coin
coinage
coincide
coincided
coincidence
coincidental
coincidentally
coinciding
coined
coining
colander
cold
cold-blooded
colder
coldest
coldly
coldness
coleslaw
collaborate
collaborated
collaboration
collaborator
collage
collapse
collapsed
collapsible
collapsing
collar
collateral
colleague
collect
collected
collecting
collection
collective

collectively
college
collide
collided
colliding
collieries
colliery
collision
colloquial
colloquialism
colloquially
cologne
colon
colonel
colonial
colonies
colonise/colonize
colonised/colonized
colonising/colonizing
colony
colour
coloured
colourful
colourfully
colouring
colourless
colt
column
columnist
comb
combat
combated
combating
combination
combine

colon This is the punctuation mark (:).
It is usually used in these two ways:

1. **Before a list of options or possibilities:**
'The menu included: fish and chips, pasta,
salad and baked potatoes.'

2. **To add an explanation:** 'She hated Tom:
he had taken her favourite toy.'

combined
combining
combustible
combustion
come
comedian
comedies
comedy
comet
comfort
comfortable
comfortably
comforted
comforting
comic

comical
coming
comma
command
commanded
commander
commanding
commandment
commando
commemorate
commemoration
commemorative
commence
commenced
commencement

comma This is the punctuation mark (,).
A comma can be used:

1. **To mark a pause after the beginning
of a sentence:** 'Although the sun had set,
the air was still warm.'

2. **To create a break between parts of a
sentence:** 'Mum liked curry, if it was not too hot.'

3. **To separate items in a list:** 'She wore a
red dress, blue cardigan and yellow tights.'

4. **To separate words inside speech marks:**
"Anna," he said, "don't you understand?"

coincidence
Memory-jogging phrases can help you remember
spellings. Try thinking 'two 'i's and three 'c's' to
help you spell 'coincidence' correctly, for example.

collapsible
It's easy to confuse '-ible' and '-able'. Try to remember
that most words ending in an '-se', such as 'collapse'
and 'reverse', drop the final '-e' and take '-ible'.

collectively; comparatively; compassionately, etc.
Notice that you keep the final '-e' of these words
when you add the ending '-ly' to make an adverb.

collieries; commodities; communities, etc.
Remember that words that end with a consonant
and a '-y' change to '-ies' in the plural.

colonel is a military officer, but a 'kernel'
(which sounds the same) is the inside of a nut.

column
You only find a silent '-n' after an 'm', as here in
'column'. 'Autumn' and 'hymn' also follow this pattern.

'com-'/'con-'
Words beginning with 'com-' or 'con-' often
mean 'with' or 'together with', e.g. 'combine'.

C

commencing	commoner	comparison	complementing
commend	commonest	compartment	complete
commendable	commonly	compass	completed
commendation	commonplace	compassion	completely
commended	commotion	compassionate	completing
commending	communal	compassionately	completion
comment	commune	compatibility	complex
commentaries	communicate	compatible	complexes
commentary	communication	compel	complexion
commentator	communicative	compelled	complexities
commented	communion	compelling	complexity
commenting	communism	compensate	compliance
commerce	communist	compensated	compliant
commercial	communities	compensating	complicate
commercialisation/	community	compensation	complicated
commercialization	commute	compensatory	complicating
commercialised/	commuted	compete	complication
commercialized	commuter	competed	complied
commercially	commuting	competence	complies
commiserate	compact	competent	compliment
commiserated	compacted	competing	complimentary
commiserating	compacting	competition	complimented
commiseration	companies	competitive	complimenting
commission	companion	competitively	comply
commissioned	companionable	compilation	complying
commissioning	companionably	compile	component
commit	companionship	compiled	compose
commitment	company	compiling	composed
committal	comparable	complacency	composing
committed	comparably	complacent	composition
committee	comparative	complain	compost
committing	comparatively	complained	composure
commodities	compare	complaining	compound
commodity	compared	complement	compounded
common	comparing	complementary	compounding

comb has a silent '-b' after the 'm', as do the words
'climb', 'crumb', 'dumb', 'lamb', 'limb' and 'numb'.

commit

Rhymes help with tricky spellings. Try saying 'one 'c',
two 'm's, one 't'', to remember how to spell 'commit'.

complement *vs* **compliment**

If something 'complements' another thing, it goes well
with it or completes it, e.g. 'mustard complements the
flavour of roast beef'. If you 'compliment' someone or
are 'complimentary' about them, you say something nice
about them. 'Complimentary' also means 'given for free'.

complimentary
complementary
mustard

MUSTARD

You
look well
done!

C

comprehend	concealing	concoction	confederation
comprehended	concealment	concourse	confer
comprehending	concede	concrete	conference
comprehension	conceded	concur	conferred
comprehensive	conceding	concurred	conferring
comprehensively	conceit	concurrent	confess
compress	conceited	concurrently	confessed
compressed	conceivable	concurring	confesses
compressing	conceivably	condemn	confessing
compression	conceive	condemnation	confession
comprise	conceiving	condemned	confessional
comprised	concentrate	condemning	confetti
comprising	concentrated	condensation	confidant
compromise	concentrating	condense	confidante
compromised	concentration	condensed	confide
compromising	concept	condensing	confided
compulsion	conception	condescending	confidence
compulsive	conceptual	condiment	confident
compulsively	conceptually	condition	confidential
compulsory	concern	conditional	confidentiality
computer	concerned	conditioned	confidentially
computerisation/	concerning	conditioner	confidently
computerization	concert	conditioning	confides
computerise/	concerted	condolence	confiding
computerize	concession	condom	confine
computerised/	concise	condone	confined
computerized	conclude	condoned	confinement
computerising/	concluded	condoning	confining
computerizing	concluding	conducive	confirm
computing	conclusion	conduct	confirmation
comrade	conclusive	conducted	confirmed
con	conclusively	conducting	confirming
conceal	concoct	conductor	confiscate
concealed	concocted	cone	confiscated
concealer	concocting	confectionery	confiscating

C

conjunctions
'Conjunctions' **link different parts of
a sentence or different words together**,
and are also known as 'linking words'. They
include 'but', 'and', 'either', 'or', 'neither',
'nor', 'because', 'if', and 'until'. You can find
a longer list of conjunctions on page 214.

confiscation	congratulatory
conflict	congregate
conflicted	congregated
conflicting	congregating
conform	congregation
conformed	congress
conforming	conical
conformist	conifer
confront	conjunction
confrontation	conjurer
confronted	conker
confronting	connect
confuse	connected
confused	connecting
confusing	connection
confusion	connective
congeal	conning
congealed	connoisseur
congealing	connotation
congenial	conquer
congeniality	conquered
congested	conquering
congestion	conqueror
congratulate	conquest
congratulated	conscience
congratulating	conscientious
congratulations	conscientiously

conscious	considerate
consciously	consideration
consciousness	considered
consecrate	considering
consecrated	consign
consecration	consigned
consecutive	consigning
consecutively	consignment
consensus	consist
consent	consisted
consented	consistencies
consenting	consistency
consequence	consistent
consequential	consistently
consequently	consisting
conservation	consolation
conservatism	console
conservative	consoled
conservatively	consolidate
conservatories	consolidated
conservatory	consolidating
conserve	consolidation
conserved	consoling
conserving	consonant
consider	consort
considerable	consortium
considerably	conspicuous

consonants **are the 21 letters in the
alphabet which are not vowels** ('a', 'e', 'i', 'o'
and 'u'). When consonants come together in
a word, they can create different sounds: 'dg'
make a 'j' sound ('fudge'); 'gh' an 'f' sound
('cough') and 'ti' a 'sh' sound ('nation'), for
instance. 'Y' can be a vowel or a consonant.

confidant/confidante
A male friend is a 'confidant'; a female, a 'confidante'.
confinement
Notice that when you add the ending '-ment'
to 'confine', you need to keep the silent '-e'.
conker *vs* **conquer**
A 'conker' is the hard seed of a horse chestnut
tree, but to 'conquer' means to 'take control of
a person or place'.
connoisseur means 'an expert', and it comes
from an Old French word meaning 'to know'.

conscience; conscious
The letters 'sci' often make a 'sh' sound in the
middle of words, as they do here. Look out for
this spelling pattern, as it comes up in lots of
words and can be easy to misspell.
consign
You'll usually find a silent 'g' followed by an
'n' in English words: 'consign', 'gnat', 'align'.
consortium
This means 'several businesses working together'.
The plural can be 'consortiums' or 'consortia'.

C

conspicuously
conspiracies
conspiracy
conspirator
conspire
conspired
conspiring
constable
constabularies
constabulary
constancy
constant
constantly
constellation
consternation
constipated
constipating
constipation
constituencies
constituency
constituent
constitute
constituted
constituting
constitution
constitutional
constitutionally
constrained
constraint
constrict
constricted
constricting
constriction
constrictor
construct

construction
constructive
constructively
consul
consulate
consult
consultancies
consultancy
consultant
consultation
consultative
consultatively
consulted
consulting
consume
consumed
consumer
consumerism
consuming
consummate
consummated
consummating
consummation
consumption
contact
contactable
contacted
contacting
contagious
contain
contained
container
containing
containment
contaminate

contaminated
contaminating
contamination
contemplate
contemplated
contemplating
contemplation
contemplative
contemporaries
contemporary
contempt
contemptible
contemptuous
contemptuously
contend
contended
contender
contending
content
contented
contentedly
contention
contest
contestant
contested
contesting
context
continent
continental
contingencies
contingency
contingent
continual
continually
continuation

continue
continued
continuing
continuity
continuous
continuously
contorted
contour
contraception
contraceptive
contract
contracted
contracting
contraction
contractor
contractual
contradict
contradicted
contradicting
contradiction
contradictory
contrary
contrast
contrasted
contrasting
contravene
contravening
contravention
contribute
contributed
contributing
contribution
contributor
contrivance
contrive

---

conspire → conspiring, etc.
Here, you drop the final '-e' when you add '-ing'.
Lots of words follow this pattern, so try to learn it.

constitutionally; continually; coolly; cordially
When you add '-ly' to these words ending in
'-l', notice that you keep that first 'l' too.

constrictor; consumer, etc.
Words that end in '-or' and '-er' usually mean
'the person who does whatever the verb means'.
A 'constrictor' constricts (squeezes), and a 'consumer'
consumes. Check which ending you need, though.

consume → consumption
Look at how the verb 'consume' changes when it
becomes a noun, 'consumption'. Other words, such
as 'absorb/absorption', 'presume/presumption' and
'assume/assumption' follow this pattern, too.

contemptible and **corruptible** are exceptions
to the guideline that, if a word makes sense without
'-ible' or '-able', it's more likely to end with '-able'.

'contra-'
Words beginning with 'contra-' often mean 'against',
as it is the Latin word for 'against', e.g. 'contradiction'.

contrived	coolest	cormorant	corrode
contriving	coolly	corn	corroded
control	coolness	corner	corroding
controlled	cooped-up	cornered	corrosion
controlling	cooperate	cornering	corrosive
controversial	cooperated	cornet	corrugated
controversially	cooperating	cornflour	corrupt
controversies	cooperation	cornflower	corrupted
controversy	cooperative	cornice	corruptible
conundrum	cooperatively	cornier	corrupting
convalesce	coordinate	corniest	corruption
convalescence	coordination	corny	corset
convalescent	cop	coronation	cosier
convey	cope	coroner	cosiest
conveyed	coped	corporal	cosily
conveying	copied	corporate	cosiness
conveyor	copier	corporation	cosmetic
convict	copies	corpse	cosmic
convicted	coping	correct	cosmology
convicting	copious	corrected	cosmonaut
conviction	copper	correcting	cosmopolitan
convince	copse	correction	cosmos
convinced	copy	correctly	cosset
convincing	copying	correctness	cosseted
convincingly	copyright	correlate	cosseting
convoluted	coral	correlated	cost
convoy	cord	correlating	costing
cook	cordial	correlation	costlier
cooked	cordiality	correspond	costliest
cooker	cordially	corresponded	costly
cookery	cordon	correspondence	costume
cookie	corduroy	correspondent	cosy
cooking	core	corresponding	cot
cool	cork	correspondingly	cottage
cooler	corkscrew	corridor	cotton

controlled; controlling
When you add '-ed' or '-ing' to a word of more than one syllable that ends in a vowel and an '-l' (as 'control' does), remember to double the final '-l'.

convalescence
The ending '-scence' usually means 'a state of being'. 'Convalescence' is the time when an ill person recovers, and 'adolescence' is when a child becomes an adult.

cooperate; coordinate
These words are pronounced 'co operate' and 'co ordinate'. They can also be written with a hyphen.

cord is a length of strong string or rope, but a 'chord' is a combination of musical notes, and begins with a hard 'ck' sound, as in 'crown', not a 'ch' sound, as in 'chair'.

cornflour vs cornflower
'Cornflour' is used to thicken sauces in cooking. A 'cornflower' is a blue wildflower.

cosmos comes from 'kosmos', the Ancient Greek word for 'in good order' or 'well-organized'. It's used to describe the order of our universe. 'Cosmology' is the word for detailed study of the universe.

C

couch	coup	coward	cram
couches	couple	cowardice	crammed
cough	coupled	cowardly	cramming
coughed	coupling	cowboy	cramp
coughing	coupon	cower	cramped
could	courage	cowered	cramping
council	courageous	cowering	cranberries
councillor	courageously	co-worker	cranberry
counsel	courgette	coy	crane
counselled	courier	coyly	craned
counselling	course	coyote	craning
counsellor	court	crab	crank
count	courted	crack	cranked
countdown	courteous	cracked	cranking
counted	courteously	cracker	cranky
countenance	courtesy	cracking	crannies
counter	courtier	crackle	cranny
counteract	courting	crackled	crash
counteracted	courtship	crackling	crashed
counteracting	courtyard	cradle	crashing
countered	cousin	cradled	crate
counterfeit	cove	cradling	crated
counterfeited	covenant	craft	crater
counterfeiting	cover	craftier	cravat
countering	coverage	craftiest	crave
counterpart	covered	crafting	craved
countess	covering	craftsman	craving
countesses	covert	craftsmanship	crawl
counties	covertly	craftsmen	crawled
counting	cover-up	craftswoman	crawler
countless	covet	crafty	crawling
countries	coveted	crag	crayfish
country	coveting	craggier	crayon
countryside	covetous	craggiest	craze
county	cow	craggy	crazier

---

cough
The letters 'gh' can make an 'f' sound, as here; a 'g' sound, as in ghost, or they can be silent, as in 'weigh'.

councillor vs counsellor
A 'councillor' is a person who makes decisions and plans, but a 'counsellor' advises and guides someone.

countries; cranberries; crannies
Many words that end in '-y' take '-ies' in the plural.

courageous
Note that if you add '-ous' to a word ending with a silent '-e', you keep it. It keeps the 'g' sound soft.

A **course** can be a route or a programme of study or medical treatment: 'a course of antibiotics'. 'Coarse' means 'rough' or 'unrefined'.

courtyard; cover-up; cowboy, etc.
Some compounds are joined into one word, such as 'courtyard' and 'cowboy', and others are linked with a hyphen, such as 'cover-up'.

cram → crammed
Notice that you double the final consonant of 'cram' when you add an ending that starts with a vowel. This is a very common spelling pattern in English.

C

craziest	creepy	crises	cross-country
crazily	cremate	crisis	crosser
craziness	cremated	crisp	crosses
crazy	cremating	crisper	crossest
creak	cremation	crispest	cross-examination
creaked	crematoria	criss-cross	cross-examine
creakier	crematorium	criteria	cross-eyed
creakiest	crept	criterion	crossfire
creakily	crescent	critic	cross-hatching
creaking	cress	critical	crossing
cream	crest	critically	crossly
creamy	crested	criticise/criticize	crossness
crease	cresting	criticised/criticized	crossroad
creased	crevice	criticising/criticizing	cross-section
creasing	crew	criticism	crosswind
create	crib	croak	crosswise
created	cribbed	croaked	crossword
creating	cribbing	croaking	crotch
creation	crick	crock	crotches
creative	cricket	crockery	crouch
creatively	cricketer	crocodile	crouched
creator	cried	crocus	crouches
creature	cries	crocuses	crouching
crèche	crime	croissant	crow
credence	criminal	crook	crowbar
credentials	crimson	crooked	crowd
credibility	crinkle	croon	crowded
credible	crinkled	crooned	crowding
credit	crinklier	crooning	crowed
creditable	crinkliest	crop	crowing
creditor	crinkling	cropped	crown
creed	crinkly	cropping	crowned
creek	cripple	cross	crowning
creep	crippled	crossbar	crucial
creeping	crippling	crossbow	crucially

cravat
A 'cravat' is a smart, scarf-like man's tie. It comes from the Serbo-Croat word for a Croat, 'Hrvat'. Croatian soldiers wore cravats in the Thirty Years' War (1618-1648), and gave their name to this kind of tie.

crèche means 'a place where babies are cared for while their parents work'. It is an Old French word for a 'crib', and needs the accent on the first 'e'.

crises; crocuses; crosses; crotches, etc.
Most words ending in an '-s', '-ss', '-ch' or other hissing sounds, take '-es' in the plural.

criteria/criterion
A 'criterion' is a vital component. It's often used in the plural, 'criteria': 'What are the criteria for success?'

croissant
A 'croissant' is a sweet bread roll, which is originally from France. It is crescent-shaped, as the moon can be, and 'croissant' means 'crescent' in French.

crucial
The second 'c' in 'crucial' makes a soft, 'sh' sound, as it's followed by an 'i'. If 'c' comes before a letter other than 'e', 'i' or 'y', it usually makes a hard sound.

C

crucified	crusade	cuffed	curdling
crucifix	crusader	cuffing	cure
crucifixes	crush	cul-de-sac	curfew
crucifixion	crushed	culinary	curiosities
crucify	crushing	cull	curiosity
crucifying	crust	culled	curious
crude	crusty	culling	curiously
crudely	crutch	culminate	curl
cruder	crutches	culminated	curled
crudest	crux	culminating	curlew
cruel	cry	culmination	curling
crueller	crypt	culprit	curly
cruellest	cryptic	cult	currant
cruelly	crystal	cultivate	currencies
cruise	crystallise/	cultivated	currency
cruised	crystallize	cultivating	current
cruiser	crystallised/	cultivation	currently
cruising	crystallized	cultural	curriculum
crumb	crystallising/	culture	curried
crumble	crystallizing	cultured	curries
crumbled	cub	cunning	curry
crumblier	cubbyhole	cunningly	curse
crumbliest	cube	cup	cursed
crumbling	cubed	cupboard	cursing
crumbly	cubic	cupful	cursor
crumpet	cubicle	cupped	curtain
crumple	cuboid	cupping	curtsies
crumpled	cuckoo	curate	curtsy
crumpling	cucumber	curator	curvature
crunch	cuddle	curb	curve
crunches	cuddled	curbed	curved
crunchier	cuddling	curbing	curving
crunchiest	cuddly	curd	cushion
crunching	cue	curdle	cushioned
crunchy	cuff	curdled	cushioning

---

cruising; crumbling; crumpling; cultivating, etc.
Most words that end with a silent '-e' drop it before you add an ending that starts with a vowel.

crumb
Look out for the silent '-b' here. You will usually find one after an 'm' in a word, e.g. 'bomb', 'lamb'.

cryptic means 'with a secret, hidden meaning', and it comes from the Greek word for 'hidden', 'kryptikos'.

cue means 'the time to speak, or do something', but a 'queue' is a line of people waiting their turn: 'The queue for the exhibition went around the corner.'

curb means 'put a limit on something or someone': 'She managed to curb her enthusiasm.' A 'kerb' is the edge of a road or pavement: 'Mind the kerb!'

currant vs current
A 'currant' is a dried grape used in baking, but 'current' means 'up-to-date', and a 'current' is an electrical force, or the direction water is flowing in.

curriculum means 'list' in Latin. A 'curriculum' is what's taught at school, or college. A 'curriculum vitae' is a 'list' of life experiences, sent to employers. The plural can be 'curriculums' or 'curricula'.

C

custard	customized	cutter	cylinder
custodial	customising/	cutting	cylindrical
custody	customizing	cycle	cymbal
custom	cut	cycled	cynic
customarily	cute	cyclic	cynical
customary	cuter	cyclical	cynically
customer	cutest	cycling	cynicism
customise/	cuticle	cyclist	cypher
customize	cutlery	cyclone	cypress
customised/	cutlet	cygnet	cypresses

custard is a sweet yellow sauce served with hot puddings. Take care, as the informal word for 'covered in custard' ('custardy') sounds like 'custody', which means 'given responsibility for': 'She got custody of Fido,' or 'Ben was in police custody.'

cygnet
A 'cygnet' is a young swan, but a 'signet ring' is a ring with a person's initials engraved into it.

cymbal
A 'cymbal' is a flat, metal percussion instrument. A 'symbol' is a sign, such as a tick (✓).

a cycling soldier

Quick tip

'C' or 'S'?
A lot of spellers get confused between the soft 'c' sound, as in 'cycle', and the 's' sound, as in 'soldier', as they sound the same. **If you can't find the word you want on the 'c' pages, check the 's' ones as well** (and the other way round).

Some tricky words to spell that start with a 'c'

Here are some words beginning with 'c' that are particularly tricky to spell. See how many you can get right. There are some tips to help you on page 7.

calendar	coalesce	conscientious
camouflage	coincidence	conscious
campaign	collaborate	conspicuous
canoe	colleague	contagious
carriage	commemorate	controversial
catastrophe	commiserate	convalescence
cauliflower	comparison	courteous
cemetery	comprehend	criticise/criticize
champagne	concede	crucial
character	condemnation	curiosity
choir	conscience	cylinder

Dd

This cow keeps a dairy diary.

Confusing words
Take care not to confuse words that look very similar. For instance, 'dairy' (where cows are milked) looks a lot like 'diary' (a book to write events in).

dab
dabbed
dabbing
dabble
dabbled
dabbling
dachshund
dad
daddies
daddy
daddy-longlegs
daffodil
daft
dafter
daftest
dagger
daily
daintier
daintiest
daintily
dainty
dairies
dairy
daisies
daisy
dam
damage
damaged

damaging
dame
damn
damned
damp
dampen
dampened
dampening
dance
danced
dancer
dancing
dandelion
dandruff
danger
dangerous
dangerously
dangle
dangled
dappled
dare
dared
daredevil
daring
dark
darken
darkened
darkening

darker
darkest
darkly
darkness
darling
darn
darned
darning
dart
darted
darting
dash
dashboard
dashed
dashes
dashing
data
date
dated
dating
daub
daubed
daubing
daughter
daughter-in-law
daughters-in-law
daunt
daunted

daunting
dawn
dawned
dawning
day
daybreak
daydream
daydreamed
daydreamer
daydreaming
daylight
day-to-day
daze
dazed
dazzle
dazzled
dazzling
deacon
deaconess
dead
deadlier
deadliest
deadline
deadlock
deadlocked
deadly
deadpan
deaf

dab → dabbed
You double the final '-b' when adding an ending that starts with a vowel to 'dab'. This happens in words of one syllable that have a short vowel and a consonant.

dabbling; dazzling; debating, etc.
If you add an ending that starts with a vowel to a word ending in a silent '-e', you usually drop the '-e'.

dachshund
This unusual word means 'badger dog' in German, and is the name for a small dog with a long, thin body. Dachshunds are also known as 'sausage dogs'.

dam vs damn
A 'dam' is a barrier built to contain water. To 'damn' means 'to condemn someone', or it can be a mild swear-word.

daughters-in-law
To make 'daughter-in-law' plural, add an '-s' to the main noun, 'daughter'.

dear vs deer
'Dear' can mean 'cherished', or 'expensive'. A 'deer' is an animal that lives in parks or woodlands and is very shy.

999.99

a dear deer

d

deafening	decamp	deceptively	decomposing
deafness	decamped	decibel	decorate
deal	decamping	decide	decorated
dealer	decant	decided	decorating
dealing	decanted	decidedly	decoration
dealt	decanting	deciding	decorator
dear	decapitate	deciduous	decorum
dearer	decapitated	decimal	decoy
dearest	decapitating	decimalisation/	decrease
dearly	decathlon	decimalization	decreased
dearth	decay	decimalise/	decreasing
death	decayed	decimalize	decree
deathly	decaying	decimalised/	decreed
debase	deceased	decimalized	decreeing
debased	deceit	decimalising/	decrepit
debasing	deceitful	decimalizing	dedicate
debatable	deceive	decipher	dedicated
debate	deceived	deciphered	dedicating
debated	deceiving	deciphering	dedication
debating	decelerate	decision	deduce
debilitating	decelerated	decisive	deduct
debit	decelerating	decisively	deducted
debrief	decency	decisiveness	deductible
debriefing	decent	deck	deduction
debris	decently	deckchair	deed
debt	decentralisation/	declaration	deep
debtor	decentralization	declare	deepen
debug	decentralise/	declared	deepened
debugged	decentralize	declaring	deepening
debugging	decentralised/	decline	deeper
début	decentralized	declined	deepest
decade	decentralising/	declining	deeply
decadence	decentralizing	decode	deer
decadent	deception	decompose	deface
decaffeinated	deceptive	decomposed	defaced

debris, which means 'rubble' or 'remains', is pronounced 'deb-ree'. It is originally a French word.

decade; decathlon
Many words beginning with 'dec-' or 'deca-' are to do with '10'. A 'decade' is 10 years, for instance.

decamp
If you see 'de-' before a word, it's often negative. 'Decamp' means 'pack up and move on', for example.

deceit
Notice that 'deceit' follows the pattern: 'i' before 'e' except after 'c', where the letters make the 'ee' sound.

decent means 'good' or 'honest'. Don't confuse it with 'descent', which means 'going down'.

deception; decide, etc.
The letter 'c' is soft, making an 's' sound, when it is followed by an 'e' or an 'i', as in these two words.

decipher
The letters 'ph' are one of four ways of spelling the 'f' sound in English. The other three are 'f', as in 'frog'; 'ff', as in 'giraffe' and 'gh', as in 'cough'.

decorum means 'with good manners' or 'with dignity', and is originally a Latin word.

d

defacing	defiantly	defusing	deleting
default	deficiencies	defy	deletion
defaulted	deficiency	defying	deliberate
defaulting	deficit	degenerate	deliberated
defeat	defies	degenerated	deliberately
defeated	define	degenerating	deliberation
defeating	defined	degeneration	delicacies
defecate	defining	degradation	delicacy
defecated	definite	degrade	delicate
defecating	definition	degraded	delicately
defecation	definitive	degrading	delicatessen
defect	definitively	degree	delicious
defected	deflate	dehydrate	deliciously
defecting	deflated	dehydrated	delight
defection	deflating	dehydrating	delighted
defective	deflation	dehydration	delightful
defector	deflect	de-ice	delightfully
defence	deflected	de-icer	delighting
defenceless	deflecting	deign	delinquent
defend	deflection	deigned	delirious
defendant	deform	deigning	delirium
defended	deformation	deities	deliver
defender	deformed	deity	deliverance
defending	deforming	déjà-vu	delivered
defensible	defraud	dejected	deliveries
defensive	defrauded	dejection	delivering
defensively	defrauding	delay	delivery
defensiveness	defrost	delayed	dell
defer	deft	delaying	delta
deference	defter	delectable	delude
deferential	deftest	delegate	deluded
deferred	deftly	delegated	deluding
deferring	defunct	delegation	deluge
defiance	defuse	delete	deluged
defiant	defused	deleted	deluging

---

defenceless
The ending '-less' does not mean 'less of', it means 'without', so 'defenceless' means 'without defences'.
defensively; definitively; densely
When you add '-ly' to word that ends with an '-e', you usually keep the '-e'. Words that end with '-le', such as 'gentle', drop it, however: 'gently', 'idly'.
definite is often misspelt (usually as 'definate'). To remember the '-nite' at the end, you could try thinking of a silly phrase that begins with the same letters, such as **'not in that egg'.**

defuse
'Defuse' means 'to remove danger from a situation' or 'to stop a bomb exploding', but 'diffuse' means 'widespread' or 'scattered'.
deign means 'lowering yourself to do something', and the letters 'ei' make an 'ai' sound, to rhyme with 'rain'. They can also make an 'ee' sound, as in 'ceiling'.
déjà-vu means 'already seen' in French. It's used to describe the sensation of feeling you've already experienced exactly the same thing before.
delight has a silent 'gh' before the '-t', so take care.

d

delusion
delusional
delve
delved
delving
demand
demanded
demanding
demean
demeaned
demeaning
demeanour
demented
demise
demist
demisted
demisting
demo
democracies
democracy
democrat
democratic
democratically
demographic
demography
demolish
demolished
demolishes
demolishing
demolition
demon
demonic
demonstrate
demonstrated
demonstrating

demonstration
demonstrator
demoralise/
demoralize
demoralised/
demoralized
demoralising/
demoralizing
demote
demoted
demotion
demure
demurely
den
denial
denies
denigrate
denigrated
denigrating
denigration
denim
denomination
denominator
denote
denoted
denoting
denounce
denounced
denouncing
dense
densely
denser
densest
densities
density

dent
dental
dented
denting
dentist
dentistry
denunciation
deny
denying
deodorant
depart
departed
departing
department
departure
depend
dependable
dependant
dependence
dependent
depict
depicted
depicting
depiction
deplorable
deplore
deplored
deploring
deploy
deployed
deploying
deployment
deport
deportation
deported

deportee
deporting
deportment
depose
deposed
deposing
deposit
deposited
depositing
deposition
depot
depraved
depress
depressant
depressed
depressing
depression
deprivation
deprive
deprived
depriving
depth
deputation
deputies
deputise/deputize
deputy
deranged
derelict
deride
derided
deriding
derision
derivation
derive
derived

---

demo is a shortened form of 'demonstration'.
Most languages use abbreviations like this at times.
democracy
A 'democracy' gives people the right to choose their
own laws and rulers. It comes from the Greek words
'demos' (ordinary people), and 'kratos' (power).
demoralise/demoralize; deputise/deputize
You can use an 's' or a 'z' in most words and be
correct, but there's a list of the words that can
only be spelt with one or the other on page 4. These
include 'seize', 'capsize', 'surprise' and 'exercise'.

dependant vs **dependent**
The word 'dependant' is a noun: 'Mrs Jones has
four dependants – her husband and three children.'
'Dependent' is an adjective: 'She is totally dependent
on me.' Take care with the '-ant' and '-ent' endings.
deportee
Words that end with '-ee' often mean 'a person that
something has happened to': a 'deportee' has been
deported and an 'amputee' has had an amputation.
derelict ends in '-ct'. You'll never see '-kt' used
in an English word.

d

deriving
derogatory
descend
descendant
descended
descending
descent
describe
described
describing
description
descriptive
descriptively
desert
deserted
deserting
desertion
deserve
deserved
deserving
design
designate
designated
designation
designed
designing
desirability
desirable
desire
desired
desiring
desist
desisted
desisting
desk

desktop
desolate
desolation
despair
despaired
despairing
despatch
despatched
despatches
despatching
desperate
desperately
desperation
despicable
despicably
despise
despised
despising
despite
despondency
despondent
dessert
destination
destined
destinies
destiny
destitute
destitution
destruction
destructive
destructiveness
desultoriness
desultory
detach
detachable

detached
detaching
detail
detailed
detain
detained
detaining
detect
detectable
detected
detecting
detection
detective
detention
deter
detergent
deteriorate
deteriorated
deteriorating
deterioration
determination
determine
determined
determinedly
determining
deterrence
deterrent
deterring
detest
detestable
detested
detesting
detonate
detonated
detonating

detonator
detour
detract
detracted
detracting
detriment
detrimental
deuce
devaluation
devalue
devalued
devaluing
devastate
devastated
devastating
devastation
develop
developed
developer
developing
development
developmental
developmentally
deviant
deviate
deviated
deviating
device
devil
devious
deviously
deviousness
devise
devised
devising

---

deriving; describing; deserving, etc.
When you add an ending that starts with a vowel to these words ending with a silent '-e', you drop the '-e'.
descent means 'downward journey' but 'decent' means 'good', 'honest'. Take care not to mix them up.
desert *vs* dessert
'Desert' can mean either 'a big, sandy area' or 'to abandon someone'. A 'dessert' is a pudding.
design; designate
In 'design', the 'g' is silent, but in 'designate', which means 'to allot a task to someone', you say 'des-ig-nate'.

despatches
Remember that words that end with '-tch', '-s', '-ss', '-x' or '-z' usually take '-es' in the plural.
desultoriness
When you add '-ness' to a word of more than one syllable ending in a '-y', you change the 'y' to an 'i'.
device *vs* devise
A 'device' is a tool or implement, but to 'devise' something is to invent it: 'We devised the game.'
dew is droplets of water on the ground in the morning. 'Due' means 'expected': 'The train is due.'

d

devoid	diary	diffusing	din
devolution	dice	diffusion	diner
devote	diced	dig	dinghies
devoted	dicing	digest	dinghy
devoting	dictate	digested	dingier
devotion	dictated	digestible	dingiest
devotional	dictating	digesting	dingo
devour	dictation	digestion	dingoes
devoured	dictator	digger	dingy
devouring	dictatorial	digging	dinner
devout	diction	digit	dinosaur
devoutly	dictionaries	digital	dint
dew	dictionary	digitally	diocese
dexterity	did	dignified	dip
dextrous	die	dignify	diploma
diabolical	died	dignity	diplomacy
diagnose	dies	dilapidated	diplomat
diagnosed	diesel	dilapidation	diplomatically
diagnosing	diet	dilemma	dipped
diagnosis	dietary	diligence	dipping
diagnostic	dietician	diligent	dire
diagonal	differ	diligently	direct
diagonally	difference	dilute	directed
diagram	different	diluted	directing
diagrammatic	differentiate	diluting	direction
dial	differentiation	dimension	director
dialect	differently	diminish	directorate
dialled	differing	diminished	directorial
dialling	difficult	diminishes	directories
dialogue	difficulties	diminishing	directory
diameter	difficulty	diminution	direr
diamond	diffident	diminutive	direst
diaries	diffidently	diminutively	dirge
diarist	diffuse	dimple	dirt
diarrhoea	diffused	dimpled	dirtier

dial → dialled
When you add an ending that starts with a vowel to a word ending in '-l', you double the 'l'.

die
To 'die' means 'to stop living', but to 'dye' is to use pigment to colour things. You keep the final '-e' when you add to 'dye': 'dyeing', but 'die' becomes 'dying'.

dietician
The ending '-cian', pronounced 'shan', implies a professional person. A 'dietician' is an expert on diet, and an 'optician' cares for eyes, for instance.

diffuse
'Diffuse' means 'widespread' or 'scattered' but 'defuse' means 'to remove danger or stress from a situation', or 'to stop a bomb from exploding'.

dig → digging; dip → dipped
Notice that when you add an ending that starts with a vowel to 'dig' or 'dip', you double the '-g' or the '-p'.

dingoes
Most words ending in '-o' just add an '-s' in the plural, but some, including 'dingoes' (wild dogs of Australia), 'tomatoes', 'potatoes' and 'echoes', add '-es'.

d

'dis-' at the beginning of a word **often gives that word a negative meaning**. To be disadvantaged means 'not to have advantages or chances'; to disagree means 'not to agree' and to disapprove means 'not to approve', for example.

dirtiest	disaster	disconcerted	discriminate
dirtiness	disastrous	disconcerting	discriminated
dirty	disastrously	disconnect	discriminating
disabilities	disband	disconnected	discrimination
disability	disbanded	disconnecting	discriminatory
disadvantage	disbanding	disconnection	discus
disadvantaged	disc/disk	discontent	discuss
disadvantageous	discard	discontented	discussed
disaffected	discarded	discontentedly	discussing
disagree	discarding	discontinue	discussion
disagreeable	discern	discontinued	disdain
disagreement	discerned	discontinuing	disdainful
disappear	discernible	discord	disease
disappearance	discerning	discount	diseased
disappeared	discharge	discounted	disembark
disappoint	discharged	discounting	disembarked
disappointed	discharging	discourage	disembarking
disappointing	disciple	discouraged	disembodied
disappointment	discipline	discouragement	disenchanted
disapproval	disciplined	discouraging	disfigure
disapprove	disciplining	discourse	disfigured
disapproved	disclose	discoursed	disfiguring
disapproving	disclosed	discoursing	disgrace
disarm	disclosing	discover	disgraced
disarmament	disclosure	discoverable	disgraceful
disarmed	disco	discovered	disgracefully
disarming	discomfort	discovering	disgracing
disarray	disconcert	discovery	disguise
		discredit	disguised
		discredited	disguising
		discrediting	disgust
		discreet	disgusted
		discrete	disgusting
		discretion	dish
		discretionary	disheartened

disadvantageous
When you add '-ous' to a word that ends in '-ge', such as 'disadvantage' or 'outrage', you keep the '-e'.
disagreement; disappointment, etc.
Adding the ending '-ment' doesn't change how most words are spelt. ('Disarmament' is an exception.)
disapproving; discharging; disclosing, etc.
If you add '-ing' to a word that ends in a silent '-e', you usually need to drop the '-e'.
discern
Notice the 'sc' in this word, pronounced 'ss'.

disc/disk
A 'disc' is a flat, round thing, such as a CD (compact disc). Computers take discs (which can also be spelt 'disks'). There's a list of 'computing words' on page 204.
discreet vs discrete
'Discreet' means 'tactful and sensitive', but 'discrete', pronounced the same, means 'separate' or 'complete'.
discus vs discuss
A 'discus' is a flat round object that athletes throw in a competition. 'Discuss' means 'to talk about': "Shall we discuss the matter privately?"

d

dishes
dishevelled
dishonest
dishonesty
disillusioned
disillusionment
disinfectant
disintegrate
disintegrated
disintegrating
disintegration
disinterest
disinterested
disjointed
dislike
disliked
disliking
dislocate
dislocated
dislocating
dislocation
dislodge
dislodged
dislodging
dismal
dismally
dismantle
dismantled
dismantling
dismay
dismayed
dismaying
dismember
dismembered
dismembering

dismiss
dismissal
dismissed
dismissing
dismissive
dismissively
disobey
disobeyed
disobeying
disorder
disordered
disordering
disorganisation/
disorganization
disorganised/
disorganized
disown
disowned
disowning
disparagement
disparaging
disparate
disparities
disparity
dispatch
dispatched
dispatches
dispatching
dispel
dispelled
dispelling
dispensaries
dispensary
dispense
dispensed

dispenser
dispensing
dispersal
disperse
dispersed
dispersing
displace
displaced
displacement
displacing
display
displayed
displaying
displease
displeased
displeasing
displeasure
disposable
disposal
dispose
disposed
disposing

disprove
disproved
disproving
dispute
disputed
disputing
disqualification
disqualified
disqualifies
disqualify
disquiet
disquieting
disregard
disregarded
disregarding
disrepair
disrespect
disrespectful
disrupt
disrupted
disrupting
disruption

'-able' *and* '-ible'

It's easy to mix up these endings, as they sound similar and have almost the same meaning: 'able to' or 'do-able'. **Try seeing if the word makes sense without the ending.**

– If it does make sense, it's likely to be '-able'. For example, 'disagree' makes sense without the '-able' of **disagreeable**.

– If it doesn't make sense without the ending, it's more likely to be '-ible'. 'Poss' (in 'possible') is not a word without '-ible', for instance.

However, **discernible** breaks this rule, so always check words with these endings.

disgraceful; disgracefully
When you add '-ful' or '-fully' to a word that ends in a silent '-e', you keep the '-e': 'hateful', 'shamefully'.

disguise
The letters 'ui' can cause problems. Here, they make a long 'i' sound, but they can make a short 'i' sound, as in 'guilt', or a 'wi' sound, as in 'anguish'.

disillusionment, meaning 'the feeling of seeing through something, and being disappointed in it', is very tricky to spell. Try breaking it down into parts - 'dis-ill-u-sion-ment', to help you remember each letter.

dismal
In medieval times, some people believed that two days of each month were 'unlucky'. The word 'dismal' (sad, or gloomy), is from the Latin for 'evil days', 'dies mali'.

disparities; dispensaries, etc.
Note that the '-y' changes to '-ies' in the plural.

dispelled
When adding an ending that starts with a vowel to a word that ends in a vowel and an '-l', double the 'l'.

disqualify; disquiet, etc.
You'll find that a 'q' is always followed by a 'u'.

d

54

ditto

This is the mark („). **It means 'the same as is written above'.** People often say 'ditto' if they agree with what you've just said:
"I get travel sick a lot," said Ali.
"Ditto," answered Sam, miserably.

disruptive
dissatisfaction
dissatisfied
dissect
dissected
dissecting
dissection
dissent
dissented
dissenting
dissertation
disservice
dissident
dissimilar
dissipate
dissipated
dissipation
dissolution
dissolve
dissolved
dissolving
distance
distant
distil
distillation
distilled
distilleries
distillery

distilling
distinct
distinctive
distinctively
distinctly
distinguish
distinguishable
distinguished
distinguishing
distort
distorted
distorting
distract
distracted
distracting
distraction
distraught
distress
distressed
distressing
distribute
distributed
distributing
distribution
distributor
district
distrust
distrusted

distrustful
distrusting
disturb
disturbed
disturbing
ditch
ditches
dither
dithered
dithering
ditto
diva
dive
dived
diver
diverge
divergent
diverse
diversification
diversifies
diversify
diversion
diversity
divert
diverted
diverting
divide
divided
dividend
dividing
divine
divined
diving
divining
divinities

divinity
division
divisional
divisive
divorce
divorcé
divorced
divorcée
divorcing
dizzier
dizziest
dizzy
do
docile
dock
docked
docker
docking
doctor
doctoral
doctored
doctoring
doctrinal
doctrine
document
documentaries
documentary
documentation
documented
documenting
dodge
dodged
dodging
dodgy
dodo

diva

Words ending in an '-a' are all from other languages. A 'diva' is a female show business idol, and is the Latin for 'goddess'.

divorcé; divorcée

A man who is divorced is a 'divorcé'. A divorced woman is a 'divorcée'. This follows a French spelling pattern, as 'divorce' comes from a French word.

a doe makes dough

doe vs dough

A 'doe' is the female of several species of animal, including deer, rabbits and mice. 'Dough' is the mixture of yeast, sugar and flour used to make bread.

does

The plural of 'doe' is 'does', and rhymes with 'goes'. 'Does', when it's pronounced to rhyme with 'buzz', is part of the verb 'to do'. Take care with these words.

doldrums

To be 'in the doldrums' means 'to lack energy'. The doldrums are a calm area of ocean near the Equator.

d

doe	don	double	downloaded
does	donate	double-cross	downloading
dog	donated	double-crossed	downpour
dog-eared	donating	double-crossing	downright
dogged	donation	doubled	downsize
dogma	done	double-decker	downsizing
dogmatic	donkey	doubling	downstairs
dogmatically	donned	doubly	downstream
dogmatism	donning	doubt	down-to-earth
doing	donor	doubted	downtrodden
doldrums	doodle	doubtful	downturn
dole	doodled	doubtfully	downward
doled	doodling	doubting	downwards
doling	doom	dough	downwind
doll	doomed	doughnut	dowries
dollar	doomsday	dour	dowry
dollop	door	douse	doze
dolorous	doorway	doused	dozed
dolphin	dope	dousing	dozen
domain	doped	dove	dozing
dome	doping	dovetail	dozy
domed	dormant	dovetailed	drab
domestic	dormitory	dovetailing	drabber
domesticated	dormouse	dowager	drabbest
domesticity	dosage	dowdier	drably
dominance	dose	dowdiest	drabness
dominant	dosed	dowdy	draft
dominate	dosing	down	drafted
dominated	dossier	downcast	drafting
dominating	dot	downfall	drag
domination	dote	downgrade	dragged
domineering	doted	downgraded	dragging
dominion	doting	downgrading	dragon
domino	dotted	downhill	dragonflies
dominoes	dotting	download	dragonfly

domestic; domesticated; domesticity
These words are all to do with the home, and how we live, as they are based on the Latin word 'domus', which means 'house' or 'home'.

doubt
Look out for the silent 'b' in 'doubt'.

dove
Remember that 'v' is always followed by a vowel or a 'y'.

down-to-earth means 'sensible' or 'balanced'.
Many compound words mean exactly what they say. Others, like this one, have a more subtle meaning.

downward; downwards
These words are often interchangeable, and can be either adjectives ('The downward journey was very steep'), or adverbs ('He fell downwards').

dowries; dragonflies, etc.
Don't forget that words which have a consonant before the final '-y' change to '-ies' in the plural.

draft
A 'draft' is a rough written version of something. A 'draught' is a cold breeze. 'Draughts' is a board game played with black and white counters.

d

drain	dreading	drinkable	drowsy
drainage	dreadlocks	drinker	drug
drained	dream	drinking	drugged
draining	dreamed/dreamt	drip	drum
drainpipe	dreamer	dripped	drummed
drake	dreaming	dripping	drummer
drama	dreamy	drive	drumming
dramatic	drearier	drivel	drumstick
dramatically	dreariest	driven	drunk
dramatist	dreary	driver	dry
drank	dregs	driving	dry-clean
drape	drench	drizzle	dry-cleaned
draped	drenched	drizzled	dry-cleaning
draping	drenches	drizzling	dryer
drastic	drenching	drone	dryness
drastically	dress	droned	dual
draught	dressed	droning	dub
draughtier	dresser	drool	dubbed
draughtiest	dressing	drooled	dubbing
draughtsman	dressmaker	drooling	dubious
draughtsmen	drew	droop	dubiously
draughty	dribble	drooped	duchess
draw	dribbled	drooping	duchesses
drawback	dribbling	drop	duchies
drawbridge	dried	droplet	duchy
drawer	drier	dropped	duck
drawing	dries	dropping	ducked
drawl	drift	drought	ducking
drawled	drifted	drove	duckling
drawling	drifting	drown	duct
drawn	driftwood	drowned	dud
dread	drill	drowning	due
dreaded	drilled	drowsier	duel
dreadful	drilling	drowsiest	duet
dreadfully	drink	drowsiness	dug

She draws drawers.

draught
A 'draught' is a chilly breeze. 'Draughts' is a board game. A 'draft' is a rough written version of a document.

draw vs drawer
To 'draw' means 'to create pictures'. A 'drawer' is a box that slots into a chest for storing things.

dreamed/dreamt
You might see either of these spellings for the past tense of 'dream': 'Last night, I dreamed/dreamt about chocolate.' Both of them are correct.

dregs means 'scrapings' or 'leftovers', and is always used in the plural: 'She drank the dregs of the wine.'

drilled; dripped
If you're unsure whether to double the consonant in a word, say it aloud. 'Driled' would rhyme with 'piled', and 'driped' with 'wiped', which don't sound right. It's not foolproof, but it's a tip worth trying.

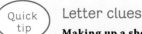 **Quick tip**

Letter clues

Making up a short saying with some of the letters in a word can help you remember it. This technique works even better if the saying has something to do with the meaning of the word. For instance:

- To remember the **double 'r'** in **'deterrent'** (something stopping you from doing wrong) think:

'rarely right'

- To remember the **'astr'** in the middle of the word **'disastrous'** (something terrible, or very wrong) try thinking :

'a sad thing really'

Keep a list of words you find especially tricky to spell, and then add short sayings that help you remember them. Experts say that this technique can help 'fix' the spelling of a word in your memory, so see if it works for you.

dugong	dune	dusk	dwell
dugout	dung	dusky	dwelled/dwelt
duke	dungarees	dust	dwelling
dull	dungeon	dustbin	dwindle
duller	dunk	dusted	dwindled
dullest	dunked	duster	dwindling
dullness	dunking	dustier	dye
dully	duo	dusting	dyed
duly	dupe	dustman	dyeing
dumb	duped	dusty	dying
dumber	duping	duties	dyke
dumbest	duplicate	dutiful	dynamic
dumbfounded	duplicated	dutifully	dynamically
dummies	duplicating	duty	dynamite
dummy	duplication	duty-free	dynamo
dump	durability	duvet	dynastic
dumped	durable	dwarf	dynasties
dumping	duration	dwarfed	dynasty
dumpling	duress	dwarfing	dyslexia
dunce	during	dwarfs/dwarves	dyslexic

droplet
The ending '-let' usually means 'small' or 'very young'. A 'droplet' is a small drop, a 'notelet' is a small note, and a 'piglet' is a baby pig.

dual *vs* **duel**
'Dual' means 'something that does two things at once, or has two parts': 'His car has dual control.' A 'duel' is a fight between two people.

due
'Due' means 'expected' ('Bob is due now'), but 'dew' is droplets of water on the ground in the morning.

dungarees
This word comes from rough, cheap cloth called 'dungri' that was used to make workers' clothes in an area of India.

dwarfs or **dwarves** is the plural of 'dwarf'. See page 5 for other words that follow this pattern.

A **dye** is a pigment used to change the colour of something. To 'die' is to stop living.

dyslexia comes from two Greek words, meaning 'bad' and 'words'. People who are 'dyslexic' find spelling difficult, and need specialist teaching.

Plurals

Quick tip

Making a word plural can sometimes cause spellers problems, as there are several ways of doing it and it can be hard to know which word does what. (You can find out more about plurals on page 5.)

Words that just add an '-s'
Most words just add an '-s' to become plural. If a plural spelling isn't listed in this dictionary, you can assume that it is made by adding an '-s'.

Words ending in '-y'
Words that end in a vowel and '-y' add an '-s', as in 'monkeys' and 'turkeys'. Words with a consonant before the '-y' take '-ies', so 'pony' becomes 'ponies', for example.

Words ending in '-o'
Words ending in '-o' usually add '-s', especially if there's a vowel before the '-o', so 'video' becomes 'videos'.

Words ending in '-o' that add '-es'
If a word has a consonant before the final '-o', as 'potato' and 'tomato' do, you often need to add '-es' to make the plural: 'potatoes'; 'tomatoes'. These plurals are often misspelt.

Words ending in an '-f'
Many words that end in an '-f' or '-fe' add '-s' in the plural, but some words change the 'f' to a 'v' and then add '-es', as 'elf' becomes 'elves'. A few words can follow either spelling pattern and still be correct, such as 'dwarfs/dwarves' and 'scarfs/scarves'.

Always check your spellings if you are unsure.

Some tricky words to spell that start with a 'd'

Here are some words beginning with 'd' that can be tricky to spell. See how many of them you can get right. There are some tips to help you on page 7.

daughter	desperate	disappear
debt	despondent	disastrous
decapitate	detach	discern
deciduous	deterrent	discretion
decrepit	deuce	disillusionment
definite	device	disintegrate
deflect	devise	disparaging
degenerate	diagnosis	dissimilar
delicious	differentiate	distinguish
demeanour	digital	divergent
denunciation	diminutive	dosage
derogatory	dinghy	dumb

Ee

Don't wear cookware, anywhere!

'-ware'
This ending on a word means **a kind of product**. Don't mix it up with 'wear' ('I wear clothes'), or 'where' ('Where are we?'). Earthenware describes things made of a particular type of clay, for instance.

e

each	earthworm	ebullient	edgiest
eager	earthy	eccentric	edging
eagerly	earwig	eccentrically	edgy
eagerness	ease	eccentricities	edible
eagle	eased	eccentricity	edibly
ear	easel	ecclesiastical	edifice
earache	easier	echelon	edit
earlier	easiest	echo	edited
earliest	easily	echoes	editing
early	easing	echoing	edition
earmark	east	eclipse	editor
earmarked	easterly	ecological	editorial
earmarking	eastern	ecologically	editorially
earn	eastward	ecologist	editorship
earned	eastwards	ecology	educate
earner	easy	economic	educated
earnest	eat	economically	educating
earnestly	eaten	economics	education
earning	eating	ecosystem	educational
earphones	eave	ecstasies	educationally
earring	eavesdrop	ecstasy	educator
earshot	eavesdropped	ecstatic	eel
earth	eavesdropping	ecstatically	eerie
earthenware	ebb	eddies	eerier
earthier	ebbed	eddy	eeriest
earthiest	ebbing	edge	eeriness
earthly	ebony	edged	effect
earthquake	ebullience	edgier	effective

e

e.g.

If you need to write 'for example', you can write 'e.g.' instead: 'That vet only treats small animals, *e.g.* cats and dogs.' It comes from the Latin words 'exempli gratia', which mean 'for the sake of example'.

effectively	ejecting	electrically	eliminated
effectiveness	ejection	electrician	eliminating
effeminate	elaborate	electricity	elimination
effervescence	elaborated	electrification	elite
effervescent	elaborately	electrified	elitist
efficiency	elaborating	electrifies	elk
efficient	elaboration	electrify	elm
efficiently	elastic	electrifying	elocution
effort	elasticity	electrocute	eloquence
effortless	elated	electrocuted	eloquent
effortlessly	elatedly	electrocuting	eloquently
egalitarian	elation	electrocution	elsewhere
egalitarianism	elbow	electronic	elude
egg	elbowed	electronically	eluded
ego	elbowing	electronics	eluding
egocentric	elder	elegance	elusive
egocentrically	elderberries	elegant	elves
egocentricity	elderberry	elegantly	email
eight	elderly	element	emailed
eighteen	eldest	elementary	emailing
eighteenth	elect	elephant	emancipate
eighth	elected	elevate	emancipated
eighthly	electing	elevated	emancipating
eightieth	election	elevating	emancipation
eighty	electoral	elevation	embankment
either	electorate	elevator	embark
eject	electric	eleven	embarkation
ejected	electrical	eleventh	embarked
		elf	embarking
		elicit	embarrass
		elicited	embarrassed
		eliciting	embarrassing
		eligibility	embarrassment
		eligible	embassies
		eliminate	embassy

ego is Latin for 'I', so words beginning with 'ego-' are usually to do with the self. Your 'ego' is your view of yourself and your worth, and you are 'egocentric' if you focus on yourself more than anyone else.

eight
You usually find a silent 'gh' before a 't', as here in 'eight', and in 'daughter' and 'sight', for example.

elaborating; electrocuting; elevating, etc.
Most words that end with an '-e' drop it when you add an ending that starts with a vowel, such as '-ing'. Remember: 'Drop the '-e' when you add '-ing'.'

electrifying
When you add an ending that begins with an 'i' to a word that ends with a '-y', you keep the 'y'. Many words follow this spelling pattern.

elf/elves
The final '-f' of 'elf' changes to '-ves' in the plural. There are lists of other words that follow this pattern, just add an '-s', or can be spelt either way, on page 5.

elicit means 'to extract': 'He elicited the truth.' The word 'illicit' means 'illegal': 'They made illicit alcohol.' Make sure you use the right word.

e

embed	empathetic	encircle	endorsement
embedded	empathy	encircled	endorsing
embedding	emperor	encircling	endowed
embers	emphasis	enclave	endowment
emblem	emphasise/	enclose	endurance
embrace	emphasize	enclosed	endure
embraced	emphasised/	enclosing	endured
embracing	emphasized	enclosure	enduring
embroider	emphasising/	encore	enemies
embroidered	emphasizing	encounter	enemy
embroideries	emphatic	encountered	energetic
embroidering	emphatically	encountering	energetically
embroidery	empire	encourage	energies
embryo	employ	encouraged	energy
emerald	employed	encouragement	enforce
emerge	employer	encouraging	enforceable
emerged	employing	encyclopaedia/	enforced
emergencies	employment	encyclopedia	enforcement
emergency	empress	encyclopaedic/	enforcing
emerging	emptier	encyclopedic	engage
emigrant	emptiest	end	engaged
emigrate	emptily	endanger	engagement
emigrated	emptiness	endangered	engaging
emigrating	empty	endangering	engine
emigration	emu	endear	engineer
eminence	emulsion	endeared	engineered
eminent	enable	endearing	engineering
eminently	enabled	endearingly	engrave
emission	enabling	endearment	engraved
emit	enamel	ended	engraver
emitted	encampment	ending	engraving
emitting	enchant	endless	engross
emotion	enchanted	endlessly	engrossed
emotional	enchanting	endorse	engrossing
emotionally	enchantment	endorsed	engulf

eligible means 'entitled to' or 'suitable for' something: 'He is eligible for a bus pass.' 'Illegible' means 'unreadable': 'The note was written in an illegible scrawl.'

embedded; emitted
Notice that the final consonant in these words is doubled when you add an ending that starts with a vowel, such as '-ed'.

An emigrant is a person who is leaving a country. An 'immigrant' is a person who is entering it.

empty → emptiness
When you add '-ness' to a two-syllable word that ends in a '-y', you usually change the 'y' to an 'i'.

encore is French for 'more'. It's pronounced 'on-kor'. In Britain, audiences shout it when they think a show or performer was exceptionally good.

encouragement; engagement
When adding an ending that starts with a consonant, such as '-ment', to a word ending in '-ge', '-ce', '-se' or '-te', you usually keep the silent '-e'.

enforceable keeps the silent '-e' when you add '-able'.

e

engulfed	enriching	entrant	epigraph
engulfing	enrichment	entreat	episode
enhance	ensemble	entreated	episodic
enhanced	ensue	entreaties	epistle
enhancement	ensued	entreating	epitaph
enhancing	ensuing	entreaty	epithet
enigma	ensure	entrepreneur	epitome
enigmatic	ensured	entries	epoch
enigmatically	ensuring	entrust	equal
enjoy	entangle	entrusted	equalities
enjoyable	entangled	entrusting	equality
enjoyed	entanglement	entry	equalled
enjoying	entangling	envelop	equalling
enlarge	enter	envelope	equally
enlarged	entered	enveloped	equate
enlargement	entering	enveloping	equated
enlarging	enterprise	enviable	equating
enlist	enterprising	enviably	equation
enlisted	entertain	envies	equator
enlisting	entertained	envious	equatorial
enmity	entertainer	enviously	equestrian
enormity	entertaining	environment	equilibrium
enormous	entertainment	environmental	equinox
enormously	enthusiasm	environmentalist	equinoxes
enough	enthusiast	envisage	equip
enquire	enthusiastic	envisaged	equipment
enquired	entire	envisaging	equipped
enquiries	entirety	envoy	equipping
enquiring	entitle	envy	equivalence
enquiry	entitled	envying	equivalent
enrage	entitlement	ephemeral	era
enraged	entitling	epic	eradicate
enraging	entrance	epidemic	eradicated
enrich	entranced	epigram	eradicating
enriched	entrancing	epigrammatic	eradication

---

enigma means 'something or someone mysterious'.
It comes from the Latin 'aenigma', meaning 'riddle'.

enquiries; entreaties; entries; equalities, etc.
Remember that most words that end in a consonant
and a '-y' change to '-ies' when they become plural.

An enquiry is a question, but an 'inquiry' is usually
a more formal investigation, e.g. 'a police inquiry'.

entrepreneur
This means 'someone who makes bold business
decisions'. It's from a French word, 'entreprendre',
which means 'to undertake to do something'.

environment
Take care not to forget the 'n' in 'environment'. Try
thinking 'natural matter' to help you remember 'nm'.

equinoxes
Words that end in '-x', '-s', '-ch' or other hissing
sounds nearly always end in '-es' in the plural.
'Oxen', the plural of 'ox', is an exception, however.

ermine (pronounced 'er-min') is a luxurious white
fur. Notice, however, that the silent '-e' on the end
of it does not make the 'i' sound long, as it does
in 'line', 'mine', 'time' and many other words.

e

erase	escaped	eternal	evading
erased	escapee	eternally	evaluate
erasing	escaping	eternities	evaluated
erasure	escapism	eternity	evaluating
erect	escapist	ether	evaluation
erected	escort	ethereal	evanescence
erecting	escorted	ethereally	evanescent
erection	escorting	ethical	evangelical
ermine	especially	ethically	evangelism
erode	espionage	ethics	evangelist
eroded	espouse	ethnic	evaporate
eroding	espoused	ethnically	evaporated
erosion	espousing	ethnicity	evaporating
erotic	espresso	etymology	evaporation
erotically	essay	eucalyptus	evasion
eroticism	essence	euphemism	evasive
err	essential	euphemistic	evasiveness
erratic	essentially	euphemistically	eve
erratically	establish	euro	even
erred	established	evacuate	evened
erring	establishing	evacuated	evening
erroneous	establishment	evacuating	evenly
error	estate	evacuation	evenness
erudite	esteem	evacuee	event
erudition	estimate	evade	eventful
erupt	estimated	evaded	eventfully
erupted	estimating		
erupting	estimation		
eruption	estranged		
escalate	estrangement		
escalated	estuaries		
escalating	estuary		
escalator	etch		
escapade	etched		
escape	etching		

etymology is the study of words, where they come from and how they change over time. English contains words from many languages, including Latin, Greek, French, German, Italian, Hindi, Dutch and Malay. The Greek word 'etymos' means 'true'. The ending '-ology' means 'to do with an area of study', and is from another Greek word, 'logia', which means 'the study of'.

err; erratic; error, etc.
These words are all to do with making mistakes. They come from the Latin word 'erro', which means 'to wander' or 'go the wrong way'.

error; erupt
One 'r' sounds exactly the same as a double 'r' in a word, as 'error' and 'erupt' show. You just have to learn which words have one 'r', and which have two.

escapee; evacuee
Words ending in '-ee' often mean 'a person who has done something, or has had it done to them', as here.

espresso is an Italian word for very strong coffee made by forcing hot water through tightly-compressed ground coffee.

evanescence; evanescent
The ending '-scence' means 'a state of being': 'The star's evanescence was breathtaking.' 'Evanescent' is an adjective: 'The vision was evanescent.'

even → evenness
Notice that you keep the final '-n' when you add the ending '-ness'. If you add '-ness' to a word that ends in '-y', you change it to an 'i': 'lonely → loneliness'.

eventual	exacerbating	excelling	excursion
eventualities	exact	except	excusable
eventuality	exactly	exception	excusably
eventually	exactness	exceptional	excuse
ever	exaggerate	exceptionally	excused
evergreen	exaggerated	excerpt	excusing
everlasting	exaggerating	excess	execute
evermore	exaggeration	excesses	executed
every	exalt	excessive	executing
everybody	exaltation	excessively	execution
everyday	exalted	exchange	executioner
everyone	exalting	exchanged	executive
everything	exam	exchanging	exemplary
everywhere	examination	excitable	exempt
evict	examine	excitably	exemption
evicted	examined	excited	exercise
evicting	examiner	excitedly	exercised
eviction	examining	excitement	exercising
evidence	example	exciting	exert
evident	exasperate	exclaim	exerted
evidently	exasperated	exclaimed	exertion
evil	exasperating	exclaiming	exhalation
evilly	exasperation	exclamation	exhale
evocation	excavate	exclamatory	exhaled
evoke	excavated	exclude	exhaling
evoked	excavating	excluded	exhaust
evoking	excavation	excluding	exhausted
evolution	exceed	exclusion	exhausting
evolutionary	exceeded	exclusive	exhaustion
evolve	exceeding	exclusively	exhibit
evolved	exceedingly	excrement	exhibited
evolving	excel	excrete	exhibiting
ewe	excelled	excreted	exhibition
exacerbate	excellence	excreting	exhibitor
exacerbated	excellent	excretion	exhort

---

eventually; evilly; exceptionally, etc.
You keep the final '-l' of a word when you add '-ly'
to make it into an adverb: 'She arrived eventually.'

eviction; evolution; exclusion; excursion, etc.
Many nouns end with '-tion', which is pronounced
'shun'. Take care not to mix it up with the ending
'-sion', however, which sounds the same.
A ewe is a female sheep. 'You' means 'not me'.

'ex-'
If you see 'ex-' (with a hyphen) in front of a word, it
means 'former': 'ex-wife'. Don't forget the hyphen.

except vs excerpt
The word 'except' means 'excluding': 'The children
had all eaten, except Ella.' An 'excerpt' is a small
part of a longer piece of music or writing: 'We read
an excerpt from *Alice in Wonderland*.'

excitably; exclusively; excusably; expensively
Words that end in '-le' drop the 'e' when you add a
'-y', as in 'excitably' or 'excusably'. Words that end in
a silent '-e' without an 'l' usually keep it: 'exclusively',
'expensively'. These are all adverbs that describe how
things are done: 'She ate exclusively at The Ritz.'

e

exhorted	expense	explorer	externally
exhorting	expensive	exploring	extinct
exile	expensively	explosion	extinction
exiled	experience	explosive	extinguish
exiling	experienced	export	extinguished
exist	experiencing	exported	extinguishing
existed	experiment	exporter	extort
existence	experimental	exporting	extorted
existing	experimentally	expose	extorting
exit	experimentation	exposed	extortion
exited	expert	exposing	extortionate
exiting	expertise	exposure	extortionately
exorcism	expertly	express	extra
exorcist	expire	expressed	extract
exorcise/exorcize	expired	expressing	extracted
exorcised/exorcized	expiring	expression	extracting
exorcising/exorcizing	expiry	expressive	extraction
exotic	explain	expressively	extraordinarily
exotically	explained	expulsion	extraordinary
expand	explaining	exquisite	extraterrestrial
expanded	explanation	exquisitely	extravagance
expanding	explanatory	exquisiteness	extravagant
expanse	explicit	extend	extravagantly
expansion	explicitly	extended	extravaganza
expect	explode	extending	extreme
expectant	exploded	extension	extremely
expectantly	exploding	extensive	extremism
expectation	exploit	extensively	extremist
expected	exploitation	extent	extremities
expecting	exploited	exterior	extremity
expedition	exploiting	exterminate	extricate
expel	exploration	exterminated	extricated
expelled	exploratory	exterminating	extrovert
expelling	explore	extermination	exuberance
expenditure	explored	external	exuberant

exhale; exit; extrovert, etc.
Many words beginning with 'ex' (with no hyphen) have
something to do with 'out' or 'away'. To 'exhale' means
'to breathe out'; an 'exit' is a way out, and an 'extrovert'
is an outward-looking and confident person.

explode → explosion
Look at how the verb 'explode' changes when it becomes
a noun. Many words follow this pattern, e.g. 'collide'
becomes 'collision' and 'deride' becomes 'derision'.

exquisite
Remember that a 'q' is always followed by a 'u'.

exterminate means 'to wipe out' or 'destroy'.
It's based on the Latin verb 'exterminare',
which means 'to drive out'.

extraordinary; extraterrestrial; extravagant
Words that start with 'extra' are often to do with
things that are unusual, as the Latin 'extra' means
'outside' or 'beyond'. For example, 'extraordinary'
means 'beyond ordinary', and 'extraterrestrial'
means 'beyond the Earth'.

extravaganza is an Italian word for 'extravagance'.
Only words from other languages end in an '-a'.

e

exuberantly	eyeball	eyeing	eyesight
exude	eyeballed	eyelash	eyesore
exuded	eyeballing	eyelashes	eyewitness
exuding	eyebrow	eyelid	eyewitnesses
eye	eyed	eyepiece	eyrie

eyeball; eyebrow; eyeing, etc.
When you add to words that end in '-ye', they stay the same, and keep the final '-e'. This rule also applies to words ending in '-oe' ('hoeing') and '-ee' ('fleeing').

eyelashes; eyewitnesses
Remember that words that end in '-sh', '-ss' or other hissing sounds add '-es' when they become plural. Just adding an '-s', as many other words do, would make them difficult to pronounce.

An eyrie is the nest of a bird of prey, such as an eagle. 'Eerie' means 'spooky': 'The house was eerie.'

an eerie eyrie

etc.
For a list of similar things, you can write 'etc.'. It means 'and the rest'. For example: 'He loves sport - football, tennis, *etc.*' It's a shortened version of 'et cetera', which is rarely written, so is not in the word list. Don't forget the (.) after the 'c' though.

Quick tip

Word families
It's a good idea to **think of words that have the same 'root' as word families**. For instance, many of the words at the top of this page have 'eye' in them, so making sure you spell that 'root' part correctly will help you spell all the other words in that word family.

Some tricky words to spell that start with an 'e'

Here are some words beginning with 'e' that are particularly tricky to spell correctly. See how many of them you can get right. There are some tips to help you on page 7.

ebullient	enormous	exhibition
eccentric	ensure	expense
echo	envelop	extension
edge	envisage	exterior
effervescence	erroneous	extinct
eighth	euphemism	extinguish
elasticity	excel	extortion
eloquence	exercise	extrovert
embarrass	exhaustion	exuberant

Try looking for words that start with an 'f' sound on the 'ph' pages if you can't find them here.

fable — fang

Ff

Felix's fad for vintage fashion was beginning to fade.

fad; fade
Adding '-e' to a word can change both its sound and its meaning. For instance, 'fad' (a short-lived craze) has a short 'a' sound, and 'fade' (get weaker), a long one.

fable	faculties	faithful	fame
fabled	faculty	faithfully	famed
fabric	fad	faithfulness	familial
fabricate	fade	fake	familiar
fabricated	faded	faked	familiarise/
fabricating	fading	faker	familiarize
fabrication	fail	faking	familiarised/
fabulous	failed	falcon	familiarized
fabulously	failing	falconry	familiarising/
façade	failure	fall	familiarizing
face	faint	fallacious	familiarity
faced	fainted	fallacy	families
facet	fainter	fallen	family
facetious	faintest	falling	famine
facial	faint-hearted	fallout	famished
facially	fainting	fallow	famous
facilitate	faintly	false	famously
facilitated	faintness	falsehood	fan
facilitating	fair	falsely	fanatic
facilities	fairer	falsification	fanatical
facility	fairest	falsified	fanatically
facing	fairground	falsifies	fanaticism
fact	fairies	falsify	fancier
factor	fairly	falsifying	fancies
factories	fairness	falsity	fanciest
factory	fairway	falter	fancy
factual	fairy	faltered	fanfare
factually	faith	faltering	fang

façade
This French word means 'the side of a building', or 'a mask' or 'image': 'He had a very confident façade.' You can leave out the accent, and still be correct.

face; faced; facing, etc.
Notice that 'c' sounds soft, like an 's', when 'e' or 'i' come after it. When it's followed by most other letters, 'c' usually makes a hard sound, as in 'fact' and 'faculty'.

facilities; factories; fairies; families; fancies
When a word ends in a consonant and a '-y', remember that it takes '-ies' in the plural.

fair
A 'fair' is a collection of rides and stalls. The adjective 'fair' means 'just' or 'equally shared'. A 'fare' can be 'the price of a journey' or 'a range of food and drink'.

faithful; faithfully
When you add '-ful' to a word, to mean 'full of', it has one 'l': 'faithful'. When you add '-ly' to a word to make it into an adverb, it has two: 'faithfully'.

fallout is a compound word, made up of 'fall' and 'out'. Together, they form a new word with its own meaning - 'consequences': 'The fallout was huge.'

fanned	fastened	favourite	feed
fanning	fastener	favouritism	feedback
fantasies	fastening	fawn	feeding
fantastic	fasting	fax	feel
fantastically	fat	faxed	feeler
fantasy	fatal	faxes	feeling
far	fatalities	faxing	feet
faraway	fatality	fear	feline
farce	fatally	feared	fell
fare	fate	fearful	felled
fared	father	fearfully	felling
farewell	fathered	fearing	fellow
far-fetched	fatherhood	fearless	fellowship
farm	fathering	fearlessly	felt
farmed	father-in-law	fearsome	female
farmer	fatherly	feasibility	feminine
farmhouse	fathers-in-law	feasible	feminism
farming	fathom	feast	feminist
farmyard	fathomed	feat	fen
farther	fathoming	feather	fence
farthest	fatigue	feathered	fenced
fascinate	fatigued	feathery	fencing
fascinated	fatiguing	feature	fend
fascinating	fatter	featured	fended
fascination	fattest	featureless	fender
fascism	fault	featuring	fending
fascist	faulted	fed	ferment
fashion	faulting	federal	fermentation
fashionable	faultless	federalism	fermented
fashionably	faulty	federation	fermenting
fashioned	favour	fee	fern
fashioning	favourable	feeble	ferocious
fast	favourably	feebler	ferociously
fasted	favoured	feeblest	ferocity
fasten	favouring	feebly	ferret

fanned
Words of one syllable, with a short vowel and a consonant, such as 'fan', double that final consonant before an ending that starts with a vowel is added.

farther vs father
'Farther' means 'a greater distance': 'He walked farther than me.' A 'father' is a male parent: 'My father is very fond of peppermints.'

fascism; fashion
In 'fascism', the letters 'sci' make a 'sh' sound, as the 'sh' does in 'fashion'. These words are easy to misspell.

fashionably; favourably; fearfully, etc.
The ending '-ly' is often found on the end of an adverb, which describes how something is done.

fate vs fête
'Fate' is a force some people believe governs our lives. A 'fête' is a summer fair, usually held outside.

faultless; fearless
The ending '-less' does not mean 'less of', it means 'without', so 'faultless' means 'without fault'.

fawn can mean 'a baby deer', 'light brown', or 'to grovel to someone powerful'.

Try looking for words that start with an 'f' sound on the 'ph' pages if you can't find them here.

ferried — firearm

ferried	fiancée	fifth	finale
ferries	fiasco	fiftieth	finalist
ferry	fib	fifty	finality
ferrying	fibbed	fig	finally
fertilisation/	fibbing	fight	finance
fertilization	fibre	fighter	financed
fertilised/fertilized	fibrous	fighting	financial
fertiliser/fertilizer	fickle	figurative	financially
fertilising/fertilizing	fiction	figuratively	financier
fertility	fictional	figure	financing
fervent	fictitious	figured	finch
fervently	fiddle	figurehead	finches
fervour	fiddled	figuring	find
festival	fiddler	filament	finder
festive	fiddling	file	finding
festivities	fiddly	filed	findings
festivity	fidelity	filing	fine
festooned	fidget	fill	finely
festooning	fidgeted	filled	finer
fetch	fidgeting	filler	finest
fetched	field	fillies	finger
fetching	fielded	filling	fingered
fête	fielder	filly	fingering
feud	fielding	film	fingernail
feudal	fieldwork	filmed	fingerprint
feudalism	fiend	filming	fingerprinted
feuded	fierce	filter	fingerprinting
feuding	fiercely	filtered	finish
fever	fiercer	filtering	finished
feverish	fiercest	filth	finishes
feverishly	fierier	filthier	finishing
few	fieriest	filthiest	finite
fewer	fiery	filthy	fir
fewest	fifteen	fin	fire
fiancé	fifteenth	final	firearm

feat *vs* feet

A 'feat' is a big achievement: 'Winning the race was a real feat.' 'Feet' is the plural of 'foot'.

female; feminine; feminism; feminist

These words are all to do with women, and they come from the Latin word 'femina', which means 'woman'.

A **ferret** is a small animal that hunts mice, rats and rabbits. It comes from the Old French word 'furet', which means 'little thief'.

feud means 'a disagreement' or 'quarrel', and it rhymes with 'chewed'.

fiancé/fiancée

Use 'fiancé' to describe a man who is engaged to be married, and 'fiancée' for a woman. This follows a French spelling pattern, as does 'divorcé/divorcée'.

fidget

In 'fidget', 'dg' makes a 'j' sound. This sound is also spelt 'j' (as in 'jug') or 'g' (as in 'generous').

fifteenth, **fifth** and **fiftieth** are ordinal numbers, used for putting things in order. 'We live on the fifteenth floor'; 'He came fifth in the race.'

fir is a tree, but 'fur' is an animal's warm coat.

fired
fire-extinguisher
firefighter
fireflies
firefly
fireman
firemen
fireplace
fireproof
firewood
firework
firing
firm
firmer
firmest
firmly
firmness
first
firstly
fish
fished
fisherman
fishermen
fishier
fishiest
fishing
fishmonger
fishy
fist
fit
fitness
fitted
fitter
fittest
fitting

five
fix
fixed
fixes
fixing
fixture
fizz
fizzed
fizzier
fizziest
fizzing
fizzle
fizzled
fizzling
fizzy
flabbergasted
flabbier
flabbiest
flabby
flaccid
flag
flagged
flagging
flagpole
flagship
flagstone
flail
flailed
flailing
flair
flake
flaked
flakier
flakiest
flaking

flaky
flamboyance
flamboyant
flamboyantly
flame
flamed
flaming
flamingo
flamingoes/
flamingos
flammable
flan
flank
flanked
flanking
flannel
flap
flapped
flapping
flare
flared
flaring
flash
flashback
flashed
flashier
flashiest
flashing
flashy
flask
flat
flatly
flatness
flatten
flattened

flattening
flatter
flattered
flattering
flattery
flattest
flatulence
flatulent
flaunt
flaunted
flaunting
flavour
flavoured
flavouring
flaw
flawed
flawless
flawlessly
flea
fleck
flecked
fled
flee
fleece
fleeced
fleecier
fleeciest
fleecing
fleecy
fleeing
fleet
fleeting
flesh
fleshier
fleshiest

firing; fizzling; flaking, etc.
Words that end in a consonant and a silent '-e' usually drop the '-e' before you add an ending that starts with a vowel, such as '-ing'.
fish can mean 'one fish' or 'lots of fish'. You may see 'fishes', but 'fish' is a more common plural. The word 'fishy' can mean 'like fish', e.g. 'It smelt fishy', or 'suspicious': 'There's something fishy going on.'
flair *vs* **flare**
A 'flair' is a talent. A 'flare' is a flash of light, or a firework, and 'flares' are wide-legged trousers.

flamboyant; flamingo
These words are spelt just as they sound, which is rare: 'flam-boy-ant'; 'fla-min-go'. Note that the plural of 'flamingo' can be correctly spelt 'flamingos' or 'flamingoes'.
flaw *vs* **floor**
A 'flaw' is a weakness, or blemish, but a 'floor' is the indoor surface you walk on: 'The muddy floor'.

a flamboyant flamingo
with a flair for flares

Try looking for words that start with an 'f' sound on the 'ph' pages if you can't find them here.

fleshy — folder

fleshy	flirtatious	flotation	fluorescent
flew	flirted	flounder	fluoride
flex	flirting	floundered	flurries
flexed	flit	floundering	flurry
flexibility	flitted	flour	flush
flexibly	flitting	flourish	flushed
flexing	float	flourished	flushing
flick	floated	flourishes	flustered
flicked	floating	flourishing	flustering
flicker	flock	floury	flute
flickered	flocked	flow	flutter
flickering	flocking	flowed	fluttered
flicking	flog	flower	fluttering
flies	flogged	flowered	fly
flight	flogging	flowering	flying
flimsier	flood	flowerpot	flyover
flimsiest	flooded	flowery	foal
flimsy	floodgate	flowing	foam
flinch	flooding	flown	foamed
flinched	floodlight	flu	foaming
flinches	floodlit	fluctuate	focus
flinching	floor	fluctuated	focused
fling	floorboard	fluctuating	focuses
flinging	floored	fluctuation	focusing
flint	flooring	flue	fodder
flinty	flop	fluency	foe
flip	flopped	fluent	fog
flippancy	floppier	fluff	foggier
flippant	floppiest	fluffier	foggiest
flippantly	flopping	fluffiest	foggy
flipped	floppy	fluffy	foil
flipper	flora	fluid	foiled
flipping	floral	fluke	fold
flirt	florist	flung	folded
flirtation	floss	fluorescence	folder

flea *vs* **flee**
A 'flea' is a tiny, biting insect. To 'flee' means 'to run away': 'The fleas were fleeing the flea spray.'

flew *vs* **flu** *vs* **flue**
'Flew' is the past of the verb 'fly'. 'Flu' is a viral illness, and short for 'influenza'. A 'flue' is a chimney or vent which smoke or fumes go out of.

flipped; flitted; flogged; flopped
Words such as 'flip', 'flit', 'flog' and 'flop', have a short vowel and a consonant. You double that final consonant before adding an ending that begins with a vowel.

flour *vs* **flower**
The word 'flour' means 'ground grain used in baking', but a 'flower' is part of a plant, which often has petals and contains pollen.

fluorescence means 'the state of giving off a bright light'. The ending '-scence' often conveys this idea: 'adolescence' is 'the state of becoming an adult', and 'pubescence' is 'the state of puberty', for instance.

focuses is the most common plural of 'focus', but you may see 'foci', which follows the Latin spelling rule for words that end in '-us'.

f

'fore-'

The prefix 'fore-' at the start of a word **means 'in advance of' or 'before something'**. For instance, a weather forecast tells us what kind of weather lies ahead. On its own, fore means 'front' or 'conspicuous position': 'He came to the fore in 1920.'

folding
foliage
folk
folklore
follow
followed
follower
following
fond
fonder
fondest
fondly
fondness
food
fool
fooled
foolhardiness
foolhardy
fooling
foolish
foolishly
foolishness
foolproof
foot
footage
football
footballer

footnote
footpath
footprint
footstep
for
forbade
forbid
forbidden
forbidding
force
forced
forceful
forcefully
forcible
forcibly
forcing
ford
forded
fording
fore
forearm
forebear
foreboding
forecast
forecasted
forecasting
forecourt

forefather
forefinger
forefront
forego/forgo
foregoing
foregone
forehand
forehead
foreign
foreigner
foreman
foremen
foremost
forensic
forerunner
foresaw
foresee
foreseeable
foreseeing
foreseen
foresight
forest
forested
forestry
foretaste
foretell
foretelling
foretold
forever
forewarn
forewarned
forewarning
foreword
forfeit
forfeited

forfeiting
forgave
forge
forged
forger
forgeries
forgery
forget
forgetful
forgetfulness
forget-me-not
forgetting
forging
forgive
forgiven
forgiveness
forgiving
forgone
forgot
forgotten
fork
forked
forking
forlorn
forlornly
form
formal
formalities
formality
formally
format
formation
formative
formed
former

fondness; foolhardiness; foolishness
These nouns all end with '-ness', but notice that the '-y' of 'foolhardy' changes to an 'i' before it's added.

for vs fore vs four
'For' is a preposition, which is a word that links other words together. It has different meanings, depending on the words it's used with. Take care not to mix it up with 'four' (4), or 'fore', which means 'front'.

foreign; forfeit
These words don't follow the "i before 'e' except after 'c'" pattern, as 'ei' doesn't make an 'ee' sound in them.

forfeit → forfeiting; forget → forgetting
As the first part of the word 'forfeit' is emphasized, you just add '-ing' to make 'forfeiting'. The second part of 'forget' is emphasized, however, so you must double the '-t': 'He's forgetting his name, these days.'

forgiving
The letter 'v' is never doubled before an ending is added. Neither are 'h', 'j', 'k', 'q', 'w', 'x' or 'y'.

fort vs fought
A 'fort' is a heavily-protected base for military forces. 'Fought' is the past tense of the verb 'fight'.

Try looking for words that start with an 'f' sound on the 'ph' pages if you can't find them here.

formerly — freshest

formerly
formidable
forming
formula
formulaic
formulate
formulated
formulating
forsake
forsaken
forsook
fort
forth
forthcoming
forthright
forties
fortieth
fortification
fortitude
fortnight
fortnightly
fortress
fortresses
fortuitous
fortunate
fortunately
fortune
forty
forum
forward
forwarded
forwarding
fossil
fossilised/fossilized
foster

fostered
fostering
fought
foul
fouler
foulest
fouling
found
foundation
founder
foundered
foundering
foundries
foundry
fountain
four
fourteen
fourteenth
fourth
fourthly
fowl
fox
foxed
foxes
foxglove
foxhound
foxing
foxy
foyer
fraction
fractionally
fracture
fractured
fracturing
fragile

fragility
fragment
fragmentary
fragmentation
fragmented
fragmenting
fragrance
fragrant
frail
frailer
frailest
frailties
frailty
frame
framed
framework
framing
franchise
frank
franker
frankest
frankly
frankness
frantic
frantically
fraternal
fraternities
fraternity
fraud
fraudulent
fraught
fray
frayed
fraying
freak

freckle
freckled
free
freedom
freehand
freehold
freeing
freelance
freely
freer
free-range
freest
freestyle
freewheel
freewheeled
freewheeling
freeze
freezer
freight
freighter
frenzied
frenzies
frenzy
frequencies
frequency
frequent
frequented
frequenting
frequently
fresh
freshen
freshened
freshening
fresher
freshest

f

---

forth *vs* **fourth**
'Forth' means 'out' or 'forwards': 'He set forth.' The word 'fourth' comes from the number 'four': 'He came fourth in the race.' It's called an ordinal number.

foul *vs* **fowl**
The word 'foul' means 'smelly' or 'dirty', but 'fowl' are birds kept for their meat and/or eggs, such as chickens, ducks and geese.

foul fowl

foundation; fragmentation, etc.
The letters '-tion' (pronounced 'shun') are found on the end of many nouns, such as these two. Remember that some nouns end with '-sion', though, which sounds just the same, so you need to take care.

fraternal means 'brotherly', and comes from 'frater', the Latin word for 'brother'.

freckle
If you hear the sound 'ul' at the end of a word, it's most likely to be spelt '-le'. In a few words, such as 'angel', 'symbol' and 'magical', it's spelt differently.

freshly
freshness
freshwater
fret
fretful
fretfully
fretted
fretting
friar
friaries
friary
friction
fridge
fried
friend
friendless
friendliness
friendly
friendship
fries
frieze
frigate
fright
frightened
frightening
frightful
frightfully
frigid
frill
frilled
frillier
frilliest
frilly
fringe
fringed

frisk
frisked
friskier
friskiest
frisking
frisky
fritter
frivolities
frivolity
frivolous
frizzier
frizziest
frizzy
frock
frog
frogman
frogmen
frolic
frolicked
frolicking
from
frond
front
frontage
frontal
fronted
frontier
fronting
frost
frostbite
frostbitten
frosted
frosting
froth
frothier

frothiest
frothy
frown
frowned
frowning
froze
frozen
frugal
frugality
frugally
fruit
fruitful
fruitfully
fruitier
fruitiest
fruitless
fruity
frustrate
frustrated
frustrating
frustration
fry
fudge
fudged
fudging
fuel
fuelled
fuelling
fug
fuggier
fuggiest
fuggy
fugitive
fulfil
fulfilled

fulfilling
fulfilment
full
full-blooded
full-blown
fullness
full-time
fully
fully-fledged
fulsome
fumble
fumbled
fumbling
fume
fumed
fuming
fun
function
functional
functioned
functioning
fund
fundamental
fundamentally
funded
funding
funeral
funereal
funfair
fungi
fungus
funnel
funnelled
funnelling
funnier

---

fret → fretted; fretting
Notice how 'fret', a one-syllable word with a short vowel and a consonant, doubles its final consonant before an ending beginning with a vowel is added.

frolicked
To keep the hard 'c' sound at the end of 'frolic', you need to add a 'k' before adding an ending. Without it, the last part of the word would be '-iced', as cakes are.

fuelled; fulfilled; funnelled
Remember to double the 'l' when you add an ending that starts with a vowel to a word that ends in an '-l'.

funeral vs funereal
Take care not to confuse 'funeral' (the ceremony at someone's death) with 'funereal' (an adjective, meaning 'very slow'): 'The bus went at a funereal pace.'

fur is the warm, hairy coat many animals have. A 'fir' is an evergreen tree (which is one that keeps its leaves all year). Make sure you use the right word.

a furry fir

Try looking for words that start with an 'f' sound on the 'ph' pages if you can't find them here.

funniest — fuzzy

funniest	furnished	furtive	fussy
funnily	furnishes	furtively	futile
funny	furnishing	fury	futilely
fur	furniture	fuse	futility
furious	furore	fused	future
furiously	furrow	fuselage	futuristic
furl	furry	fusing	fuzz
furled	further	fusion	fuzzier
furling	furthered	fuss	fuzziest
furlong	furthering	fussier	fuzzily
furnace	furthermore	fussiest	fuzziness
furnish	furthest	fussily	fuzzy

Quick tip

Same sounds

Many English words sound very similar, and may even be spelt almost identically, but have different meanings.

For example, 'fizzy', 'frizzy', 'fussy' and 'fuzzy' are easy to mix up. **Try keeping a list of words you come across that sound like other words.** This means you can double-check how to spell the word you need, when you need it.

I'm so fussy about my frizzy, fuzzy hair.

Some tricky words to spell that start with an 'f'

Here are some words beginning with 'f' that are particularly tricky to spell. See how many you can get right. There are some tips to help you on page 7.

fabulous	fatigue	fluoride
facet	favourite	foliage
facetious	ferocious	formulaic
facilitate	fibrous	fortuitous
faculty	figurative	foyer
falcon	fixture	fraudulent
fallacy	flabbergasted	freight
falsify	flaccid	frivolous
fanaticism	flammable	fulfil
fascinate	fluctuate	function

Gg

a gambolling gambler

gamble *vs* **gambol**
To 'gamble' means 'to take a risk' or 'place a bet', but to 'gambol' is to run and leap in a carefree way. Notice that you double the 'l' in **gambolled** and **gambolling**.

gabble	gallop	gaoler	garrison
gabbled	galloped	gap	garter
gabbling	galloping	gape	gas
gable	gallows	gaped	gaseous
gabled	galore	gaping	gash
gadget	galoshes	garage	gashed
gadgetry	galvanise/galvanize	garb	gashes
gag	galvanised/	garbage	gashing
gagged	galvanized	garbled	gasoline
gagging	galvanising/	garden	gasp
gaiety	galvanizing	gardened	gasped
gaily	gambit	gardener	gasping
gain	gamble	gardening	gassed
gained	gambled	gargle	gasses
gaining	gambler	gargled	gassing
gala	gambling	gargling	gate
galactic	gambol	gargoyle	gateau
galaxies	gambolled	garish	gateaux
galaxy	gambolling	garishly	gatecrash
gale	game	garland	gatecrashed
gallant	gamely	garlanded	gatecrasher
gallantly	gammon	garlic	gatecrashing
gallantry	gander	garlicky	gateway
galleon	gang	garment	gather
galleries	gangplank	garnish	gathered
gallery	gangster	garnished	gatherer
galley	gannet	garnishes	gathering
gallon	gaol	garnishing	gauche

gabble; gable
Notice that the 'a' sound is short in 'gabble', but in 'gable', it makes a long sound. The double 'b' changes the sound of the vowel completely.

gadgetry; gallantry; geometry
If you see '-ry' on the end of a word, it often means 'to do with'. For instance 'gadgetry' means 'to do with gadgets', and 'gallantry', 'to do with being gallant'.

gag → gagged; gas → gassed; gel → gelled
For these one-syllable words, remember to double the final consonant before adding '-ed' or '-ing'.

galaxies; galleries; gipsies/gypsies
When a word ends in a consonant and '-y', remember that it changes to '-ies' in the plural.

galloped
'Gallop' is an exception to the spelling rule that you double the final '-p' in a word when you add an ending that starts with a vowel. Lots of rules have exceptions.

gargoyle
A 'gargoyle' is a grotesque carved waterspout, added to cathedrals and colleges by medieval stonemasons. It comes from an Old French word for 'throat', 'gargouille'.

g

gaudier	generalizing	geranium	giddiness
gaudiest	generally	gerbil	giddy
gaudiness	generate	germ	gift
gaudy	generated	germinate	gifted
gauge	generating	germinated	gig
gauged	generation	germinating	gigantic
gauging	generator	germination	giggle
gaunt	generosity	gesticulate	giggled
gauntlet	generous	gesticulated	giggling
gave	generously	gesticulating	giggly
gay	genial	gesture	gild
gayer	genially	gestured	gilded
gayest	genie	gesturing	gilding
gaze	genius	get	gill
gazed	geniuses	getaway	gilt
gazelle	genre	getting	gimmick
gazing	gentle	geyser	gimmicky
gear	gentleman	ghastlier	ginger
geared	gentlemanly	ghastliest	gingerbread
gearing	gentlemen	ghastly	gingerly
geese	gentleness	gherkin	gipsies/gypsies
gel	gentler	ghetto	gipsy/gypsy
gelding	gentlest	ghost	giraffe
gelled	gently	ghostlier	gird
gelling	genuine	ghostliest	girder
gem	genuinely	ghostly	girding
gender	geographer	ghoulish	girdle
general	geographical	ghoulishly	girl
generalisation/	geographically	giant	girlhood
generalization	geography	gibberish	girlish
generalise/	geological	gibbon	girth
generalize	geologist	gibe	gist
generalised/	geometric	giddier	give
generalized	geometrical	giddiest	given
generalising/	geometry	giddily	giving

gateau is a French word for a luxurious cake. The correct plural is 'gateaux', but you may see 'gateaus'.

gauge
This word, meaning 'measure', is tricky to spell, as it's pronounced 'gaydge'. Try visualizing 'a' before 'u'.

gel; gem; general, etc.
Notice that the letter 'g' is soft, like a 'j', when it's followed by an 'e', as in these words.

gibe
This word, meaning 'a taunt' or 'insult', can also be spelt 'jibe', though 'gibe' is more common.

generosity drops the 'u' from the word 'generous'.

gently
When you add '-ly' to 'gentle', you replace '-le' with '-ly'. 'Idly' and 'subtly' also follow this pattern.

geyser means 'a jet of hot water and steam that comes from underground'. It's from an Old Norse word 'geysa', meaning 'to gush'.

ghastly; gherkin; ghetto; ghost, etc.
It's easy to miss the silent 'h' in these words.

gild means 'to cover with a thin layer of gold', but a 'guild' is the name for a group of craftspeople.

g

glacial	glided		
glaciation	glider		
glacier	gliding		
glad	glimmer		
gladder	glimmered		
gladdest	glimmering		
glade	glimpse		
gladiator	glimpsed		
gladly	glimpsing	gloss	gnat
gladness	glint	glossaries	gnaw
glamorous	glinted	glossary	gnawed
glamour	glinting	glossed	gnawing
glance	glisten	glossier	gnome
glanced	glistened	glossiest	gnu
glancing	glistening	glossing	go
glare	glitter	glossy	goad
glared	glittered	glove	goaded
glaring	glittering	glow	goading
glass	gloat	glowed	go-ahead
glasses	gloated	glower	goal
glassy	gloating	glowered	goalkeeper
glaze	global	glowering	goat
glazed	globalisation/	glowing	gobbledygook
glazing	globalization	glue	go-between
gleam	globally	glued	goblet
gleamed	globe	gluing	goblin
gleaming	gloom	glum	god
glean	gloomier	glumly	godchild
gleaned	gloomiest	glummer	godchildren
gleaning	gloomily	glummest	goddaughter
glee	gloomy	glut	goddess
gleeful	glorified	glutton	goddesses
gleefully	glorify	gluttonous	godparent
glen	glorious	gluttony	godson
glide	glory	gnarled	goes

glossary

A 'glossary' is **a list of words and their meanings.** Many books have glossaries to explain difficult or specialist words that occur in the text. If you are unsure about the meaning of a word you come across in a factual book, check it in the glossary.

glamorous

When you add to words that end in '-our', such as 'glamour' and 'humour', you need to drop the 'u', to make 'glamorous' and 'humorous'.

glasses; goddesses; governesses; grasses

Remember that words that end with a hissing sound, such as '-ss', '-z', '-ch' or '-sh', take the ending '-es' when they become plural.

gleefully; globally; gracefully; gradually, etc.

You keep the '-l' on the ends of these adjectives when you add the ending '-ly' to make adverbs.

globalisation/globalization

For most words, either 's' or 'z' is correct. Words which can only have one or the other are on page 4.

gluing

Notice that 'glue' drops its final '-e' before an ending that starts with a vowel is added. This is quite an unusual spelling pattern, and is easy to get wrong.

gnarled; gnat; gnaw, etc.

A silent 'g' before the letter 'n' in English words may come at the beginning of a word, as here, or at the end, as in 'assign', 'design', 'foreign' and 'sign'.

g

goggles
going
gone
gong
good
goodbye
goodies
good-looking
good-natured
goodness
goodwill
goody
goose
gooseberries
gooseberry
gore
gorge
gorged
gorgeous
gorgeously
gorging
gorier
goriest
gorilla
gorse
gory
gosling
gospel

gossip
gossiped
gossiping
got
gouge
gouged
gouging
goulash
gourd
gourmet
govern
governed
governess
governesses
governing
government
governmental
governor
gown
grab
grabbed
grabbing
grace
graced
graceful
gracefully
gracing
gracious

graciously
grade
graded
gradient
grading
gradual
gradually
graduate
graduation
graffiti
graft
grafted
grafting
grain
grammar
grammatical
grammatically
gramophone
grand
grandad
grandchild
grandchildren
granddaughter
grander
grandest
grandeur
grandfather
grandiose
grandly
grandma
grandmother
grandpa
grandparent
grandstand
granite

grannies
granny
grant
granted
granting
granular
granulated
granule
grape
grapefruit
grapevine
graph
graphic
graphically
graphite
grapple
grappled
grappling
grasp
grasped
grasping
grass
grasses
grasshopper
grassy
grate
grated
grateful
gratefully
grater
gratify
gratifying
grating
gratis
gratitude

'-ling'
Words ending in '-ling'
are usually young animals.
A gosling is a young goose,
a 'duckling' is a young duck
and a 'fledgling' is a baby bird.

a gosling

gnu
Unusually, the 'g' in 'gnu' is not silent. A 'gnu' is an
African antelope and the word is pronounced 'guh-noo'.
Only words from other languages end with a '-u'.
gobbledygook means 'nonsense'. It was first
used by a US Congressman in 1944 to describe
information given out by the US government.
gorilla
A 'gorilla' is the largest of the apes. A 'guerrilla'
fights in a small, often unofficial, army.
grab doubles the '-b' before '-ed' or '-ing' are added.

government has an 'n', which is easy to forget.
Think of 'the people who govern us' to remind you.
grammar is the set of rules a language follows.
There's more about English grammar on page 3,
and more detail on pages 210–215.
grate means 'to shred food with a grater'. A 'grate' is
also where a fire is lit in a house. If something 'grates
on you', it annoys you. The word 'great', however,
means 'big' or 'fantastic': 'The food was great.'
gratis means 'for free', and is a shorter version of the
Latin word, 'gratiis', which means 'for nothing'.

g

gratuitous	greedily	grim	groove
gratuitously	greediness	grimace	grooved
grave	greedy	grimaced	groovy
gravel	green	grimacing	grope
gravelled	greener	grime	groped
gravely	greenery	grimly	groping
graver	greenest	grimmer	gross
gravest	greenflies	grimmest	grosser
gravestone	greenfly	grimy	grossest
graveyard	greengrocer	grin	grossly
gravitate	greenhouse	grind	grotesque
gravitated	greet	grinding	grotesquely
gravitating	greeted	grinned	ground
gravitation	greeting	grinning	grounded
gravitational	gregarious	grip	grounding
gravity	grenade	gripped	groundless
gravy	grew	gripping	groundsheet
graze	grey	grislier	groundsman
grazed	greyed	grisliest	group
grazing	greyer	grisly	grouped
grease	greyest	grit	grouping
greased	greyhound	gritted	grouse
greaseproof	greying	gritting	grove
greasier	grid	gritty	grovel
greasiest	grief	grizzled	grovelled
greasing	grievance	grizzly	grovelling
greasy	grieve	groan	grow
great	grieved	groaned	grower
greater	grieving	grocer	growing
greatest	grievous	groceries	growl
great-grandfather	grievously	grocery	growled
great-grandmother	grill	groin	growling
greed	grille	groom	grown
greedier	grilled	groomed	grown-up
greediest	grilling	grooming	growth

greaseproof
The ending '-proof' means 'resistant to', 'able to repel'. 'Greaseproof' paper is used on baking trays to stop grease soaking through, and water cannot get through something that is 'waterproof', for instance.

great means 'big' or 'fantastic'. To 'grate' is to shred food, using a grater. A 'grate' is also where a fire is lit inside a house.

greenflies; groceries; gullies, etc.
Remember that words that end with a consonant and a '-y' change to '-ies' in the plural.

grenade means 'a small, hand-held bomb'. It comes from the Spanish word 'granada', which is the name for the seed-filled fruit, a pomegranate.

grief; grievance, etc.
Remember: 'i' before 'e' except after 'c' when the letters 'ie' make an 'ee' sound, as they do in these two words. Most words stick to this spelling pattern, but there's a list of the ones that don't on page 4.

grill vs grille
To 'grill' food is to cook it under dry heat. A 'grille' is a mesh of bars over a door or window.

g

grub	guerrilla	gunfire	gutter
grubbier	guess	gunned	guttering
grubbiest	guessed	gunning	gutting
grubby	guessing	gunpowder	guttural
grudge	guesswork	gunshot	guy
grudged	guest	gurgle	guzzle
grudging	guidance	gurgled	guzzled
grudgingly	guide	gurgling	guzzling
gruelling	guided	gush	gym
gruesome	guidelines	gushed	gymkhana
gruff	guiding	gushes	gymnasium
gruffer	guild	gushing	gymnast
gruffest	guillotine	gust	gypsies/gipsies
gruffly	guilt	gusto	gypsy/gipsy
grumble	guiltier	gusty	gyrate
grumbled	guiltiest	gut	gyrated
grumbler	guiltily	gutted	gyrating
grumbling	guilty		
grumpier	guinea		
grumpiest	guise		
grumpily	guitar		
grumpiness	guitarist		
grumpy	gulf		
grunt	gull		
grunted	gullet		
grunting	gullibility		
guarantee	gullible		
guaranteed	gullies		
guaranteeing	gully		
guarantor	gulp		
guard	gulped		
guarded	gulping		
guardian	gum		
guardianship	gummed		
guarding	gun		

> **Quick tip**
>
> ## Two ways
>
> From time to time, you'll come across **a word that can be spelt in two slightly different ways, both of which are correct**. Often, one spelling is more common than the other, but it's best to try to learn both versions of the word, so that you always recognize it.
>
> These three words beginning with 'g' can be spelt in two ways, for example:
>
> ## 'gaol/jail'
> ## 'gipsy/gypsy'
> ## 'gibe/jibe'

a guerrilla gorilla

grim; grime
Adding a silent '-e' to the word 'grim' (serious or stern) changes its sound and meaning. 'Grime', with a long 'i' to rhyme with 'climb', means 'dirt' or 'filth'.

grinned; gripped; gritted, etc.
One-syllable words that end in a short vowel and a consonant, such as 'grin', 'grip' and 'grit', double the final consonant before an ending is added. Try to learn this common spelling pattern.

groove and **groovy** prove the rule that a 'v' is always followed by a vowel or a 'y'.

grisly vs grizzly
The word 'grisly' means 'gory', but 'grizzly' means 'grumpy'. It is also a type of bear.
A **guerrilla** is a soldier in a small, often unofficial, army. A 'gorilla' is the largest of the apes.
guild means 'a group of craftspeople'. To 'gild' is to cover something with a thin layer of gold.

Quick tip

Grammar

The rules that govern how a language is spoken and written are called grammar. These include how sentences are put together, how they are divided up, or punctuated, and what types of words are used in them. You'll find more detail about grammar on pages 3 and 210–215, but here's a reminder of the different kinds of words, and what they do:

Adjectives

These are **describing words**, such as 'happy', 'sad' and 'beautiful'. They always accompany a noun or pronoun and tell you more about it: 'She was a *generous* person.'

Adverbs

These **describe how an action is done**, such as singing 'tunefully'. A lot of adverbs end with '-ly', but many do not, such as 'He ate *fast*', or 'She speaks French *well*'.

Conjunctions

These **link words together in a sentence**, and include 'and', 'but', 'because' and 'while'. You could say that conjunctions form the 'glue' in a language, sticking the different parts of it together.

Nouns

These words are **things, or objects**, such as 'chair', 'car', 'house' and 'book'. Languages have many thousands of nouns.

Pronouns

These words include 'he', 'she', 'it', 'you' and 'we'. They are **words you use instead of a noun** (a person or thing): '*He* says *he* loves *me*'; 'That book is *mine*'. There are several different kinds of pronoun.

Verbs

These are **action, or 'doing' words**, such as 'laugh', 'run', 'skip' and 'sing'. Verbs have a different 'tense' to describe when in time an action takes place. The main ones are the past, present and future tenses.

Some tricky words to spell that start with a 'g'

See how many of these tricky words beginning with 'g' you can spell correctly. There are some spelling tips to help you on page 7.

genuine	granite	guard
ghastly	granulated	guardian
ghost	graphic	guess
gigantic	gratuitous	guide
giraffe	grievance	guillotine
gist	grievous	guilt
gluttonous	grotesque	guitar
gouge	gruesome	gullible
grandeur	guarantee	gymkhana

Hh

a hanger
hangar

hangar *vs* **hanger**
Aircraft are stored in a 'hangar',
but you hang clothes on a 'hanger'.
One letter makes a big difference.

h

habit	hairiness	hamburger	handled
habitat	hairline	hammer	handling
habitual	hairstyle	hammered	handmade
habitually	hairy	hammering	handout
hack	hake	hammock	hand-picked
hacked	half	hamper	handshake
hacker	half-baked	hampered	handsome
hacking	half-hearted	hampering	handsomely
hacksaw	half-heartedly	hamster	handwriting
had	half-time	hand	handy
haddock	halfway	handbag	hang
haemorrhage	halibut	handbook	hangar
haemorrhaged	hall	handcuff	hanged
haemorrhaging	hallucinate	handcuffed	hanger
hag	hallucinated	handed	hanger-on
haggard	hallucinating	handful	hangers-on
haggle	hallucination	hand-held	hang-glider
haggled	hallucinatory	handicap	hanging
haggling	halo	handicapped	hangman
hail	haloes	handicapping	hangover
hailed	halt	handicraft	hang-up
hailing	halted	handier	hanker
hailstone	halter	handiest	hankered
hair	halting	handing	hankering
haircut	halved	handiwork	haphazard
hairdresser	halves	handkerchief	haphazardly
hairier	halving	handle	hapless
hairiest	ham	handlebar	happen

haemorrhage
This tricky word can be a verb (to haemorrhage) or
a noun (a haemorrhage). It means 'to bleed heavily'
or 'a serious bleed', and is pronounced 'hem-er-ij'.

hair
A 'hare' is a mammal a bit like a large rabbit,
but with longer ears. 'Hair' grows on our heads.
hall can mean 'a very large room' or 'the passageway
between rooms in a house'. To 'haul' is to pull
something heavy: 'He hauled the sack across the floor.'

hallucinate: remember two 'l's, one 'c' and an 'n'.

haloes
Some words ending in '-o' change to '-oes'
in the plural, though many just add an '-s'.

handbag; handcuff; hand-held; hand-picked, etc.
Compounds are made up of two words. Some have
a hyphen between them ('hand-held', 'hand-picked'),
but many join into one word ('handbag', 'handcuff').

handy → handicraft; handiwork
Notice that the '-y' at the end of 'handy' changes
to 'i' before an ending is added. This is a common
spelling pattern, so learn it if you can.

h

happened	harking	hash	haunch
happening	harlequin	hassle	haunches
happier	harm	hassled	haunt
happiest	harmed	hassling	haunted
happily	harmful	haste	haunting
happiness	harmfully	hasten	have
happy	harming	hastened	haven
happy-go-lucky	harmless	hastening	having
harangue	harmonic	hastier	havoc
harangued	harmonica	hastiest	hawk
haranguing	harmonies	hastily	hawked
harass	harmonious	hastiness	hawking
harassed	harmoniously	hasty	hawthorn
harassing	harmony	hat	hay
harassment	harness	hatch	haymaking
harbour	harnessed	hatchback	haystack
harboured	harnesses	hatched	hazard
harbouring	harnessing	hatches	hazardous
hard	harp	hatchet	haze
hardback	harped	hatching	hazel
harden	harping	hate	hazier
hardened	harpist	hated	haziest
hardening	harpoon	hateful	haziness
harder	harpsichord	hatefully	hazy
hardest	harrow	hating	he
hardness	harsh	hatred	head
hard-nosed	harsher	hat-trick	headache
hard-wearing	harshest	haughtier	headdress
hardwood	harshly	haughtiest	headdresses
hare	harvest	haughtily	headed
hared	harvested	haughty	header
harem	harvester	haul	heading
haring	harvesting	haulage	headland
hark	has	hauled	headless
harked	has-been	hauling	headlight

hare hair

hare
A 'hare' is a mammal, slightly larger than a rabbit. To 'hare' means 'to run very fast'. 'Hair' grows on our heads.

harlequin
A 'q' is always followed by a 'u' in English words.

harmful; harmless
The ending '-ful' means 'full of'; '-less' means 'without any'.

harnesses; hatches; haunches, etc.
Notice that words that end in '-ch', '-s', '-ss' or other hissing sounds take '-es' in the plural.
has-been means 'someone who was famous, but now isn't': 'He is such a has-been.'

haughty
The 'au' in 'haughty' is only one way of spelling the sound 'aw'. Others are 'aw' ('straw'); 'a' ('ball'); 'ou' ('ought'); 'al' ('walk'), 'oa' ('oar') and 'or' ('sword').

haul means 'to pull something heavy', but a 'hall' is a large room, or a passageway between rooms in a house.

headline
headlong
headmaster
headmistress
head-on
headphones
headquarters
headroom
headstone
headstrong
headteacher
headway
headwind
heady
heal
healed
healer
healing
health
healthier
healthiest
healthy
heap
heaped
heaping
hear
heard
hearing
hearsay
hearse
heart
heartache
heartbreak
heartbreaking
heartbroken

heartburn
heartening
heartfelt
hearth
heartier
heartiest
heartily
heartless
heart-rending
heart-throb
heart-to-heart
hearty
heat
heated
heater
heath
heathen
heather
heating
heatwave
heave
heaved
heaven
heavenly
heavier
heaviest
heavily
heaviness
heaving
heavy
heavy-duty
heavy-handed
heavyweight
heckle
heckled

heckler
heckling
hectic
hedge
hedged
hedgehog
hedgerow
hedging
hedonism
hedonistic
heed
heeded
heeding
heel
heeled
heftier
heftiest
hefty
height
heighten
heightened
heightening
heinous
heir

heiress
heiresses
heirloom
held
helicopter
hell
hell-bent
hellish
helm
helmet
helmeted
helmsman
help
helped
helper
helpful
helpfully
helping
helpless
helplessly
helplessness
hem
hemisphere
hemmed

h

A rule, or not a rule?
Many words break spelling rules. Take the guideline: 'i' before 'e' except after 'c' when the letters make an 'ee' sound, for example: heighten follows the rule as 'ei' make an 'i' sound in this word, not an 'ee' sound. heinous (meaning 'terrible') is pronounced 'heenuss', but it breaks the rule anyway. heir (pronounced 'air'), follows the rule, as the 'ei' sounds like 'ai', not 'ee'.

---

haven; heave; heaved; heavy, etc.
Notice that the letter 'v' is always followed by a vowel. A 'y' often counts as a vowel, as it does in 'heavy'.

headphones; headquarters
Notice that these are both plural nouns. They are almost always only used in the plural.

heal *vs* **heel**
To 'heal' is to make better, or cure. A 'heel' is the back part of a foot. Make sure you use the right word. hear means 'to sense sound', but 'here' is an adverb, meaning 'in, at or to this place'.

heard is the past tense of the verb 'hear'. A large group of animals such as cows is called a 'herd'. Take care not to mix them up.

hedonism
This is the practice of experiencing as much pleasure as possible in life. It comes from the Greek word 'hedone', which means 'pleasure'.

hemmed
If you add '-ed' to a word of one syllable with a short vowel and a consonant (e.g. 'hem'), double the final consonant (except 'h', 'j', 'k', 'q', 'v', 'w', 'x' or 'y').

hemming	herring	highest	hinging
hemp	herself	highland	hint
hence	hesitant	highlight	hinted
henceforth	hesitantly	highlighted	hinting
henchman	hesitate	highlighter	hip
her	hesitated	highlighting	hippies
herald	hesitating	highly	hippo
heralded	hesitation	high-rise	hippopotami/
heralding	hessian	highway	hippopotamuses
herb	heterosexual	highwayman	hippopotamus
herbal	heterosexuality	highwaymen	hippy
herbivore	hexagon	hijack	hire
herd	hexagonal	hijacked	hired
herded	heyday	hijacker	hiring
herding	hibernate	hijacking	his
here	hibernated	hike	hiss
hereafter	hibernating	hiked	hissed
hereby	hibernation	hiker	hissing
hereditary	hiccup	hiking	historian
herein	hiccupped	hilarious	historic
heresies	hiccupping	hilarity	historical
heresy	hid	hill	historically
heretic	hidden	hillier	histories
herewith	hide	hilliest	history
heritage	hide-and-seek	hillside	hit
hermit	hideous	hilly	hit-and-run
hermitage	hideously	hilt	hitch
hero	hideout	him	hitched
heroes	hiding	himself	hitches
heroic	hierarchies	hind	hitching
heroically	hierarchy	hinder	hitting
heroin	hieroglyphics	hindered	hive
heroine	higgledy-piggledy	hindering	hoard
heroism	high	hinge	hoarded
heron	higher	hinged	hoarding

henceforth means 'after this point in time'. It's a little old-fashioned, but it's still used.

herbivore
Words that end in '-vore' are types of animal. A 'carnivore' eats meat, a 'herbivore' eats plants and an 'omnivore' eats everything.

herd means 'a group of animals', such as cows. 'Heard' is the past tense of 'to hear'.

The herd didn't want to be heard.

Shh   shhhh

hereafter; hereby; herein; herewith
These compound words, based on the adverb 'here', are quite formal, and are more commonly used in written English than in everyday speech.

heroin vs heroine
'Heroin' is an addictive, illegal drug. A 'heroine' is a lead female character.

hiccup is sometimes spelt 'hiccough', but 'hiccup' is much more common.

hoarse
hoarsely
hoarser
hoax
hoaxes
hob
hobbies
hobble
hobbled
hobbling
hobby
hockey
hoe
hoed
hoeing
hog
hoist
hoisted
hoisting
hold
holdall
holder
holding
hole
holed
holey
holiday
holidaymaker
holier
holiest
holiness
holing
hollies
hollow
hollowed

hollowing
holly
holocaust
holster
holy
homage
home
homeland
homeless
homelessness
homely
homeowner
homesick
homesickness
homespun
homestead
homeward
homewards
homework
homicide
homing
homograph
homonym
homophone
homosexual
homosexuality
hone
honed
honest
honestly
honesty
honey
honeycomb
honeycombed
honeymoon

honeysuckle
honing
honk
honked
honking
honorary
honour
honourable
honoured
honouring
hood
hooded
hoof
hook
hooked
hooking
hooligan
hooliganism
hoop
hooped
hoot
hooted
hooting
hoover
hoovered
hooves
hop

hope
hoped
hopeful
hopefully
hopeless
hopelessly
hopelessness
hoping
hopped
hopper
hopping
horde
horizon
horizontal
horizontally
hormonal
hormone
horn
horned
hornet
horoscope
horrendous
horrible
horribly
horrid
horrific
horrifies

h

homophones **are words that sound the same, but are spelt differently, and have different meanings**. e.g. 'red/read'; 'would/wood'; homographs **have the same spelling, but a different sound and meaning**, e.g. 'row' (which can mean 'move with oars' or 'argument'). They are both homonyms.

higgledy-piggledy **means 'messy' or 'chaotic':** 'Her clothes were tossed higgledy-piggledy all over the floor.' Other compound words following this pattern include 'topsy-turvy', 'hurly-burly' and 'tittle-tattle'.

hinging **looks as if it should rhyme with 'singing', but the 'g' still makes the soft 'j' sound, as in 'hinge'. Most words ending in '-ge' drop the 'e' when you add '-ing', but 'singeing' and 'whingeing' don't.

hoard vs horde
To 'hoard' is to stockpile things in case they run out. A 'horde' is a big group, e.g. 'a horde of visitors'.

hoarse **means 'croaky' or 'husky-voiced':** 'You sound a little hoarse today.' A 'horse' is a large mammal.

hold vs holed
To 'hold' can mean 'to grasp', or 'the storage area of a ship'. If something is 'holed', it has a hole in it.

hole
A 'hole' is a pit in the ground or gap: 'I have a hole in my sock.' 'Whole' means 'all of': 'The whole thing.'

holey vs holy
Something 'holey' is full of holes, but 'holy' means 'to do with a religion'.

horrify
horrifying
horror
horse
horseback
horsepower
horseradish
horseshoe
horticultural
horticulture
hose
hosed
hosiery
hosing
hospice
hospitable
hospital
hospitality
host
hosted
hostess
hostesses
hostile
hostilities
hostility
hosting
hot
hotel
hotly
hotter
hottest
hound
hounded
hounding
hour

hourly
house
housed
household
householder
housekeeper
housekeeping
housewife
housewives
housework
housing
hovel
hover
hovercraft
hovered
hovering
how
however
howl
howled
howling
hub
hubbub
huddle
huddled
huddling
hue
huff
hug
huge
hugely
huger
hugest
hugged
hugging

hulk
hulking
hull
hum
human
humane
humanely
humanism
humanitarian
humanity
humanly
humble
humbled
humbling
humbly
humbug
humdrum
humid
humidity
humiliate
humiliated
humiliating
humiliation
humility
hummed
humming
hummingbird
humorous
humour
humoured
humouring
hump
humped
humping
hunch

hunchback
hunched
hunches
hunching
hundred
hundredth
hung
hunger
hungered
hungering
hungrier
hungriest
hungrily
hungry
hunk
hunt
hunted
hunter
hunting
hurdle
hurdled
hurdling
hurl
hurled
hurling
hurly-burly
hurricane
hurried
hurries
hurry
hurt
hurting
hurtle
hurtled
hurtling

cough

a hoarse horse

horse
A 'horse' is a large mammal, but 'hoarse' means 'husky-voiced'.
horticulture means 'growing things in a garden', and it comes from the Latin word for 'garden', 'hortus'.

host; hostess
The male version of this word is 'host', and the female has '-ess', to make 'hostess'. This is a common spelling pattern, that 'waiter/waitress'; 'tempter/temptress' also follow.

hostesses; hunches; hutches
Words ending with '-ss', or other hissing sounds such as '-ch', '-s', '-sh' or '-z' take the ending '-es' in the plural.

hour
Be careful not to confuse 'hour', which means 'a period of 60 minutes', with 'our', which means 'belonging to us': 'Our house is always busy.'

housewife → housewives
Most words ending in '-f' or '-fe' just add an '-s' in the plural, but some change to '-ves', as here.

husband	hutch	hypnotic	hypocrite
husbandry	hutches	hypnotise/hypnotize	hypocritical
hush	hybrid	hypnotised/	hypocritically
hushed	hyena	hypnotized	hypotheses
huskier	hygiene	hypnotising/	hypothesis
huskiest	hygienic	hypnotizing	hypothetical
husky	hymn	hypnotism	hypothetically
hustle	hyperactive	hypnotist	hysteria
hustled	hyperbole	hypochondria	hysterical
hustling	hyphen	hypochondriac	hysterically
hut	hypnosis	hypocrisy	hysterics

hug; huge
To 'hug' means 'hold in your arms', and is from an Old Norse word for 'comfort', 'hugga'. Adding a silent '-e' makes 'huge', which means 'very big'.

humorous
Notice that if you are adding '-ous' to a word ending in '-our', the 'u' is dropped: 'humorous'; 'glamorous'.

hurdle; hurtle
The letters 'ur' in these words are one of the ways of spelling the sound 'er'. The other are 'ea' ('earn'); 'er' ('her'); 'ir' ('bird'); 'or' ('word'), and 'our' ('journey').

hymn
Remember the silent '-n' after the 'm'.

'hyper-'/'hypo-'
'Hyper-' at the beginning of a word means 'a great deal' or 'very much': 'hyperactive' means 'very, very active', for instance. Don't confuse it with 'hypo-', which is from the Greek for 'under' or 'beneath'.

hypnosis; hypnotic; hypnotist, etc.
Words that begin with 'hypno-' are something to do with sleep, as these three words are. They all come from the Greek word for 'sleep', 'hypnos'.

hyphens are the symbol (-). You will see them used in these three ways:

1. **To form compound words:**
'half-hearted'; 'heavy-duty'; 'high-handed'.

2. **To separate awkward letter combinations:**
're-educate'; 'de-activate'; 'pre-eminent'.

3. **To show that a word continues on the line below:** If, as shown here, a word has to be divided into two parts to fit onto a line.

Quick tip

Break it down
Try sounding each part of long, or tricky, words out loud:

'ha-bit-u-al'
and
'hap-haz-ard'

Many words aren't spelt exactly as they sound, but this technique can make it easier to hear each part of a word, before you put them all back together to spell it.

Some tricky words to spell that start with an 'h'

Here are some words beginning with 'h' that are particularly tricky to spell.
See how many you can get right. There are some tips to help you on page 7.

haemorrhage	havoc	hierarchy
handicap	height	hoax
harangue	hemisphere	hoeing
harass	hideous	hygiene

I i

This rabbit's a little long in the tooth.

idioms are **phrases that mean something different from the words they contain**. For example, 'long in the tooth' means 'getting old'. This idiom comes from the traditional way of calculating the age of a horse: by looking at its teeth.

ibis
ibises
ice
iceberg
ice cream
ice cube
iced
ice-skating
icicle
icier
iciest
icing
icon
iconic
icy
idea
idealism
idealise/idealize
idealised/idealized
idealising/idealizing
idealist
idealistic
ideally
identical
identically
identification
identifies
identify

identifying
identities
identity
idiom
idiomatic
idiosyncrasies
idiosyncrasy
idiot
idiotic
idle
idled
idleness
idling
idly
idol
idolatry
idolise/idolize
idolised/idolized
idolising/idolizing
idyll
idyllic
igloo
igneous
ignite
ignited
igniting
ignition
ignominious

ignominiously
ignominy
ignorance
ignorant
ignorantly
ignore
ignored
ignoring
iguana
ill
illegal
illegality
illegally
illegibility
illegible
illegitimacy
illegitimate
ill-fated
illicit
illiteracy
illiterate
illness
illnesses
illogical
illogically
ill-treat
ill-treated
ill-treating

ill-treatment
illuminate
illuminated
illuminating
illumination
illusion
illusory
illustrate
illustrated
illustrating
illustration
illustrative
illustrator
illustrious
image
imagery
imaginary
imagination
imaginative
imaginatively
imagine
imagined
imagining
imbalance
imbalanced
imbecile
imitate
imitated

an idle idol

idle *vs* **idol**
Idle means 'lazy', but an 'idol' is worshipped or admired by others.

idolise/idolize
Most words can be correctly spelt with an 's' or a 'z', but some words are only ever spelt '-ise', or only with '-ize'. You'll find a list on page 4.

'il-', 'im-', 'in-', 'ill-'
When these letters are added to the beginning of a word, they may make it mean its opposite: 'impossible' means 'not possible', for example. When 'ill-' comes before a word, it has a negative meaning: 'ill-fated'.

identification; illumination; illusion, etc.
Many words end with '-tion' (pronounced 'shun'), but the ending '-sion' sounds the same, so spell with care.

ignorance; impertinence; importance, etc.
It's easy to get the endings '-ence' and '-ance' mixed up. Always check the spelling if you are unsure.

imitating	immune	imperfection	implication
imitation	immunity	imperfectly	implicit
imitative	imp	imperial	implicitly
imitator	impact	imperialism	implied
immaculate	impair	imperialist	implore
immaculately	impaired	imperious	implored
immaterial	impairing	impersonal	imploring
immature	impale	impersonally	imply
immaturity	impaled	impersonate	implying
immediate	impaling	impersonated	impolite
immediately	impart	impersonating	impolitely
immemorial	imparted	impersonation	import
immense	impartial	impersonator	importance
immensely	impartiality	impertinence	important
immensities	impartially	impertinent	importantly
immensity	imparting	impertinently	importation
immerse	impasse	impetuosity	imported
immersed	impassioned	impetuous	importer
immersing	impassive	impetuously	importing
immersion	impassively	impetus	impose
immigrant	impatience	impinge	imposed
immigration	impatient	impinged	imposing
imminent	impatiently	impinging	impossibility
imminently	impeccable	impish	impossible
immobile	impeccably	implacable	impossibly
immobilise/	impede	implacably	imposter/impostor
immobilize	impeded	implant	impotence
immobilised/	impediment	implanted	impotent
immobilized	impeding	implanting	impotently
immobilising/	impel	implausible	impound
immobilizing	impelled	implausibly	impounded
immobility	impending	implement	impounding
immoral	impenetrable	implementation	impoverished
immortal	imperative	implemented	impractical
immortality	imperfect	implementing	impregnable

---

illicit means 'illegal', and 'elicit' means 'extract' or 'draw out': 'Her question elicited a swift response.'

illustrator; imitator; impersonator, etc.
Here, the ending '-or' means 'person who does it', e.g. an 'imitator' imitates, and an 'illustrator' illustrates.

immediately
When you add an ending that starts with a consonant, such as '-ly', to 'immediate', keep the '-e'. If the word ends in '-le' ('gentle', 'idle'), drop the '-e': 'gently', 'idly'.
immigrant means 'a person who enters a country'. An 'emigrant' is someone who leaves it.

immoral means 'going against or disregarding moral standards', but 'amoral' means 'having no moral standards at all'.

impair
The letters 'air' in 'impair' are only one way of spelling this sound. The others are 'are' ('hare'), 'ear' ('bear'), 'ere' ('there') and 'eir' ('heir'), so take care.

impasse is originally a French word, meaning 'dead end', and is used in English to mean 'a situation without a solution'.

impregnate	impure	inch	incomparable
impregnated	impurities	inched	incompatibility
impregnating	impurity	inches	incompatible
impress	inabilities	inching	incompetence
impressed	inability	incidence	incompetent
impressing	inaccessibility	incident	incompetently
impression	inaccessible	incidental	incomprehensible
impressionable	inaccuracies	incidentally	inconceivable
impressionism	inaccuracy	incinerate	inconceivably
impressionist	inaccurate	incinerated	inconclusive
impressive	inadequacies	incinerating	inconclusively
impressively	inadequacy	incinerator	incongruous
imprint	inadequate	incipient	incongruously
imprinted	inadequately	incision	inconsiderate
imprinting	inadvertent	incisive	inconsiderately
imprison	inadvertently	incisively	inconsistencies
imprisoned	inane	incite	inconsistency
imprisoning	inanely	incited	inconsistent
improbabilities	inanimate	incitement	inconsistently
improbability	inappropriate	inciting	inconspicuous
improbable	inappropriately	inclination	inconspicuously
improbably	inarticulate	incline	inconvenience
impromptu	inaudible	inclined	inconvenienced
improper	inborn	inclining	inconveniencing
improperly	incapable	include	inconvenient
improve	incapacity	included	inconveniently
improved	incendiary	including	incorporate
improvement	incense	inclusion	incorporated
improving	incensed	inclusive	incorporating
impudence	incentive	incognito	incorrect
impudent	inception	incoherence	incorrectly
impudently	incessant	incoherent	increase
impulse	incessantly	incoherently	increased
impulsive	incest	income	increasing
impulsively	incestuous	incoming	increasingly

incredible	indigestion	industrial	infamously
incredulity	indignant	industrialist	infamy
incredulous	indignantly	industries	infancy
incubate	indignation	industrious	infant
incubated	indignities	industriously	infantry
incubation	indignity	industry	infatuated
incubator	indigo	inedible	infatuation
incurable	indirect	ineffective	infect
incurably	indirectly	ineffectively	infected
indebted	indiscriminate	ineffectual	infecting
indecency	indiscriminately	ineffectually	infection
indecent	indispensable	inefficiencies	infectious
indecently	indistinct	inefficiency	infer
indeed	indistinctly	inefficient	inference
indefinite	individual	inefficiently	inferior
indefinitely	individualist	inept	inferiority
indelible	individualistic	ineptitude	infernal
indelibly	individuality	inequalities	infernally
indemnity	individually	inequality	inferno
indent	indoctrinate	inert	inferred
indentation	indoctrinated	inertia	inferring
indented	indoctrinating	inevitability	infertile
indenting	indoctrination	inevitable	infertility
independence	indoor	inexhaustible	infest
independent	indoors	inexorable	infestation
independently	induce	inexorably	infested
index	induced	inexpensive	infesting
indexes	inducement	inexpensively	infidelities
indicate	inducing	inexperience	infidelity
indicated	induction	inexperienced	infighting
indicating	indulge	inexplicable	infiltrate
indication	indulged	inexplicably	infiltrated
indicative	indulgence	infallibility	infiltrating
indicator	indulgent	infallible	infiltration
indigestible	indulgently	infamous	infinite

i

incorrect; indirect; infect
You'll never find a 'k'
before a 't'. It's always a
'c' that makes a 'ct' sound.

indebted
Remember the silent 'b' before the 't' in 'indebted'.

indemnity; indignant; indiscriminate
Many words are not spelt as they sound in English, but
many are. Try breaking these tricky words down into
parts: 'in-dem-ni-ty'; 'in-dig-nant'; 'in-dis-crim-in-ate'.
It may help you hear, and remember, every letter.

indoor; indoors
The word 'indoor' is an adjective, describing a noun:
'The indoor fireworks were fantastic.' 'Indoors' is
an adverb, describing a verb: 'We ate indoors.'

inertia
The letters 'ti' often make a 'sh' sound, as here
in 'inertia' (lack of energy). This pattern appears
often, e.g. 'initial', 'insatiable' and 'initiate'.

infernal; inferno
'Infernal' means 'awful': 'He was an infernal liar.'
An 'inferno' is a fierce fire, from the Italian for 'Hell'.

infinitely	informatively	inherited	in-law
infinitive	informed	inheriting	inlay
infinity	informer	inheritor	inlet
infirm	informing	inhibit	inmate
infirmaries	infrastructure	inhibited	inn
infirmary	infringe	inhibiting	innards
infirmities	infringed	inhibition	innate
infirmity	infringement	inhospitable	innately
inflamed	infringing	inhuman	inner
inflaming	infuriate	inhumane	innermost
inflammable	infuriated	inhumanity	innings
inflammation	infuriating	inimitable	innocence
inflammatory	infuse	initial	innocent
inflate	infused	initially	innocuous
inflated	infusing	initiate	innocuously
inflating	infusion	initiated	innovation
inflation	ingenious	initiating	innovator
inflection	ingeniously	initiative	innovatory
inflexibility	ingenuity	inject	innuendo
inflexible	ingrain	injected	innumerable
inflict	ingrained	injecting	input
inflicted	ingraining	injection	inquest
inflicting	ingredient	injunction	inquire
influence	inhabit	injure	inquired
influenced	inhabitant	injured	inquiring
influencing	inhabited	injuries	inquiry
influential	inhabiting	injuring	inquisition
influx	inhalation	injury	inquisitive
inform	inhale	injustice	inquisitively
informal	inhaled	ink	inroads
informalities	inhaling	inked	insane
informality	inherent	inking	insanely
informally	inherently	inkling	insanitary
information	inherit	inlaid	insanity
informative	inheritance	inland	insatiable

infirmities; informalities; injuries, etc.
Remember that words that end in a consonant and a '-y' change to '-ies' in the plural.

inflammable; inflammation
A phrase might help you remember the two 'm's in these words. '**M**elting **m**atter' might make you think of 'inflammable' and '**my m**uscles' of 'inflammation'.

innocence; innocent; insignificance; insignificant
It's hard to hear a difference between '-ence' and '-ance', and '-ent' and '-ant'. Whatever pattern a word follows, it will stick to it in all its variations.

informatively; inquisitively; insensitively, etc.
If you remember that 'v' always has a vowel or a 'y' after it, it will remind you to keep the 'e' in these adverbs.

infringement; infringing
If you add an ending that starts with a vowel to a word with a silent '-e' on the end, you usually drop it: 'infringing'. If the ending starts with a consonant, you keep the '-e': 'infringement'.

inhabit vs inhibit
It's easy to mix these words up. 'Inhabit' means 'live in'. 'Inhibit' means to 'limit' or 'hold back'.

inscribe	insolence	instilling	integral
inscribed	insolent	instinct	integrate
inscribing	insolently	instinctive	integrated
inscription	insolubility	instinctively	integrating
inscrutable	insoluble	institute	integration
insect	insolvency	instituted	integrity
insecticide	insolvent	instituting	intellectual
insecure	inspect	institution	intellectually
insecurities	inspected	institutional	intelligence
insecurity	inspecting	instruct	intelligent
insensitive	inspection	instructed	intelligently
insensitively	inspector	instructing	intelligibility
insensitivity	inspiration	instruction	intelligible
insert	inspire	instrument	intend
inserted	inspired	instrumental	intended
inserting	inspiring	insufficiencies	intending
insertion	instability	insufficiency	intense
inshore	install	insufficient	intensely
inside	installation	insufficiently	intensified
insight	installed	insular	intensify
insignificance	installing	insulate	intensifying
insignificant	instalment	insulated	intensity
insincere	instance	insulating	intensive
insincerely	instant	insulation	intensively
insinuate	instantaneous	insulator	intent
insinuated	instantaneously	insult	intention
insinuating	instantly	insulted	intentional
insinuation	instead	insulting	intentionally
insipid	instigate	insurance	intently
insist	instigated	insure	interact
insisted	instigating	insured	interacted
insistence	instigation	insuring	interaction
insistent	instigator	insurrection	interactive
insistently	instil	intact	intercept
insisting	instilled	intake	intercepted

inkling means 'an idea' or 'a hint'. The ending '-ling' usually means 'small' or 'baby', e.g. 'duckling'.

innuendo
An 'innuendo' is a way of referring to something rude without saying it directly. It's from the Latin 'innuere', which means 'to tell with a nod'.

inquire
'Inquire', meaning 'to ask for information about something', can also be correctly spelt 'enquire'.

inquiry usually describes a formal investigation such as a 'police inquiry'. An 'enquiry' is a simple question.

insistence/insistent, etc.
'Insistence' is a noun and 'insistent' is an adjective. You'll spot the '-ence/-ent' pattern again and again.

instalment
This noun from the verb 'install' is often misspelt. Don't forget to drop one 'l' before you add '-ment'.

instil → instilled
Double the final '-l' when you add '-ed' to 'instil'.

insure means 'to pay for protection against harm with insurance'. To 'ensure' means to 'make sure': 'She ensured that her seat belt was fastened.'

interjections are often used in everyday speech to **express a feeling, such as surprise or disbelief**. They can be used on their own, e.g. *'Hooray!'*, *'Wow!'*, *'No way!'*, or as part of a sentence, separated by a commas and/or dashes: 'She turned the key and, *thank goodness*, the door opened.'

intercepting
interception
interchange
interchangeable
intercom
intercourse
interest
interested
interesting
interestingly
interfere
interfered
interference
interim
interior
interjection
interlude
intermediaries
intermediary
intermediate
interminable
interminably
intermission
intermittent
intermittently
internal
internally

international
internationally
interplay
interpret
interpretation
interpreted
interpreter
interpreting
interrogate
interrogated
interrogating
interrogation
interrogator
interrupt
interrupted
interrupting
interruption
intersect
intersected
intersecting
intersection
interspersed
interval
intervene
intervened
intervening
intervention

interview
interviewed
interviewing
intimacies
intimacy
intimate
intimately
intimation
intimidate
intimidated
intimidating
intimidation
intolerable
intolerably
intolerant
intonation
intone
intoned
intoning
intoxicate
intoxicated
intoxicating
intoxication
intractability
intractable
intrepid
intrepidly
intricacies
intricacy
intricate
intricately
intrigue
intrigued
intriguing
intrinsic

intrinsically
introduce
introduced
introducing
introduction
introductory
introvert
introverted
intrude
intruder
intruding
intrusion
intrusive
intrusively
intuition
intuitive
intuitively
inundated
inundating
invade
invaded
invader
invading
invalid
invalidate
invalidity
invaluable
invariably
invasion
invective
invent
invented
inventing
invention
inventive

'inter-' at the beginning of a word conveys the idea of going between two things, or people, e.g. 'intercept', 'intercourse'. It is the Latin word for 'between'.

interrupt
To help you remember the double 'r' in 'interrupt', think '**r**eally **r**ude' (which interrupting someone is).

intrigue
You'll find '-gue' at the end of several words, such as 'catalogue', 'dialogue', 'fatigue' and 'vague'. Remember you need to drop the '-e' when you add '-ing' to most verbs, to make 'cataloguing' and 'fatiguing'.

invalid
When you emphasize the first syllable of 'invalid', it means 'a very ill person'. When you stress the second syllable, 'va', it means 'not valid': 'an invalid licence'.

inward/inwards
'Inward' means 'inside' or 'within yourself': 'My inward thoughts were gloomy.' 'Inwards' means 'moving further inside': 'The miners burrowed inwards.'

isle is another word for 'island'. An 'aisle' is the passageway in a church or theatre. All three words have a silent 's', so take care when spelling them.

inventor
inventories
inventory
inverse
invert
inverted
inverting
invest
invested
investigate
investigated
investigating
investigation
investigative
investing
investiture
investment
investor
invincibility
invincible
invincibly
invisibility
invisible
invisibly
invitation
invite
invited
inviting
invoice
involve
involved
involvement

involving
inward
inwards
irascible
irate
iris
irises
iron
ironed
ironic
ironical
ironically
ironies
ironing
irony
irrational
irrationality
irrationally
irregularities
irregularity
irregularly
irrelevance
irrelevant
irrepressible
irresistible
irresistibly
irrespective
irresponsibility
irresponsible
irresponsibly
irrigate
irrigated

irrigating
irrigation
irritable
irritant
irritate
irritated
irritating
irritation
island
islander
isle
isolate
isolated
isolating
isolation
issue

issued
issuing
italics
itch
itched
itches
itching
itchy
item
itineraries
itinerary
its
it's
itself
ivory
ivy

its or it's?
Lots of spellers get confused between
'its' and 'it's'. **Just remember that:**
Its means 'belonging to it':
'*Its* tail was long.'
It's is short for 'it is' or 'it has':
'*It's* a disaster.' '*It's* been too long.'

It's got its hat on to keep warm.

Some tricky words to spell that start with an 'i'

How many of these tricky 'i' words can you spell correctly?

idiosyncracy	impetuous	interrupt
illegitimacy	implausible	irascible
illiterate	incoherent	irrelevance
illogical	incongruous	irresponsibility
immaterial	innocence	irritable
impartial	innocuous	itinerary

Jj

A jewel may be a gem, but it starts with a 'j', not a 'g'.

The 'j' sound can be made in several ways:

1. By the letter 'j', as in the word jewel.
2. The letter 'g', when it's followed by an 'e' ('gem'), an 'i' ('giant') or a 'y' ('gym').
3. The letters 'dg', as in 'dredge' and judge.

jab	jailing	jay	jerkily
jabbed	jam	jaywalk	jerking
jabber	jammed	jaywalked	jerky
jabbering	jamming	jaywalking	jersey
jabbing	jangle	jazz	jest
jackal	jangled	jazzier	jested
jackass	jangling	jazziest	jester
jackasses	jar	jazzy	jesting
jackdaw	jargon	jealous	jet
jacket	jarred	jealously	jetted
jackpot	jarring	jealousy	jetties
jacuzzi	jasmine	jeans	jetting
jade	jaundice	jeep	jettison
jaded	jaundiced	jeer	jettisoned
jagged	jaunt	jeered	jettisoning
jaguar	jauntily	jeering	jetty
jail	jaunty	jellies	jewel
jailed	javelin	jelly	jewellers
jailer	jaw	jellyfish	jewellery
		jeopardise/	jibe
		jeopardize	jig
		jeopardised/	jigged
		jeopardized	jigging
		jeopardising/	jiggle
		jeopardizing	jiggled
		jeopardy	jiggling
		jerk	jigsaw
		jerked	jilt

jargon means **language that only the people who use it can understand easily.** There are lots of different types of jargon.

We'll downsize outgoings, to maximize throughput.

---

jabbed; jammed; jarred, etc.
Words of one syllable, with a short vowel and a consonant, double the final consonant before an ending that begins with a vowel is added (but 'h', 'j', 'k', 'q', 'v', 'w', 'x' and 'y' are almost never doubled).

jackasses; jukeboxes
Remember that words ending in '-ss', '-ch', '-z', '-x' or other hissing sounds usually take '-es' in the plural.

jail
You may occasionally see the spelling 'gaol' for this word. Both versions are correct.

jaywalk
This word means 'to cross a road without paying attention to traffic'. It may be linked to the confident, bold behaviour of birds called blue jays.

jeans; jodhpurs
You will only ever see these words used in the plural, as they are plural nouns.

jellies; jetties; juries
Notice that these words end in a consonant, and then a '-y', so they take '-ies' in the plural. This is a common spelling pattern, so try to learn it.

For words that begin with the 'j' sound, try the 'g' pages if you can't find a word you need here.

jilted — juxtaposition

jilted
jilting
jingle
jingled
jingling
jinx
jinxes
job
jobless
jockey
jodhpurs
jog
jogged
jogger
jogging
join
joined
joiner
joinery
joining
joint
jointed
jointly
joist
joke
joked
joker
joking
jokingly
jollier
jolliest
jollity
jolly
jolt
jolted

jolting
jostle
jostled
jostling
jot
jotted
jotter
jotting
journal
journalism
journalist
journalistic
journey
journeyed
journeying
joust
jousted
jousting
jovial
joviality
jovially
jowl
joy
joyful
joyfully
joyless
joyous
joyously
joyride
joyrider
joyriding
jubilant
jubilantly
jubilation
jubilee

judder
juddering
judge
judged
judgement/judgment
judgemental/
judgmental
judging
judicial
judicious
judo
jug
juggernaut
juggle
juggled
juggling
juice
juicy
jukebox
jukeboxes
jumble
jumbled
jumbling
jump
jumped
jumper
jumpier

jumpiest
jumping
jumpy
junction
jungle
junior
junk
juries
jurisdiction
juror
jury
just
justice
justification
justified
justifies
justify
justifying
justly
jut
jutted
jutting
juvenile
juxtapose
juxtaposed
juxtaposing
juxtaposition

j

Quick tip **'Special J'**
Did you know that the
letter 'j' is rather special?
Firstly, it's **always followed by a vowel**, never a consonant. Also, **you'll never see a double 'j' in an English word**, as it's never repeated.

jellyfish is also the plural of 'jellyfish', but you may, occasionally, read 'jellyfishes'. The word 'fish' follows this pattern too.

jibe can also be spelt 'gibe'. Both of these spellings are correct, but 'gibe' is more common. Both words mean a 'taunt' or an 'insult'.

jobless
The ending '-less' means 'without', not 'less of'. 'Jobless' means 'without a job', for instance.

joke → joking; jostle → jostling
Here, when you add '-ing', you drop the final '-e'.

journey; joust
Notice that the letters 'ou' make different sounds in these two words. In 'journey', they rhyme with 'turn', but in 'joust', they rhyme with 'cow'.

judgement/judgment
You can use both these spellings of this word, but most words keep the '-e' before the ending '-ment', as in 'encourage/encouragement'.

judo
Only words from other languages end in an '-o'. 'Judo' is the Japanese name for a sport.

Words with a story to tell

A lot of English words come from other languages, and have histories all of their own. Knowing a little about the origins of these words may help you remember their unusual spellings. Here are three such words that begin with the letter 'j':

1. **Jeans** are blue denim trousers, first made by Levi Strauss in the USA in the 1860s from material originally made in Genoa, in Italy. The name 'jeans', is probably adapted from the name of this Italian city.

2. **Jodhpurs** are closely-fitted riding trousers, and were originally called 'jodhpur breeches'. They are named after a former state in northern India called Jodhpur, where Indian men wore similarly-styled trousers.

3. **Juggernaut** means 'a huge lorry or truck'. It comes from a Hindu ceremony, in which believers threw themselves beneath the image of a god known as 'Jaggarnath,' as it was drawn through the town of Puri, in a procession.

British or American English?

English-speaking countries often adapt the English language. Words may be spelt the same, but pronounced differently, or one letter may change, for instance. Here are some ways British English and American English relate to each other.

- In British English, it's fine to use 's' or 'z' in words such as 'jeopardise/jeopardize', but 'z' is always used in American English.

- In North America, people tend to use 'jail' more than they use 'gaol', and they spell the word 'jewellery', 'jewelry'.

- Languages absorb words from other cultures. For instance, 'jaywalk' and 'joyride', first used in North America, are now a part of British English.

- There are times when the word is completely different, however. For example, a 'nappy' in British English is a 'diaper' in American English.

Language changes all the time, so check your spelling.

Some tricky words to spell that start with a 'j'

See how many of these tricky words beginning with 'j' you can get right.

jealous	joyous
jeopardise/jeopardize	juggernaut
jewellery	junction
jinx	jurisdiction
jodhpurs	juvenile
journey	juxtaposition

If the word you need begins with a 'k' sound, it may begin with a 'c', so check those pages too.

kaleidoscope — knack

Kk

a kiwi doing karaoke

kamikaze; karaoke; karate; karma; khaki; kimono; kiwi
English uses many words from other languages, such as those listed here. They often end in a vowel that you can hear when you say the word, such as '-a' or '-i'.

kaleidoscope	kestrel	kilometre	kink
kaleidoscopic	ketchup	kilt	kinkier
kamikaze	kettle	kimono	kinkiest
kangaroo	key	kimonos	kinky
karaoke	keyboard	kin	kinship
karate	keyed-in	kind	kiosk
karma	key-in	kinder	kip
kayak	keying-in	kindergarten	kipper
kebab	khaki	kindest	kiss
keel	kibbutz	kind-hearted	kissed
keeled	kibbutzim	kind-heartedly	kisses
keeling	kick	kindle	kissing
keen	kicked	kindling	kit
keener	kicking	kindly	kitchen
keenest	kick-off	kindness	kite
keenly	kid	king	kitsch
keenness	kidded	kingdom	kitten
keep	kidding	kingfisher	kitties
keeper	kidnap	kingly	kitty
keeping	kidnapped	kingship	kiwi
keepsake	kidnapper	king-size	knack
keg	kidnapping		
kelp	kill		
kennel	killed		
kept	killer		
kerb	killing		
kernel	kiln		
kerosene	kilogram		

 Quick tip The letters 'k' and 'c' can sound the same, so it can be easy to use the wrong one. Remember that **the letter 'k' always makes a hard sound**, as in 'kick' and 'kiss'. It never makes the soft 'ss' sound that 'c' makes in 'certain', 'circus' or 'cycle'. This may help you choose whether you need a 'k' or a 'c'.

kaleidoscope means 'a rich array', or 'a tube containing pieces of coloured plastic which form patterns when the tube is twisted'. It's from the Greek words 'kalos' (lovely), 'eidos' (shape) plus '-scope' (an instrument for looking at things, e.g. 'telescope').

kerb
A 'kerb' is the edge of a pavement. To 'curb' is to limit: 'She had to curb her liking for chocolate.'

kernel
A 'kernel' is the nut inside a nutshell, but a 'colonel' (which sounds the same) is a military officer.

key
A 'key' can open a door, be a button on a computer keyboard or a note on a piano. A 'quay', pronounced the same, is the side of a harbour, where boats tie up.

kilogram; kilometre
You will often see these measurements shortened to 'kg' and 'km': 'She weighed 70kg and ran 10km.'

kingship *vs* **kinship**
Don't mix up 'kingship', which means 'being a king', and 'kinship', which is to do with the idea of being related or in the same family.

k

knapsack

knave

knead

kneaded

kneading

knee

kneecap

kneel

kneeled

kneeling

knelt

knew

knickers

knife

knifed

knifing

knight

knighted

knighthood

knighting

knightly

knit

knitted

knitting

knives

knob

knobbly

knock

knocked

knocker

knocking

knockout

knoll

knot

knotted

knotting

knotty

know

know-how

knowing

knowingly

knowledge

knowledgable/

knowledgeable

known

knuckle

koala

kumquat

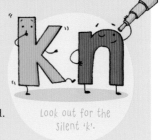

Silent letters

More than forty of the words in this section are spelt with a silent 'k-' at the beginning, always before a letter 'n'. Many of these words are very old, and have changed gradually over time. They used to sound very different.

For instance, the word 'know' is from the Old English word 'cnawan', in which the 'c' was pronounced. Centuries later, the 'k' is silent.

Look out for the silent 'k'.

knave means 'a rogue' or 'rascal', but a 'nave' is the central part of a church.

knead
To 'knead' dough means 'to prepare it for baking'. To 'need' is to have to do, or have, something: 'I need to lose weight'; 'We need food and water to survive.'

knew is the past tense of the verb 'to know': 'Freddie knew that he loved her.' Don't confuse it with 'new', which means the opposite of 'old': 'My new shoes.'

knife → **knives**
Many '-f' or '-fe' endings change to '-ves' in the plural.

knight means 'a noble warrior' in tales and legends, but 'night' is the opposite of 'day'.

knit is to make something with wool, but a 'nit' is an insect, or a fool: 'She is such a nit.'

knot
'Knot' can mean 'tied up threads', or 'the speed of a boat' e.g. '10 knots'. 'Not' makes a phrase negative: 'He will not make it in time.'

knowledgable/knowledgeable
You usually keep the '-e' before adding '-able' (to keep the 'g' sound soft), but 'knowledgable' is also correct.

Some tricky words to spell that start with a 'k'

Here are some words beginning with 'k' that are particularly tricky to spell.

kaleidoscope	kitchen	knight
keenness	knead	knock
kerb	knee	knot
ketchup	knickers	knowledge
kilometre	knife	knuckle

Ll

Practice makes perfect
Some words, such as labyrinth, lacklustre and lacquer, aren't spelt as you might expect. You need to keep practising words like these, until you know them off by heart.

label	laden	lance	lapping
labelled	ladies	lanced	lapse
labelling	ladle	lancing	lapsed
laboratories	lady	land	lapsing
laboratory	ladybird	landed	lard
laborious	ladylike	landing	larder
laboriously	ladyship	landladies	large
labour	lag	landlady	largely
laboured	lager	landlord	larger
labourer	lagged	landmark	largest
labouring	lagging	landowner	lark
labrador	lagoon	landscape	larva
labyrinth	laid	landslide	larvae
lace	lain	lane	lasagne
laced	lair	language	laser
lacing	lake	languid	lash
lack	lamb	languidly	lashed
lacked	lame	languish	lashes
lacking	lamely	languished	lashing
lacklustre	lameness	languishing	lass
laconic	lament	lankier	lasses
laconically	lamentable	lankiest	lasso
lacquer	lamented	lankiness	lassoes/lassos
lacquered	lamenting	lanky	last
lacrosse	laminated	lantern	lasted
lacy	lamp	lap	lasting
lad	lamppost	lapel	lastly
ladder	lampshade	lapped	latch

labelled; labelling
Notice that when you add an ending that starts with a vowel to a word ending in a single '-l', such as 'label', you double the 'l'.

lacing; lapsing
When you add an ending that starts with a vowel to a word that ends in a silent '-e', you usually drop the '-e'. Think: 'I drop the '-e' when I add '-ing'.'

ladies; landladies
Words that end with a consonant and then a '-y', such as 'lady', take the ending '-ies' in the plural.

lanky → lankiness
The '-y' at the end of 'lanky' changes to an 'i' before '-ness' is added. Lots of words follow this pattern.

A larva is a young insect. The plural, 'larvae', follows the Latin spelling pattern, as many mathematical and scientific words do. Don't mix it up with 'lava', which is molten rock that gushes from volcanoes.

A laser is a powerful light, used in medicine and industry. It is an acronym (a word made from the first letters of words in a phrase). 'Laser' is from '**l**ight **a**mplification by **s**timulated **e**mission of **r**adiation'.

latched	lavish	leakage	leftover
latches	lavished	leaked	leg
latching	lavishing	leakier	legacies
late	law	leakiest	legacy
lately	lawful	leaking	legal
latent	lawfully	leaky	legalise/legalize
later	lawless	lean	legalised/legalized
lateral	lawlessly	leaned/leant	legalising/legalizing
latest	lawn	leaner	legalities
lather	lawnmower	leanest	legality
latitude	lawsuit	leaning	legally
latter	lawyer	leap	legend
latterly	lax	leaped/leapt	legendary
lattice	laxative	leaping	leggings
latticed	lay	learn	legibility
laudable	layer	learned/learnt	legible
laugh	layered	learner	legion
laughable	layering	learning	legislate
laughed	laying	lease	legislated
laughing	layman	leased	legislation
laughter	laymen	leasehold	legislator
launch	layout	leash	legitimacy
launched	laze	least	legitimate
launches	lazed	leather	legitimately
launching	lazier	leathery	leisure
launder	laziest	leave	leisurely
laundered	lazing	leaves	lemon
launderette	lazy	led	lemonade
laundering	lead	leek	lend
laundry	leader	leer	lending
laurel	leadership	leered	length
lava	leading	leering	lengthen
lavatories	leaf	left	lengthened
lavatory	leaflet	left-handed	lengthening
lavender	leak	left-handedness	lengthways

---

laugh; light

Take care with the letters 'gh'. They make an 'f' sound in 'laugh'. They make a 'g' sound, as at the beginning of 'ghastly', but in 'light', they are silent.

lava

'Lava' is the molten rock that gushes out of volcanoes. A 'larva' is a young insect.

lawful; lawless

The ending '-ful' is positive: 'lawful' means 'abiding by the law'. The ending '-less' means 'without', so 'lawless' means 'without any control by the law'.

lead vs led

The words 'lead' and 'led' can be very confusing, so check your spelling before you use them, if unsure.
- The verb 'lead' means 'to guide or direct people from the front': 'She leads the procession.'
- The word 'lead', pronounced to rhyme with 'bed', is a heavy, grey metal.
- The noun 'lead', to rhyme with 'freed', is a strap or leash, often used for walking dogs.
- The word 'led' is the past tense of the verb 'to lead': 'He led me to the hotel.'

lengthy	lewdness	lied	likelihood
lenience	liabilities	lieutenant	likely
lenient	liability	life	liken
leniently	liable	lifebelt	likened
lens	liaise	lifeblood	likeness
lenses	liaised	lifeboat	likening
lent	liaising	lifeguard	likewise
lentil	liaison	lifeless	liking
leopard	liar	lifelike	lilac
leotard	libel	lifeline	lilies
less	libellous	lifelong	lily
lessen	liberal	lifestyle	limb
lessened	liberalism	lifetime	limber
lessening	liberally	lift	limbered
lesser	liberate	lifted	limbering
lesson	liberated	lifting	lime
let	liberating	lift-off	limelight
lethal	liberation	light	limerick
lethargic	liberty	lighted/lit	limestone
lethargy	librarian	lighten	limit
letter	libraries	lightened	limitation
lettering	library	lightening	limited
letting	lice	lighter	limiting
lettuce	licence	lightest	limitless
level	license	light-headed	limousine
levelled	licensed	light-hearted	limp
levelling	licensing	lighthouse	limped
lever	lichen	lighting	limpet
leverage	lick	lightly	limping
leveret	licked	lightness	line
levied	licking	lightning	lineage
levies	lid	lightweight	linear
levy	lidded	like	lined
levying	lido	likable/likeable	linen
lewd	lie	liked	liner

leak *vs* **leek**

A 'leak' is a hole or gap, which allows something to escape. A 'leek' is a green and white vegetable that tastes quite like an onion.

That leek will cause a leak.

legend; legible; legion

Notice that 'g' is soft when it is followed by an 'e' (in 'legend') or an 'i' (in 'legible' and 'legion').

lessen *vs* **lesson**

To 'lessen' means 'to make less', but a 'lesson' is a period of tuition, or teaching.

learned/learnt

You can use either 'learned' or 'learnt' for the past tense of 'learn'. The word 'learned' (say 'ler-ned') is an old-fashioned adjective used to describe someone knowledgeable: 'A learned woman.'

licence *vs* **license**

A 'licence' is a noun: 'I've got my driving licence', but 'license' is a verb: 'He's licensed to sell alcohol.' 'Advice/advise' and 'practice/practise' also follow this pattern.

linesman	listen	loaded	lodge
linesmen	listened	loading	lodged
lineswoman	listener	loaf	lodger
lineswomen	listening	loan	lodging
linger	listing	loaned	loft
lingered	listless	loaning	loftier
lingerie	listlessly	loath	loftiest
lingering	lit/lighted	loathe	lofty
lining	literacy	loathed	log
link	literal	loathing	logged
linkage	literally	loathsome	logging
linked	literary	loaves	logic
linking	literate	lob	logical
lino	literature	lobbed	logically
linoleum	litre	lobbies	logistics
lint	litter	lobbing	logo
lion	littered	lobby	loin
lioness	littering	lobbying	loiter
lionesses	little	lobster	loitered
lip	live	local	loiterer
lip-read	lived	localities	loitering
lip-reading	liveliest	locality	loll
lipstick	livelihood	locally	lolled
liqueur	liveliness	locate	lollies
liquid	lively	located	lolling
liquidate	liven	locating	lollipop
liquidated	livened	location	lolly
liquidating	livening	lock	lone
liquidation	lives	locked	lonelier
liquorice	livestock	locker	loneliest
lisp	livid	locket	lonely
lisped	living	locking	long
lisping	lizard	locksmith	longed
list	llama	locomotive	longer
listed	load	locust	longest

Quick tip

Men and women

You will sometimes come across words that end in '-man', or '-woman', e.g. **linesman/ lineswoman**. In the plural, the last part of the word changes, and these words become **linesmen/lineswomen**. You can usually use '-person' and '-people' as an ending instead. These include the sense of both men and women, e.g. 'spokesperson', 'salesperson' and 'townspeople'.

liqueur; liquid; liquidate, etc.
Notice that a 'q' is always followed by a 'u'. The 'kw' sound in a word is spelt 'qu': 'quiet', 'quell', 'quit'.

live; lived; liveliest, etc.
The letter 'v' is always followed by a vowel or a 'y'.

lively → liveliness; lovely → loveliness
Notice how the adjectives 'lively' and 'lovely' change when they become the nouns 'liveliness' and 'loveliness'. The '-y' becomes an 'i'. Only short adjectives, such as 'shy', 'sly' and 'wry' keep the '-y' and add '-ly' to make 'shyly', 'slyly' and 'wryly'.

longing	lordly	lovely	lullabies
long jump	lordship	loving	lullaby
long-range	lorries	lovingly	lulled
long-sighted	lorry	low	lulling
long-suffering	lose	lower	lumber
long-term	loser	lowered	lumbered
long-winded	loss	lowering	lumbering
look	losses	lowest	luminaries
looked	lost	lowland	luminary
looking	lot	lowliness	luminosity
lookout	lotion	lowly	luminous
loom	lotteries	loyal	lump
loomed	lottery	loyalist	lumped
looming	loud	loyalty	lumpier
loop	louder	lozenge	lumpiest
looped	loudest	lubricant	lumpiness
loophole	loudly	lubricate	lumpy
looping	loudness	lubricating	lunacy
loose	loudspeaker	lubrication	lunar
loosely	lounge	lucid	lunatic
loosen	lounged	lucidity	lunch
loosened	lounging	lucidly	lunched
looseness	louse	luck	lunching
loosening	lousier	luckier	lung
looser	lousiest	luckiest	lunge
loosest	lousily	luckily	lunged
loot	lousy	lucrative	lunging
looted	lout	ludicrous	lurch
looter	lovable	ludicrously	lurched
looting	lovably	lug	lurching
lop	love	luggage	lure
lopped	loved	lugged	lured
lopping	lovelier	lugging	lurid
lopsided	loveliest	lukewarm	luridly
lord	loveliness	lull	luridness

loan *vs* **lone**
A 'loan' is money that is lent: 'He offered me a loan of 20 Euros.' 'Lone' means 'single', e.g. 'A lone man.'

loath; loathe
'Loath', to rhyme with 'both', means 'reluctant', but 'loathe', with a much longer 'o' sound, means 'to hate'.

lobbed; logged; lopped, etc.
One-syllable words, with a short vowel and a consonant, such as 'lob', 'log' and 'lop', double that consonant to make 'lobbed', 'logged' and 'lopped'. Try to learn this spelling pattern if you can.

A **logo** is a name or symbol which represents a particular product, or brand. It comes from the Greek for 'word', 'logos'.

loose *vs* **lose**
The word 'loose' is the opposite of 'tight', but 'lose' means 'to misplace'. It's very easy to mix them up.

lunacy; lunar; lunatic
The word 'lunacy' (madness) is from the Latin for the Moon, 'luna', and the word 'lunar' means 'to do with the Moon'. For centures, people believed the Moon affected peoples' mood, and mental health.

luring	lust	luxuriance	lynched
lurk	lusted	luxuriant	lynching
lurked	lustful	luxuries	lynx
lurking	lustily	luxurious	lynxes
luscious	lusting	luxuriously	lyric
lush	lustre	luxury	lyrical
lusher	lustrous	lying	lyrically
lushest	lute	lynch	lyricism

luscious; lustrous; luxurious
It's easy to miss the 'u' out of the '-ous' ending, as you can't hear it.

luxuriance; luxuriant
Try not to confuse the endings '-ance' and '-ant'. Remember that '-ance' is usually a noun: 'The luxuriance of her hair was amazing', but '-ant' is usually an adjective: 'She has such luxuriant hair.'

lynxes
Words ending in '-x' nearly always take '-es' in the plural. 'Oxen' is an exception.

Quick tip

Ssshhh
The letters 'ci' in 'luscious' make a 'sh' sound. There are eight different ways of spelling this sound, so take care when you hear it. These ways are:

- **'ch'** ('machine')
- **'ci'** ('luscious')
- **'s'** ('sure')
- **'sh'** ('shade')
- **'si'** ('confusion')
- **'ss'** ('pressure')
- **'ssi'** ('permission')
- **'ti'** ('nation')

Some tricky words to spell that start with an 'l'

Here are some words you might find tricky to spell, that begin with 'l':

labyrinth	leopard	literature
language	liaise	litre
laugh	library	luminous
leaned/leant	limb	luscious
leisure	limousine	lustre

Breaking a tricky word down into smaller parts can help you remember how it's spelt. For example, to spell 'limousine', try thinking:

'li-mous-ine'

Imagining a 'limo with a mouse in' might help.

Mm

This is my main mane.

macabre	magically	main	malice
macaroni	magician	mainland	malicious
macaroon	magistrate	mainly	malign
mace	magnanimous	mainstay	malignancies
machete	magnanimously	mainstream	malignancy
machine	magnate	maintain	malignant
machined	magnet	maintained	mallard
machine-gun	magnetic	maintaining	mallet
machinery	magnetically	maintenance	malnutrition
machining	magnetism	maisonette	malodorous
machismo	magnificence	maize	malpractice
macho	magnificent	majestic	malt
mackerel	magnificently	majestically	mammal
mackintosh	magnifies	majesties	mammoth
mad	magnify	majesty	man
madam	magnifying	major	manacle
maddening	magnitude	majorities	manacled
madder	magnolia	majority	manage
maddest	magpie	make	manageable
made	mahogany	make-believe	managed
madly	maid	maker	management
madman	maiden	make-up	manager
madness	mail	maladjusted	manageress
madrigal	mailed	male	managing
magazine	mailing	malevolence	mandarin
maggot	maim	malevolent	mandate
magic	maimed	malfunctioned	mandatory
magical	maiming	malfunctioning	mane

m

macabre
This word, meaning 'gruesome', is pronounced 'mak-ah-br'. The unusual final '-re' also appears in 'maneouvre', 'massacre' and 'metre', so take care.

machismo means 'exaggerated masculine qualities and pride'. 'Macho' means 'manly' or 'to do with men'. These words come from the Spanish for 'male', 'macho'.

made vs **maid**
The word 'made' means 'created': 'The car was made in Britain.' A 'maid' can be a female servant, or a young, unmarried woman (though this is old-fashioned).

mail vs **male**
'Mail' is the delivery of letters and parcels. 'Male' is 'to do with men', and is the opposite of 'female'.

maize is the plant which produces sweetcorn cobs. A 'maze' is a network of paths or lines which is tricky to find a way through.

malevolence; malfunctioned, etc.
Words beginning with 'mal-' are usually to do with evil, or things not going or working well.

manageable keeps the '-e' when you add '-able', and this keeps the 'g' sound in the word soft.

manger
mangle
mangled
mangling
mango
mangoes/mangos
manhandle
manhandled
manhandling
manhole
mania
manic
manically
manicure
manicurist
manifest
manifestation
manifested
manifesting
manifesto
manipulate
manipulated
manipulating
manipulation
manipulator
mankind
manlier
manliest
manliness
manly
manna
manned
manner
manning
manoeuvrable

manoeuvre
manoeuvred
manoeuvring
manor
mansion
manslaughter
mantelpiece
mantle
manual
manually
manufacture
manufactured
manufacturer
manufacturing
manure
manuscript
many
map
maple
mapped
mapping
mar
marathon
marauder
marauding
marble
marbled
marbling
mare
margarine
margin
marginal
marginalised/
marginalized
marginally

marigold
marijuana
marina
marinade
marinaded
marinading
marinate
marinated
marinating
marine
mariner
marital
maritime
marjoram
mark
marked
markedly
market
marketing
marking
marksman
marksmen
marlin
marmalade
maroon
marooned
marooning
marquee
marquis
marred
marriage
married
marries
marring
marrow

marry
marrying
marsh
marshal
marshalled
marshalling
marshier
marshiest
marshmallow
marshy
marsupial
martial
martyr
martyrdom
marvel
marvelled
marvelling
marvellous
marvellously
marzipan
mascara
mascot
masculine
masculinity
mash
mashed
mashing
mask
masked
masking
masochism
masochist
masochistic
mason
masonry

m

mangoes/mangos
Most words ending in '-o' just add '-s' in the plural, but some add '-es'. Mango is an unusual word, as it can do either and still be correct.

manna vs manner vs manor
'Manna', in the Bible, was food sent from Heaven. A 'manner' is a way of behaving: 'She had a friendly manner.' A 'manor' is a big house in the country.

manufacture
Lots of English nouns end with '-ture' (pronounced 'choor'), including 'adventure', 'capture' and 'rapture'.

mapped; marred, etc.
One-syllable words with a short vowel before a consonant, such as 'map' and 'mar', double the final consonant before adding '-ed': 'mapped'; 'marred'.

mare vs mayor
A 'mare' is a female horse. A 'mayor' is a local official. margarine is a rare exception to the rule that 'if a 'g' is followed by an 'a', it makes a hard sound'.

marine; mariner; maritime
These three words are all to do with the sea, and come from the Latin word for 'sea', 'mare'.

masquerade
masqueraded
masquerading
mass
massacre
massacred
massacring
massage
massaged
massaging
massed
masses
massing
massive
massively
mass-produce
mass-produced
mass-producing
mass-production
mast
master
mastered
masterful
mastering
masterly
mastermind
masterminded
masterminding
masturbate
masturbated
masturbating
masturbation
mat
matador
match

matched
matches
matching
mate
mated
material
materialise/
materialize
materialised/
materialized
materialism
materialist
materialistic
materially
maternal
maternally
maternity
mathematically
mathematician
mathematics
maths
matinee
mating
matriarch
matriarchal
matrices
matrimonial
matrimony
matrix
matron
matronly
matt
matted
matter
mattered

mattering
matter-of-fact
matting
mattress
mature
matured
maturely
maturing
maturity
maudlin
maul
mauled
mauling
mausoleum
mauve
maxim
maximise/maximize
maximised/
maximized
maximising/
maximizing
maximum
may
maybe
mayhem
mayonnaise
mayor
maze
me
meadow
meal
mean
meander
meandered
meandering

meaner
meanest
meaning
meanly
meanness
meant
meantime
meanwhile
measles
measly
measure
measured
measurement
measuring
meat
meaty
mechanic
mechanical
mechanically
mechanism
medal
medallist
meddle
meddled
meddling
media
mediaeval/medieval
mediate
mediated
mediating
mediation
mediator
medical
medically
medication

m

marquee; marquis; masquerade
These words are originally French, and 'qu' is a
very common spelling pattern in that language.

marshalled; marvelled
If you are adding an ending that starts with a vowel to
a word that ends in a vowel plus an '-l', double the 'l'.

mat vs matt
A 'mat' is a floor covering, but 'matt' means 'non-shiny'.

matrix → matrices
Mathematical words ending in '-x' may become '-ces' in
the plural, e.g. 'index → indices' and 'vortex → vortices'.

A **maze** is a network of paths it's hard to find
a way through. 'Maize' is grain that people eat.

meat is animal flesh that we eat, but 'to meet' means
'to join' or 'come together': 'Let's meet for lunch.'

medal vs meddle
A 'medal' is a metal disc, given as a reward for
an achievement of some kind. To 'meddle' means
'to interfere': 'Don't meddle in my business.'

media is a plural noun meaning 'television,
radio, newspapers or social networking sites'.
It's also the materials used to create art.

medicinal
medicine
mediocre
mediocrity
meditate
meditated
meditating
meditation
medium
medley
meek
meeker
meekest
meekly
meerkat
meet
meeting
melancholy
mêlée/melee
mellow
mellowed
mellowing
mellowness
melodic
melodies
melodious
melodiously
melodrama
melodramatic
melodramatically
melody
melon
melt
melted
melting

member
membership
membrane
memento
memo
memoir
memorable
memorably
memoranda
memorandum
memorial
memories
memory
memos
men
menace
menacingly
menagerie
mend
mended
mender
mending
menial
menstruation
mental
mentalities
mentality
mentally
mention
mentioned
mentioning
mentor
menu
mercenaries
mercenary

metaphor

A 'metaphor' is **a way of describing something as if it was something else**. Metaphors can make your writing much more interesting, so use them if you can.

Here are two examples:
'She was *a pearl among women*', and
'Books are *treasure chests, to be unlocked*.'

merchandise
merchant
mercies
merciful
merciless
mercilessly
mercury
mercy
mere
merely
merge
merged
merger
merging
meringue
merit
merited
meriting
mermaid
merrier
merriest
merrily
merriment
merry
merry-go-round
mesh

meshed
meshes
meshing
mess
message
messed
messenger
messier
messiest
messing
messy
met
metal
metallic
metamorphoses
metamorphosis
metaphor
metaphorical
metaphorically
meteor
meteoric
meteorite
meteorological
meteorology
meter
method

m

Hello!

Well, hello!

meat meets meat

meet

To 'meet' is to encounter, or come into contact with someone. 'Meat' is animal flesh, that people eat.

mêlée/melee

A 'mêlée' is a throng of people, from the French word 'mêler', 'to mix'. You can leave the accents out.

memoranda is the Latin plural of 'memorandum' (a note, or reminder). However, you may also see 'memorandums' or 'memos'.

mentality → mentalities, etc.

Words that end in a consonant and a '-y' change to '-ies' in the plural.

metal vs mettle

'Metal' is a hard element, such as steel or iron. 'Mettle' is an old-fashioned word for strength of character.

meter vs metre

A 'meter' can be machine that counts time, electricity or gas. It can also be the rhythm, in music or poetry. A 'metre' is 100 centimetres.

methodical	might	mime	minimal
methodically	mightier	mimed	minimalist
meticulous	mightiest	mimic	minimally
meticulously	mightily	mimicked	minimise/minimize
metre	mighty	mimicking	minimised/
metric	migrant	mimicry	minimized
metronome	migrate	miming	minimising/
metropolis	migrated	minaret	minimizing
metropolises	migrating	mince	minimum
metropolitan	migration	minced	mining
mettle	migratory	mincing	minister
mew	mild	mind	ministerial
mewed	milder	minded	ministries
mewing	mildest	mindful	ministry
miasma	mildew	mindfulness	mink
mice	mildly	minding	minnow
microcosm	mile	mindless	minor
microphone	mileage	mine	minorities
microscope	militancy	mined	minority
microscopic	militant	minefield	minstrel
microwave	militarily	miner	mint
midday	militia	mineral	minted
middle	milk	minestrone	minting
middle-aged	milked	mingle	minus
middling	milkier	mingled	minuscule
midge	milkiest	mingling	minute
midget	milking	miniature	minutely
midnight	milky	minibus	minutiae
midriff	mill	minibuses	miracle
midst	milled		
midsummer	millennium		
midway	miller		
midwife	milling		
midwifery	million		
midwives	millionaire		

m

'mini-'
Words beginning with the prefix 'mini-'
**usually mean something to do with
smallness**, for example: miniature
and minimum.

might can be a part of the verb 'may' ('I might
come, but I might not'), and can also mean 'power'
or 'strength'. A 'mite' is a very small bug or thing.

mileage
Notice that 'mile' keeps its final '-e' when '-age' is
added. This keeps the 'i' sound long, but take care,
as it's an easy word to misspell.

mimicked
You need a 'k' after the 'c' to keep the hard 'ck' sound
when you add '-ed'. (Without a 'k', the end of this
word would be '-iced', to rhyme with 'sliced'.)

mine is a possessive pronoun, meaning 'belonging
to me'. It is also a concealed bomb, or underground
passages where minerals such as coal are excavated.

miner vs minor
A 'miner' works underground digging up coal or
other minerals. 'Minor' can mean 'not important
or serious', or 'a child that is under 18 years old'.

minute can mean '60 seconds' when 'min-' is
emphasized, but when '-nute' is emphasized
(so that the word sounds like 'my-newt'), it means
'very small indeed': 'The portions were minute.'

miraculous
miraculously
mirage
mire
mired
mirror
mirrored
mirroring
mirth
misbehave
misbehaved
misbehaving
misbehaviour
miscellaneous
mischief
mischievous
misconception
misconduct
misdemeanour
miser
miserable
miserably
miseries
miserly
misery
misfire
misfired
misfiring
misfit

misfortune
misgiving
misguided
misinform
misinformation
misinformed
misinforming
misinterpret
misinterpretation
misinterpreted
misinterpreting
misjudge
misjudged
misjudging
mislaid
mislay
mislaying
mislead
misleading
misled
misplaced
misprint
misrepresent
misrepresentation
misrepresented
misrepresenting
miss
missed
missile

missing
mission
missionaries
missionary
missive
misspell
misspelled/misspelt
misspelling
mist
mistake
mistaken
mistakenly
mistaking
misted
mister
mistier
mistiest
misting
mistook
mistreat
mistreated
mistreating
mistress
mistresses
mistrust
mistrusted
mistrusting
misty
misunderstand
misunderstanding
misunderstood
misuse
misused
misusing
mite

mitigating
mitten
mix
mixed
mixer
mixes
mixing
mixture
mix-up
moan
moaned
moat
mob
mobbed
mobbing
mobile
mobility
moccasin
mock
mocked
mockery
mocking
mode
model
modelled
modelling
moderate
moderated
moderately
moderating
moderation
modern
modernise/
modernize
modernised/

'mis-'
Words beginning with the suffix 'mis-' are usually to do with **something that has gone wrong, or is not right**, e.g. misbehaviour; misinform; misjudge and misspell.

m

---

miseries; missionaries; monarchies, etc.
Remember that words that end with a consonant, and then a '-y', change to '-ies' in the plural.

missed vs mist
'Missed' is the past tense of 'to miss'. 'Mist' is drops of water in the air, which can make it hard to see clearly.

mite is a very small bug or thing, but 'might' is part of the verb 'may': 'I might go home.' It can also mean 'power', but this is a little old-fashioned.

mob stems from a Latin phrase, 'mobile vulgus', which means 'unreliable, unpredictable commoners'.

moccasin
Native Americans wore flat, animal-skin shoes called 'mocussins', which 'moccasin' comes from.

monarch
The letters '-ch' make a hard 'k' sound in 'monarch', so you can just add an '-s' to make the plural, 'monarchs' (not '-es', as with many words ending in a soft '-ch').

'mono-'
The prefix 'mono-' conveys the idea of singleness. 'Monogamy' is when you have one partner. A 'monologue' is a speech for one actor.

modernized	momentum	monumental	moron
modernising/	monarch	monumentally	moronic
modernizing	monarchies	mood	morose
modernity	monarchy	moodier	morosely
modest	monasteries	moodiest	morsel
modestly	monastery	moodiness	mortal
modesty	monastic	moody	mortality
modification	monasticism	moon	mortally
modified	money	moonlight	mortar
modifies	moneyed	moonlit	mortgage
modify	mongrel	moor	mortgaged
modifying	monitor	moored	mortgaging
modular	monitored	mooring	mortified
module	monitoring	moose	mortifies
mohair	monk	moot	mortify
moist	monkey	mooted	mortifying
moisten	monocle	mooting	mosaic
moistened	monogamous	mop	mosque
moistening	monogamy	mope	mosquito
moister	monologue	moped	mosquitoes/
moisture	monopolies	moping	mosquitos
molar	monopoly	mopped	moss
mole	monotone	mopping	mosses
molest	monotonous	moral	mossy
molested	monotonously	morale	most
molester	monotony	moralities	mostly
molesting	monsoon	morality	moth
mollifies	monster	morally	mother
mollify	monstrosities	morbid	mothered
mollifying	monstrosity	morbidly	motherhood
molten	monstrous	more	mothering
moment	monstrously	moreover	mother-in-law
momentarily	month	morgue	mothers-in-law
momentary	monthly	moribund	motif
momentous	monument	morning	motion

m

moose
mousse

moor *vs* more
A 'moor' is a barren, often treeless landscape. It also means 'to tie up a boat'. 'More' means 'a larger quantity or number': 'He has more money than me.'

morning
'Morning' is the first half of the day. 'Mourning' is feeling very sad because someone has died.

mortgage
A 'mortgage' is money borrowed from a bank or building society to buy a house. To help you remember 'rtg', try thinking '**r**epay **t**hose **g**uys'.

moose
A 'moose' is a large mammal that lives in the northernmost areas of North America. A 'mousse' is a soft whipped dessert.

mother-in-law
This is a compound noun, made up of several words. Notice that, to make it plural, you add an '-s' to the main noun, 'mother': 'mothers-in-law'.

motioned	mourned	muffin	mural
motioning	mourner	muffle	murder
motionless	mournful	muffled	murdered
motivate	mourning	muffling	murderer
motivated	mouse	mug	murdering
motivating	mousse	mugged	murderous
motivation	moustache	mugger	murkier
motivational	mouth	muggier	murkiest
motive	mouthed	muggiest	murky
motley	mouthful	mugging	murmur
motor	mouthpiece	muggy	murmured
motorboat	movable	mule	murmuring
motorcycle	move	mull	muscle
motorcycling	moved	mulled	muscled
motorcyclist	movement	mulling	muscling
motoring	moving	multimedia	muscular
motorist	movingly	multinational	muse
motorway	mow	multiple	mused
mottled	mowed	multiplication	museum
motto	mower	multiplicity	mush
mould	mowing	multiplies	mushier
moulded	mown	multiply	mushiest
moulding	much	multitude	mushroom
mouldy	muck	mum	mushy
moult	muckier	mumble	music
moulted	muckiest	mumbled	musical
moulting	mucky	mumbling	musically
mound	mud	mummies	musician
mount	muddier	mummy	musing
mountain	muddiest	munch	musk
mountaineer	muddle	munched	musket
mountaineering	muddled	munching	musky
mounted	muddling	mundane	muslin
mounting	muddy	municipal	mussel
mourn	muesli	munitions	must

m

mustard	mute	mutual	mystery
muster	muted	mutually	mystic
mustered	mutilate	muzzle	mystical
mustering	mutilated	muzzled	mysticism
mustier	mutilating	muzzling	mystified
mustiest	mutilation	my	mystifies
musty	mutinies	myriad	mystify
mutant	mutiny	myrrh	mystifying
mutate	mutter	myself	mystique
mutated	muttered	mysteries	mythical
mutating	muttering	mysterious	mythological
mutation	mutton	mysteriously	mythology

muscle *vs* **mussel**

A 'muscle' is the tissue in our bodies that enables us to move. A 'mussel' is an edible shellfish.

muscular, and all words linked with 'muscle', come from a Latin root word, 'musculus', which means 'little mouse'. The Romans thought that the muscles rippling beneath human skin looked like mice.

Look at the muscles on that mussel!

Quick tip

Drop the '-e'

One of the most common spelling rules you will come across is **drop the silent '-e' after a consonant when you add '-ing'.** Thousands of words follow this pattern, including eleven words on these two pages alone. Can you find them? *(The answers are upside-down at the bottom of the page.)*

Memorable mnemonics

A 'mnemonic' is **a rhyme or saying that jogs your memory**. It's from the Greek word 'mnemonikos', which means 'to do with remembering'. One of the best tips for spelling a difficult word is to make up a mnemonic that uses all, or some, of the letters in that word:

1. You can invent a silly phrase in which the words start with the letters that make up that tricky word. For **myth**, how about: '**m**y **y**oung **t**ulips **h**elped'?

2. A mnemonic can help you remember the order of letters in a word: 'There are **m**any **n**ice things about autu**mn**.'

3. You can highlight particular parts of a word in a mnemonic. For example: 'I need a **pie**ce of **pie**.'

Some tricky words to spell that start with an 'm'

Here are some words that can be tricky to spell that begin with 'm':

macabre	marvellous	mileage
maintenance	mayonnaise	miniature
manoeuvre	mediocre	minuscule
marriage	meringue	miscellaneous
martyr	metamorphosis	muscle

Nn

a naval navel

nag
nagged
nagging
nail
nailed
nailing
naïve
naivelyly
naively
naïveté/naivety
naked
nakedly
nakedness
name
named
nameless
namely
naming
nannies
nanny
nap
nape
napkin
napped
nappies
napping
nappy
narrate
narrated

narrating
narration
narrator
narrow
narrowed
narrower
narrowing
narrowly
narrowness
nasal
nasally
nastier
nastiest
nastily
nastiness
nasty
nation
national
nationalism
nationalist
nationalistic
nationalities
nationality
nationally
nationwide
native
nativities
nativity

natural
naturalist
naturally
naturalness
naughtier
naughtiest
naughtily
naughty
nausea
nauseating
nauseous
nautical
naval
navel
navies
navigable
navigate
navigated
navigating
navigation
navigator
navy
near
nearby
neared
nearer
nearest
nearing

nearly
neat
neater
neatest
neatly
neatness
necessarily
necessary
necessities
necessity
neck
necklace
nectar
nectarine
need
needed
needier
neediest
needing
needle
needled
needless
needlessly
needlework
needling
needy
negate
negated

n

---

nagged; napped; nipped; nodded
One-syllable words (e.g. 'nag', 'nap', 'nip' and 'nod'), which end in a short vowel and a consonant, double that final consonant before '-ed' or '-ing' are added.

naïve; naïveté/naivety
'Naïve' means 'inexperienced' or 'innocent'. It comes from an Old French word, 'naïf'. The noun 'naïveté' can also be spelt 'naivety'.

nap; nape
Notice that adding an '-e' to 'nap' makes the 'a' sound long, in 'nape' (which rhymes with 'ape').

narrating; negotiating; nestling, etc.
Think: 'drop the silent '-e' when you add '-ing''.

nastiness
When you add '-ness' to a word ending in '-y', such as 'nasty', remember to change the 'y' to an 'i'.

naughty; night; nightie, etc.
The silent letters 'gh' are only found before the letter 't', as here, or at the end of words, such as 'weigh'.

need means 'to require' or 'feel you must have' something: 'I need a drink.' To 'knead' is to squeeze, pummel and stretch dough, ready for baking.

If you can't find the word beginning with an 'n' sound here, check the 'gn-', 'kn-' and 'pn-' pages.

negating — noiselessly

negating	nestled	next	nimblest
negation	nestling	nib	nimbly
negative	net	nibble	nine
negatively	netball	nibbled	nineteen
neglect	netting	nibbling	nineteenth
neglectful	nettle	nice	nineties
neglectfully	network	nicely	ninetieth
negligible	neuter	nicer	ninety
negotiate	neutered	nicest	ninth
negotiated	neutering	niceties	nip
negotiating	neutral	nicety	nipped
negotiation	neutralise/	niche	nippier
negotiator	neutralize	nick	nippiest
neigh	neutralised/	nicked	nipping
neighbour	neutralized	nickel	nipple
neighbourhood	neutralising/	nicking	nippy
neighbouring	neutralizing	nickname	nit
neighed	neutrality	nicknamed	nitty-gritty
neighing	never	nicknaming	nobility
neither	nevertheless	nicotine	noble
neon	new	niece	nobleman
nephew	newborn	niggle	noblemen
nerve	newcomer	niggled	nobler
nerve-racking	newer	niggling	noblest
nervous	newest	night	noblewoman
nervousness	newly	nightclub	noblewomen
nest	news	nightdress	nobodies
nested	newsagent	nightfall	nobody
nesting	newspaper	nightie	nocturnal
nestle	newt	nightingale	nod
		nightly	nodded
		nightmare	nodding
		nil	noise
		nimble	noiseless
		nimbler	noiselessly

'-ness'
Notice that the ending '-ness' makes an adjective ('She was a nervous person') into a noun ('She suffered from nervousness').

neigh
The 'ei' in 'neigh' (which rhymes with 'hay', and is the sound horses make) is one of six ways to spell the long 'a' sound. The others are 'a' ('cake'), 'ai' ('plain'), 'ay' ('crayon'), 'ea' ('steak') and 'ey' ('grey').

nerve-racking can also be correctly spelt 'nerve-wracking', but this is less commonly used.

neutralise/neutralize
Either of these spellings is correct for most words, but a few can only be spelt with an 's' or a 'z'. There's a list of these words on page 4.

night is the opposite of 'day', but a 'knight' is a noble warrior.

nimble → nimbly
'Nimble' loses the '-e' when it becomes an adverb.

nitty-gritty means 'the basics', and nobody knows its origins for certain. Some believe it first meant 'rubbish', and was connected to slavery, and others link it to a kind of jazz music named after 'grits' (ground cornmeal eaten in the United States).

Let's not niggle over the nitty-gritty.

n

noisier
noisiest
noisiness
noisy
nomad
nomadic
nominal
nominally
nomination
nominee
nonchalance
nonchalant
nonchalantly
non-drip
none
non-existent
non-fiction
non-flammable
nonplussed
non-refundable
non-returnable
nonsense
nonsensical
non-stop
noodle
nook
noon

no-one
noose
nor
norm
normal
normality
normally
north
north-east
north-easterly
north-eastern
northerly
northern
northerner
northward
northwards
north-west
north-westerly
nose
nosed
nose-dive
nose-dived
nose-diving
nosier
nosiest
nosily
nosiness

nosing
nostalgia
nostalgic
nostril
nosy
not
notable
notably
notch
notched
notches
notching
note
notebook
noted
nothing
notice
noticeable
noticeably

noticeboard
noticed
noticing
notification
notified
notifies
notify
notifying
noting
notion
notionally
notoriety
notorious
notoriously
notwithstanding
nougat
nought
noun
nourish

noun

A 'noun' is **the grammatical name for a thing, an idea, or a person**. There are three different kinds of noun:

1. **Common nouns** often name things you can touch: 'The *house* was huge.' Others name ideas, that you can't touch: 'Her *kindness* was legendary.'

2. **Proper nouns** begin with a capital letter, and name a place, person or specific thing: 'New York'; 'Caroline Young'.

3. **Collective nouns** name a group of things: 'a *herd* of cows'; 'a *flock* of geese'.

You can find out about how to make nouns plural on page 5, in the grammar section.

none *vs* nun

A 'nun' is a woman who lives in a convent, and devotes her life to God. 'None' means 'not a single one' or 'nothing': 'We had none.'

The priest has plenty of food, but the nun has none.

nor is usually used with 'neither', to show a second negative in a sentence: 'The movie star was neither blonde nor bubbly.' The positive version is 'either/or'.

northward; northwards

'Northward' is an adjective: 'We drove in a northward direction.' 'Northwards' is an adverb: 'He travelled northwards.'

not makes a phrase negative. It may go before a verb ('not go') or after it ('may not'), and can be shortened to 'n't' at the end of a word. 'Knot' can mean 'tied up threads' or 'the speed of a ship', e.g. '10 knots'.

If you can't find the word beginning with an 'n' sound here, check the 'gn-', 'kn-' and 'pn-' pages.

nourished — nymph

nourished	nuclear	numbly	nut
nourishing	nucleus	numbness	nutmeg
nourishment	nude	numeral	nutrition
novel	nudge	numerical	nutritional
novelist	nudged	numerous	nutritionist
novelties	nudging	nun	nutritious
novelty	nudist	nunnery	nutshell
novice	nudity	nurse	nuttier
now	nugget	nursed	nuttiest
nowadays	nuisance	nurseries	nutty
nowhere	null	nursery	nuzzle
noxious	numb	nursing	nuzzled
nozzle	number	nurture	nuzzling
nuance	numbered	nurtured	nylon
nubile	numbering	nurturing	nymph

notch → notches
Most words ending in '-ch', '-ss', '-sh' or other hissing sounds, add '-es' to become plural. A few words, such as 'monarch/monarchs' and 'patriarch/patriarchs', just add an '-s', as the '-ch' makes a hard 'k' sound.

noticeable
You keep the '-e' at the end of 'notice' when you add '-able'. This keeps the 'c' sound soft, like an 's'.

novelist; nutritionist
The ending '-ist' means 'a person who does something linked to the meaning of the word'.

number can mean 'more numb' when the 'b' isn't pronounced, or 'a word used to explain quantity, or to count' (such as 1, 2 or 3) when the 'b' is pronounced.

nurse
In 'nurse', the letter 'u' is pronounced to rhyme with 'search' or 'earn'. It can be easy to misspell it.

nymph usually means a young insect such as a dragonfly, but 'nymphs' were also mythical creatures. The letters 'ph' make an 'f' sound, and are based on a Greek spelling pattern.

n

Some tricky words starting with an 'n'

See how many of these tricky 'n' words you can get right:

nation	neutral
naughty	nicety
nausea	nonchalance
necessary	nuisance
negotiate	numb
neighbour	nurse
neither	nymph

(Quick tip) Say and spell
Many words are not spelt as they are said, or pronounced, which often causes spellers problems. **Two of the most common mistakes are missing out parts of words because we don't usually pronounce them, and spelling a word exactly as it sounds** (which is often incorrect). For example:

- it's easy to forget about the 'u' in **'natural'**, as we tend to say 'nat-ral'.

- it can be easy to spell the word **'nominal'** with a 'u' rather than an 'a', as we say the word 'nom-in-ul'.

The best way of making sure you spell a word correctly, however you say it, or however it sounds, is to **check the spelling in a dictionary**.

chocolate cake
really rules

occur; occurred; occurrence; occurring
These words are all easy to misspell. Try thinking of a saying, such as 'chocolate **c**ake **r**ules' for the two 'c's and an 'r' in 'occur'. For the words that stem from it, with two 'r's: 'chocolate **c**ake **r**eally **r**ules'.

oak	oblige	obstruction	odder
oar	oblong	obstructive	oddest
oases	obnoxious	obstructively	oddities
oasis	obnoxiously	obtain	oddity
oat	oboe	obtainable	oddly
oath	oboist	obtained	oddment
oatmeal	obscure	obtaining	oddness
obedience	obscurely	obtuse	odds
obedient	obscurity	obvious	ode
obediently	observance	obviously	odorous
obelisk	observation	occasion	odour
obese	observatories	occasionally	of
obesity	observatory	occult	off
obey	observe	occupancy	offal
obeyed	observed	occupant	offence
obeying	observer	occupation	offend
obituaries	observing	occupied	offended
obituary	obsess	occupy	offender
object	obsessed	occupying	offending
objected	obsessing	occur	offensive
objecting	obsession	occurred	offensively
objection	obsessive	occurrence	offer
objectionable	obsolete	occurring	offered
objective	obstacle	ocean	offering
objectively	obstinacy	o'clock	offhand
objector	obstinate	octopus	office
obligation	obstinately	octopuses	officer
obligatory	obstruct	odd	official

oases is the plural of 'oasis'. Other words that follow this pattern include 'basis → bases' and 'crisis → crises'.
obese means 'very overweight', and it comes from the Latin 'ob' (a lot) and 'edere' (to eat).

objectively; obscurely; obstinately, etc.
Many words keep the silent '-e' when '-ly' is added to make them into adverbs, e.g. 'She voted objectively.'

objector; oboist; observer
The endings '-or', '-er' and '-ist' often indicate a person who does what the word means. An 'objector' objects, an 'oboist' plays the oboe and an 'observer' observes.

obnoxious has a silent 'o' in '-ous', don't forget.

obsolete means 'no longer in use': 'This computer model is now obsolete.' It's from the Latin word 'obsoletus', which means 'worn out' or 'old'.

obtuse can mean 'an angle between 90 and 180 degrees' or 'a little awkward': 'Lara was so obtuse.'

o'clock is a shortened version of 'of the clock', and it's how people describe the time of day: 'It's four o'clock.'

oddity → oddities
Words that end in a consonant and a '-y', as 'oddity' does, change to '-ies' in the plural.

officially
officiate
officiated
officiating
offline
offset
offsetting
offshoot
offshore
offside
offspring
often
ogle
ogled
ogling
ogre
oil
oiled
oilfield
oiliness
oiling
oilskin
oily
ointment
old
older
oldest

olive
omelette
omen
ominous
ominously
omit
omitted
omitting
omnibus
omnibuses
omnipotent
omnivore
omnivorous
on
once
one
one-off
onerous
oneself
one-sided
one-way
ongoing
onion
online
onlooker
only
onomatopoeia

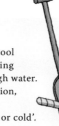

oar *or* **or?**
An 'oar' is a flat tool for making a rowing boat move through water. 'Or' is a conjunction, used for giving alternatives: 'hot or cold'.

This oar, or that oar?

onomatopoeic
onshore
onslaught
onto
onus
onward
onwards
ooze
oozed
oozing
opaque
open
opened
opener
opening
openly
opera
operate
operated
operatic
operating
operation
operator
opinion
opponent
opportunities
opportunity

oppose
opposed
opposing
opposite
opposition
oppress
oppressed
oppressing
oppression
oppressive
oppressively
oppressor
opt
opted
optical
optician
optimism
optimist
optimistic
optimistically
optimum
opting
option
optional
opulent
opus
or

O

onomatopoeia means **a word that makes the same sound as its meaning when you say it**. It comes from two Greek words, 'onoma' (name) and 'poiein' (to make up). '*Mumble*', '*hiss*', '*purr*' and '*smash*' are all examples of onomatopoeia. Words like these are said to be onomatopoeic.

odd *vs* odds
The word 'odd' can be an adjective, meaning 'strange' or 'unusual': 'She is a bit odd'. It can mean 'roughly': 'I've eaten thirty-odd apples.' The word 'odds' is always used in the plural, and is to do with gambling, or the chances of winning or losing: 'The odds on the horse winning were ten to one.'

odour → odorous
Notice that the 'u' in 'odour' is dropped to form 'odorous'. Words such as 'glamour → glamorous' and 'humour → humorous' also follow this pattern.

ogle → ogling; ooze → oozing, etc.
Remember to drop the silent '-e' when you add '-ing'.
'omni-'
Words beginning with 'omni-' are to do with 'all' or 'everything', as the Latin word for 'all' is 'omni'. An 'omnivore' eats everything, and to be 'omnipotent' is to be 'all powerful', for example.

one means 'the number 1', or 'I' in very formal language: 'One rarely shouts.' 'One-' can be added to a word to mean 'single', e.g. 'one-way'. 'Won' sounds the same as 'one', but is the past tense of 'win'.

oracle
oral
orally
orange
orang-utan
orator
oratory
orbit
orbital
orbited
orbiting
orchard
orchestra
orchestral
orchestrate
orchestrated
orchestrating
orchestration
orchid
ordain
ordained
ordaining
ordeal
order
ordered
ordering
orderliness
orderly
ordinarily
ordinary
ordination
ore
oregano
organ
organic

organically
organisation/
organization
organisational/
organizational
organise/organize
organised/organized
organising/
organizing
organism
organist
orient
oriental
orientate
orientated
orientation
orienteering
origami
origin
original
originality
originally
originate
originated
originating
originator
ornament
ornamental
ornamentation
ornate
ornately
ornithologist
ornithology
orphan
orphanage

orphaned
orthodox
orthodoxy
ostensible
ostensibly
ostentation
ostentatious
ostentatiously
ostrich
ostriches
other
otherwise
otter
ought
ounce
our
ourselves
oust
ousted
ousting
out
out-and-out
outback
outboard
outbreak
outburst
outcast
outclass
outclassed
outcome
outcries
outcry
outdid
outdo
outdoes

outdoing
outdone
outdoor
outdoors
outer
outfit
outgoing
outgrew
outgrow
outgrowing
outgrown
outing
outlast
outlasted
outlasting
outlaw
outlawed
outlawing
outlet
outlive
outlived
outliving
outlook
outlying
outnumber
outnumbered
outnumbering
outpatient
outpost
output
outrage
outraged
outrageous
outrageously
outright

O

---

oral means 'to do with mouths', but 'aural' means
'to do with ears', so take care which word you use.

ore
'Ore' is rock or earth which contains metal,
such as 'iron ore'. An 'oar' is a flat tool for moving
a boat through water. 'Or' is a conjunction, used
for giving alternatives: 'hot or cold'.

oregano; origami
Words ending in '-o' or '-i' always come from other
languages. 'Oregano', the herb, is a Spanish word.
'Origami' is the Japanese art of paper-folding.

organise/organize
Either of these spellings is correct for most words.
Check the list of '-ise/-ize' words on page 4.

ornithology is the study of birds. It's from the
Greek words 'ornis' (bird) and 'logia' (study).

ostriches
Words ending in a soft '-ch' add '-es' in the plural.

ought means 'should': 'I ought to go.'
Don't forget the silent 'gh' before the '-t'.

our means 'belonging to us'. 'Hour', pronounced
just the same, means 'a period of 60 minutes'.

outset
outshine
outshining
outshone
outside
outsider
outsize
outsized
outskirts
outspoken
outstanding
outstretched
outward
outwardly
outwards
outweigh
outweighed
outweighing
outwit

outwitted
outwitting
oval
ovaries
ovary
ovation
oven
over
overall
overawed
overbearing
overboard
overcame
overcast
overcoat
overcome
overcoming
overcrowded
overdid

overdo
overdoes
overdoing
overdone
overdose
overdosed
overdosing
overflow
overflowed
overflowing
overgrown
overhang
overhanging
overhaul
overhauled
overhauling
overhead
overhear
overheard
overhearing
overhung
overjoyed
overland
overlap
overlapped
overlapping
overleaf
overload
overloaded
overloading
overlook
overlooked
overlooking
overnight
overpower

overpowered
overpowering
overran
overrate
overrated
overrating
overreact
overreacted
overreacting
overreaction
overridden
override
overriding
overrode
overrule
overruled
overruling
overrun
oversaw
overseas
oversee
overseeing
overseen
oversight
oversleep
oversleeping
overslept
overtake
overtaken
overtaking
overthrew
overthrow
overthrown
overtime
overtook

'over-'

When you see 'over-' before a word, it often means 'to excess' or 'too much': 'an *over-cooked* dish'. 'Over' can also be joined to a word: **overawed**, **overbearing**, **overcome**.

She was overwhelmed, overcome and overjoyed.

out-and-out is a phrase that means 'completely': 'He was an out-and-out villain', for example.

'out-' before a word can mean 'be better at', e.g. 'out-perform' or 'out-manoeuvre'. It can be hyphenated, but not always, e.g. 'outclass' or 'outdo'.

outdoor; outdoors
The word 'outdoor' is an adjective: 'An outdoor toilet', but 'outdoors' is an adverb: 'They often ate outdoors.' Also see 'outward/outwards'.

outrageous
Keeping the '-e' before '-ous' keeps the 'g' sound soft.

outspoken; outstretched
You will never read 'outspeak' or 'outstretch', as these words are always adjectives, never verbs: 'She is very outspoken'; 'His outstretched hand'.

overhung; overran; overslept; overthrew; overtook
These compound words made with 'over-' follow the pattern of their main verb when they are in the past.

overlapped doubles the '-p' before you add '-ed'.

overrate; overreact; overrun, etc.
Notice that the '-r' of 'over' is not dropped when it is added to another word that begins with an 'r'.

overture	overwork	owe	owning
overturn	overworked	owed	ox
overturned	overworking	owing	oxen
overturning	overwrought	owl	oxygen
overweight	ovulate	own	oxygenated
overwhelm	ovulated	owned	oxymoron
overwhelmed	ovulating	owner	oyster
overwhelming	ovulation	ownership	ozone

overture
A lot of nouns end with '-ture', which is pronounced 'cher'. Examples include 'adventure' and 'aperture'. An 'overture' is the musical term for the beginning of a piece of music.

overturn; overwhelm; overwork, etc.
Words beginning with 'over-' often have the meaning of 'excess' or 'too much'. It's from an Old English word 'ofer', which meant 'beyond' or 'above'.

overweight; overwrought
Don't forget the silent 'gh' before the final '-t'.

ovulation is what happens when a woman or a female animal produces eggs from her ovaries. These words are from the Latin for 'egg', 'ovum'.

owe; owl; own
The letters 'ow' can make a short 'o' sound, as in 'owe' and 'own', or a long one, as in 'owl' and 'fowl'.

ox → oxen
The plural of 'ox' is 'oxen', which is an exception to the spelling rule that words ending in '-x', '-ch', '-ss' or other hissing sounds end in '-es' in the plural. Many spelling rules have exceptions like this.

oxymoron
An 'oxymoron' is **a short phrase containing two words that contradict each other**, e.g. *'a wise fool'; 'a silent scream'; 'an open secret'* and *'the living dead'*. Technically these phrases are 'wrong', but people often use them.

the living dead

Quick tip

Spelling book

Try keeping a 'spelling book' to help you practise spelling tricky words.

1. Write each word neatly at the top of its own page. Read it aloud, saying each sound in the word as you do so.

2. Now copy the word out several more times underneath the neat version at the top of the page. Again, say it aloud as you write it out.

3. From time to time, open your notebook and choose a tricky word at random. Write it out correctly six more times.

Some tricky words that start with an 'o'

Here are some tricky words that begin with 'o'. See how many of these words you can get right. There are some tips to help you on page 7.

occasion	opportunity	our
occur	opposite	overrate
odorous	orchestra	overwhelm
opponent	ordinary	oxygen

O

Pp

a pair of pears

Pick with care
A pair means 'two': 'a pair of swans'.
To 'pare' means 'reduce to a minimum':
'They pared the shortlist down to four.'
A 'pear' is a fruit. Make sure you pick
the right word.

pace	pageant	palatial	pamper
paced	pageantry	pale	pampered
pacifism	pagoda	paleness	pampering
pacifist	paid	paler	pamphlet
pacify	pail	palest	pan
pacing	pain	palette	panache
pack	pained	palindrome	pancake
package	painful	paling	panda
packaged	painfully	pall	pandemonium
packaging	painkiller	palled	pander
packed	painless	pallet	pandered
packet	painlessly	pallid	pandering
packing	painstaking	pallor	pane
pact	painstakingly	palm	panel
pad	paint	palmed	panelled
padded	paintbox	palming	panelling
padding	paintboxes	palmistry	pang
paddle	paintbrush	paltrier	panic
paddled	paintbrushes	paltriest	panicked
paddling	painted	paltry	panicking
paddock	painter	pampas	panicky
paddy	painting		
padlock	pair		
padlocked	paired		
padlocking	pairing		
paella	palace		
pagan	palatable		
page	palate		

p

palindrome
A 'palindrome' is **a word or phrase that
reads the same both forwards and backwards**.
The words 'eye', 'kayak', 'radar' and the names
'Bob', 'Eve', and 'Otto' are all palindromes.
Can you think of any more?

paella; pagoda; panda
Only words from other languages end in '-a'. 'Paella'
is a Spanish rice dish, and a 'pagoda' is a tower-shaped
Hindu or Buddhist temple. 'Panda' may come from
the Nepalese name for the black and white bear.
pail vs pale
A 'pail' is a bucket, but 'pale' means 'light in colour'.
pain vs pane
'Pain' is real physical discomfort. A 'pane'
is a thin sheet, usually of glass.
painful means 'full of pain', but '-ful' only has one 'l'.

palate vs palette vs pallet
A 'palate' is the roof of your mouth. A 'palette'
is a range of colours, and a 'pallet' is a wooden
storage platform for goods.
panda vs pander
A 'panda' is a black and
white bear that eats
bamboo shoots.
To 'pander' is 'to
indulge' or 'spoil'
someone.

He panders to
the panda.

paragraphs

Long pieces of text or writing are usually divided into 'paragraphs'. A paragraph begins on a new line, can vary in length, and often discusses one theme, or subject.

panorama	paradoxical	pardoned	partially
panoramic	paraffin	pardoning	participate
pansies	paragraph	pare	participated
pansy	parallel	pared	participating
pant	paralyse	parent	participation
panted	paralysed	parentage	particle
panther	paralysing	parental	particular
panting	paralysis	parented	particularly
pantomime	paralytic	parenting	parties
pantries	paramedic	paring	parting
pantry	parameter	parish	partition
pants	paramilitary	parishioner	partitioned
papaya	paramount	parity	partitioning
paper	paranoia	park	partly
paperback	paranoid	parka	partner
papered	paranormal	parked	partnered
papering	parapet	parking	partnering
paperwork	paraphernalia	parliament	partnership
papier-mâché	paraphrase	parliamentary	partook
paprika	paraphrased	parlour	partridge
parable	paraphrasing	parochial	part-time
parachute	parasite	parodies	party
parachutist	parasitic	parody	pass
parade	parasol	parole	passable
paraded	paratrooper	parrot	passably
parading	parcel	parsley	passage
paradise	parched	parsnip	passageway
paradox	parchment	parson	passed
paradoxes	pardon	parsonage	passenger
		part	passer-by
		partake	passers-by
		partaken	passing
		partaking	passion
		parted	passionate
		partial	passionately

papier-mâché is a craft activity involving gluing layers of strips of paper onto a mould until they harden. It actually means 'chewed paper' in French. Try not to forget the accents when you spell it.

parade → parading; partake → partaking
These words drop the final, silent '-e' when an ending that begins with a vowel is added to them. Thousands of words follow this pattern, so try to learn it.

paradoxes
Words that end in a hissing sound, such as '-x', '-ss', '-sh', '-ch' and '-tz', take '-es' in the plural.

'para-'
If you see 'para-' in front of a word, it often means 'alongside' or 'parallel to'. A 'paramedic' works alongside senior doctors and nurses, for example.

passed vs past
'Passed' is the past tense of the verb 'to pass': 'He passed me on the motorway.' 'Past' means 'time before the present': 'You can't change the past.'

pat → patted
One-syllable words ending in a short vowel and a consonant double that consonant before adding '-ed'.

passive	pathetically	pave	pearliest
passively	pathological	paved	pearly
passivity	pathologically	pavement	peasant
passport	pathos	pavilion	peasantry
password	pathway	paving	peat
past	patience	paw	pebble
pasta	patient	pawed	pebbly
paste	patiently	pawing	peck
pasted	patio	pawn	pecked
pastel	patisserie	pawnbroker	pecking
pastime	patriarch	pawned	peculiar
pasting	patriot	pawning	peculiarities
pastor	patriotic	pawpaw	peculiarity
pastoral	patriotism	pay	peculiarly
pastries	patrol	payable	pedal
pastry	patrolled	paying	pedalled
pasture	patrolling	payment	pedalling
pat	patron	payroll	pedant
patch	patronage	pea	pedantic
patched	patronise/patronize	peace	peddle
patches	patronised/	peaceful	peddled
patchier	patronized	peacefully	peddling
patchiest	patronising/	peach	pedestal
patching	patronizing	peaches	pedestrian
patchwork	patted	peacock	pedigree
patchy	patter	peak	peek
pâté	pattered	peaked	peeked
patent	pattering	peaking	peeking
patented	pattern	peal	peel
patenting	patterned	pealed	peeled
patently	patting	pealing	peeling
paternal	paunch	peanut	peep
paternity	pause	pear	peeped
path	paused	pearl	peeping
pathetic	pausing	pearlier	peer

p

patrolled; patrolling
Words of more than one syllable that end in a vowel and a single '-l', double that 'l' when you add an ending that starts with a vowel.

peace is the opposite of war, but a 'piece' is a part or slice.

peak *vs* peek
A 'peak' is the topmost point of something, such as a mountain. To 'peek' is to take a quick look.

peal *vs* peel
A 'peal' of bells is a pre-arranged series of musical notes. 'Peel' is the outer layer of something, such as an orange.

A **pear** is a fruit, but 'pair' means 'two': 'a pair of doves'. To 'pare' means 'to reduce to the minimum'.

pedal *vs* peddle
To 'pedal' a bicycle is to move it by pushing on two pedals. To 'peddle' is to sell things illegally.

peer means 'to look hard at something', and Lords and Ladies are 'peers'. A 'pier' is a walkway over the sea.

I'm just having a peek at the peak.

peered	penitent	percussionist	perishable
peering	penknife	perennial	perished
peerless	penknives	perennially	perishing
pejorative	pennant	perfect	perjure
pelican	pennies	perfected	perjured
pellet	penniless	perfecting	perjuries
pelt	penny	perfection	perjury
pelted	pension	perfectionist	perk
pelting	pensioner	perfectly	perkier
pen	pensive	perforate	perkiest
penal	pentathlon	perforated	perky
penalise/penalize	penthouse	perforation	permanence
penalised/penalized	pent-up	perform	permanent
penalising/	penultimate	performance	permanently
penalizing	peonies	performed	permissible
penalties	peony	performer	permission
penalty	people	performing	permissive
penance	peopled	perfume	permissiveness
pence	pepper	perfumed	permit
penchant	peppermint	perfuming	permitted
pencil	per	perfunctorily	permitting
pencilled	perceive	perfunctory	permutation
pencilling	perceived	perhaps	pernicious
pendant	perceiving	peril	perpendicular
pending	per cent	perilous	perpetrate
pendulum	percentage	perilously	perpetrated
penetrate	perceptible	perimeter	perpetrating
penetrated	perception	period	perpetrator
penetrating	perceptive	periodic	perpetual
penetration	perceptively	periodically	perpetually
penguin	perch	peripheral	perpetuate
peninsula	perched	peripherally	perpetuated
penis	perching	peripheries	perpetuating
penises	percolator	periphery	perpetuity
penitence	percussion	perish	perplex

p

pen comes from the Latin word for 'feather', 'penna'. Early pens were quills, made from feathers.

penalise/penalize, etc.
Most words can be correctly spelt '-ise' or '-ize'. The ones that can't are listed on page 4.

penalties; pennies; perjuries
Remember that words such as 'perjury', that end in a consonant and a '-y', change to '-ies' in the plural.

penknives
Some words that end in '-f' or '-fe' change to '-ves' in the plural. There's a full list of these words on page 5.

per means 'for each', for example: 'You can have two biscuits per person.'

perceive sticks to the spelling guideline: 'i' before 'e' except after 'c' when the letters make an 'ee' sound.

permissiveness
The letter 'v' is always followed by a vowel or a 'y', so you keep the '-e' when you add '-ness', as here.

perpetrator; persecutor
Words that end in '-or' often mean 'people who do what the word means', e.g. a 'perpetrator' perpetrates, and a 'persecutor' persecutes.

Remember that the letters 'ph' make an 'f' sound in many words.

perplexed	persuasive	pharmaceutical	photogenic
perplexing	persuasively	pharmacies	photograph
persecute	pessimism	pharmacist	photographed
persecuted	pessimist	pharmacy	photographer
persecuting	pessimistic	phase	photographing
persecution	pessimistically	phased	photography
persecutor	pest	phasing	phrase
perseverance	pester	pheasant	phrased
persevere	pestered	phenomena	phrasing
persevered	pestering	phenomenal	physical
persevering	pesticide	phenomenally	physically
persist	pestle	phenomenon	physician
persisted	pet	philanthropic	physics
persistence	petal	philanthropist	physique
persistent	petite	philanthropy	pianist
persistently	petition	philistine	piano
persisting	petitioned	philosopher	piccolo
personal	petitioning	philosophical	pick
personalities	petrified	philosophically	pickaxe
personality	petrify	philosophies	picked
personally	petrifying	philosophy	picket
personification	petrol	phobia	picketed
personifies	petted	phoenix	picketing
personify	petticoat	phoenixes	picking
personifying	pettier	phone	pickle
personnel	pettiest	phoned	pickled
perspective	petting	phonetic	pickling
perspiration	petty	phoney	pickpocket
perspire	petulance	phoning	picnic
perspired	petulant	photo	picnicked
perspiring	petulantly	photocopied	picnicking
persuade	pew	photocopier	pictorial
persuaded	pewter	photocopies	picture
persuading	phantom	photocopy	pictured
persuasion	pharaoh	photocopying	picturesque

p

persistence/persistent; petulance/petulant, etc.
Try to remember that words ending with '-ence' and '-ance' tend to be nouns: 'Her persistence was amazing.' Words ending with '-ent' and '-ant' tend to be adjectives: 'She was such a petulant girl.'

personal *vs* **personnel**
'Personal' means 'private' or 'to do with an individual'; 'personnel' means 'a group of colleagues'.

petite is the feminine form of the French word for 'small'. It's usually used in English to describe a small-framed woman, and small-sized womens' clothes.

phenomenon means 'a remarkable occurrence or event', and its correct plural is 'phenomena'.
phobia
A 'phobia' is an irrational fear. It comes from the Greek word 'phobos' (fear). Phobias include 'arachnophobia' (fear of spiders), 'claustrophobia' (fear of enclosed spaces) and 'xenophobia' (fear or strong hatred of foreigners).
phonetic means 'as it sounds'. Many English words are not spelt phonetically (pronounced 'fer-net-ic-al-ee'), so you just have to learn them.

picturing	pilloried	piping	plagiarised/
pie	pillory	piracy	plagiarized
piece	pillorying	pirate	plagiarising/
pieced	pillow	pistol	plagiarizing
piecemeal	pillowcase	piston	plagiarism
piecing	pilot	pit	plagiarist
pier	piloted	pitch	plague
pierce	piloting	pitched	plagued
pierced	pimple	pitcher	plaguing
piercing	pimpled	pitching	plaice
piety	pimply	pitfall	plaid
pig	pin	pith	plain
pigeon	pinafore	pitied	plainer
pigeonhole	pincers	pitiful	plainest
piggyback	pinch	pitifully	plainly
piglet	pinched	pittance	plaintiff
pigment	pinching	pitted	plait
pigmentation	pincushion	pity	plaited
pigsties	pine	pitying	plaiting
pigsty	pineapple	pivot	plan
pigtail	pined	pivotal	plane
pike	ping-pong	pivoted	planet
pilchard	pining	pivoting	planetary
pile	pink	pixie	plank
piled	pinned	pizza	plankton
pile-up	pinning	placard	planned
pilfer	pint	placate	planning
pilfered	pioneer	placated	plant
pilfering	pious	placating	plantation
pilgrim	piously	place	planted
pilgrimage	pip	placed	planting
piling	pipe	placid	plaque
pill	piped	placidly	plaster
pillage	pipeline	placing	plastered
pillar	piper	plagiarise/plagiarize	plasterer

piece means 'a slice, section or part': 'a piece of cake'. 'Peace' is the opposite of war.

pier
A 'pier' is a walkway over the sea. 'Peer' means 'to look at something closely', and Lords and Ladies are 'peers'.

pigeon; pilgrimage; pillage
Note the 'j' sound is made with a 'g', not a 'j', or 'dg'.

pigeonhole; piggyback; pile-up; pillowcase, etc.
Compounds are made up of two words put together. Some are joined with a hyphen (-), such as 'pile-up', but many become a new word, with its own meaning.

pining; pinning
Words of one syllable that end in a short vowel and a consonant (such as 'pin') often double the final consonant when an ending that begins with a vowel is added ('pinning'). 'Pining' (which means 'longing for') has a long 'i' sound, however, so has only one 'n'.

pitiful; pitifully
When '-ful' is added to a word to make it mean 'full of', it has only one 'l': 'It is pitiful.' When you add '-ly' to a word to make it into an adverb, it has a double 'l': 'The dog whined pitifully.' Learn this rule if you can.

p

plastering	pleasing	plucky	pocket
plastic	pleasurable	plug	pod
plate	pleasure	plugged	podium
plateau	pleat	plugging	poem
plateaus/plateaux	pleated	plum	poet
plated	pledge	plumb	poetic
plateful	pledged	plumber	poetically
platform	pledging	plumbing	poetry
platinum	plentiful	plume	poignancy
platitude	plentifully	plummet	poignant
platonic	plenty	plummeted	point
platoon	pliable	plummeting	point-blank
platter	plied	plump	pointed
platypus	pliers	plumper	pointedly
platypuses	plies	plumpest	pointer
plausibility	plight	plunder	pointing
plausible	plinth	plundered	pointless
play	plod	plunderer	pointlessly
played	plodded	plundering	poise
player	plodding	plunge	poised
playful	plop	plunged	poison
playfully	plopped	plunging	poisoned
playground	plopping	plural	poisoner
playgroup	plot	pluralism	poisoning
playing	plotted	plus	poisonous
play-off	plotter	plush	poke
playwright	plotting	ply	poked
plea	plough	plywood	poker
plead	ploughed	pneumatic	poking
pleaded	ploughing	pneumonia	polar
pleading	ploughman	poach	pole
pleasant	ploy	poached	police
pleasantly	pluck	poacher	policed
please	plucked	poaching	policeman
pleased	plucking		policemen

p

place *vs* plaice
A 'place' is a location, or spot. A 'plaice' is a flat seawater fish with orange spots.

plaice; plain; plait
In 'plaice' and 'plain', the 'a' sound is long. In the word 'plait' (strands of interwoven hair, wool or thread), the letters 'ai' make a short 'a' sound, as in 'at'. Spell with care when you see the letters 'ai' in a word.

plaque
A 'q' is always followed by a 'u' in English words.

plateaus/plateaux are both correct plurals.

pledging; plunging
These words drop the silent '-e' before an ending that starts with a vowel is added.

plum *vs* plumb
A 'plum' is a fruit. 'Plumb', with a silent '-b', means 'feel despairing': 'He plumbed the depths.' It can also mean 'exactly': 'It fell plumb in the middle.' A 'plumber' fixes central heating and bathrooms.

pole
A 'pole' is a rod, or stick. A 'Pole' is also someone from Poland. A 'poll' is an election.

policewoman
policewomen
policies
policing
policy
policyholder
polish
polished
polishing
polite
politely
politeness
politer
politest
political
politically
politician
politics
polka
poll
polled
pollen
polling
pollutant
pollute
polluted
polluting
pollution
polo
polo neck
poltergeist
polyester
polygamist
polygamous
polygamy

pomegranate
pomp
pomposity
pompous
ponder
pondered
pondering
ponderous
ponies
pony
ponytail
poodle
pool
pooled
pooling
poor
poorer
poorest
poorly
pop
popcorn
poplar
popped
poppies
popping
poppy
populace
popular
populate
populated
populating
population
porcelain
porch
porcupine

'post-' is the **Latin for 'after'.** You might see it used in front of a word, either joined with a hyphen (as in post-mortem, which is examining a body after death), or all one word (as in posthumous, which means 'after death'). Don't confuse it with the post, which means 'letters and parcels'.

pore
pored
poring
pork
pornographic
pornography
porous
porpoise
porridge
port
portable
portcullis
porter
portfolio
porthole
portion
portrait
portray
portrayal
portrayed
portraying
pose
posed
poser
posh
posher

poshest
posies
posing
position
positioned
positioning
positive
positively
posse
possess
possessed
possessing
possession
possessor
possibilities
possibility
possible
possibly
possum
post
postage
postal
postbox
postboxes
postcard
posted

polish means 'to rub something until it shines' but 'Polish' is the language spoken in Poland.
poll means 'an election', but a 'Pole' is a person from Poland and a 'pole' is a rod or stick.
A poltergeist is a spirit that returns after death and makes noise or does scary things. It's from the German words 'poltern' (to make a noise) and 'Geist' (ghost).
'poly-' at the beginning of a word means 'many' or 'much', e.g. 'polygamy' is having more than one wife.
pomegranate is a fruit full of seeds. Its name is from the Latin 'pomum granatum' ('apple of seeds').

popular is often misspelt. To remember that it ends in '-ar', not '-er', try thinking: 'popular, like a star'.
pore vs pour
To 'pore' over something is to study it very carefully. A 'pore' is a tiny hole in the skin. To 'pour' means 'to measure out liquid'.
posse is from the Latin word for power, 'posse'. It means 'a group of people, often with power or authority', and is pronounced 'poss-ee'.
potatoes is the only correct plural of 'potato'. Find out which other words ending in '-o' add '-es' on page 5.

p

poster	pounced	praised	preciously
posterity	pouncing	praising	precipice
posthumous	pound	pram	precipitate
posthumously	pounded	prance	precipitated
posting	pounding	pranced	precipitating
postman	pour	prancing	precipitation
postmark	poured	prank	precise
postmen	pouring	prattle	precisely
post-mortem	pout	prattled	precision
postpone	pouted	prattling	precocious
postponed	pouting	prawn	preconception
postponement	poverty	pray	predator
postponing	powder	prayed	predatory
posture	powdered	prayer	predecessor
posy	powdery	praying	predicament
pot	power	preach	predict
potato	powered	preached	predictable
potatoes	powerful	preacher	predictably
potency	powerfully	preaching	predicted
potent	powering	precarious	prediction
potential	powerless	precariously	predominance
potentially	powerlessly	precaution	predominant
potion	practicable	precautionary	predominantly
potted	practical	precede	predominate
potter	practically	preceded	predominated
pottered	practice	precedence	predominating
potteries	practise	preceding	pre-eminence
pottering	practised	precinct	pre-eminent
pottery	practising	precious	pre-eminently
potties	practitioner		
potting	pragmatic		
potty	pragmatically		
pouch	pragmatism		
poultry	prairie		
pounce	praise		

p

> **'pre-'**
> **Words starting with 'pre-' often mean 'before', or 'in advance'.** For example, precede means 'come before something or someone else'. 'Prae' is Latin for 'before'.

practice vs practise
Try to remember that 'practice', the noun, is spelt with a 'c': 'She does a lot of violin practice.' 'Practise', the verb, is with an 's': 'She practises every day.'
pray means 'to communicate with a spiritual being, or god'. 'Prey' is a victim, or food for a predator.
precede
Be careful not to mix up 'precede', which means 'come before' or 'go before': 'The starter usually precedes the main course', and 'proceed', which means 'carry on' or 'move forwards': 'Let's proceed to step three.'

Pray, prey!

135

pre-empt
pre-empted
pre-empting
pre-emptive
preen
preened
preening
preface
prefaced
prefacing
prefect
prefer
preferable
preference
preferential
preferred
preferring
prefix
prefixes
pregnancy
pregnant
prehistoric
prehistory

prejudice
prejudicial
preliminaries
preliminary
prelude
premature
prematurely
premier
première
premise
premises
premium
premonition
preoccupation
preoccupied
preparation
preparatory
prepare
prepared
preparing
preposition
preposterous
preposterously

> **A preposition links a noun to the other words in a sentence in some way.** It will often tell you where, when or how something happened, for example. Prepositions include 'in', 'on', 'at', 'under', 'through', 'for', 'until', 'between' and 'over', but there are many, many more. You'll find out more about prepositions, plus a list of common ones, on page 215 of this dictionary.

prerogative
preschool
prescribe
prescribed
prescribing
prescription
presence
present
presentable
presented
presenter
presenting
presently
preservation
preserve
preserved
preserving
preside
presided
presidency
president
presidential
presiding
press
pressed

pressing
pressure
pressured
pressuring
pressurised/
pressurized
pressurising/
pressurizing
prestige
prestigious
presumably
presume
presumed
presuming
presumption
presumptuous
presumptuously
previous
previously
prey
price
priced
priceless
pricier
priciest

> **A prefix is added to the beginning of a word to alter its meaning.** This doesn't change the spelling of that word, but the prefix may alter slightly, depending on the word it's attached to. For example:
>
> The prefix 'in-' becomes 'il-' in 'illegal', and 'im-' in 'impossible'.
>
> You'll find out more about prefixes and how they are used on page 210.

---

preferable; preferred
In words of more than one syllable, where the stress falls at the end of the word, as in 'prefer', the final consonant is usually doubled before an ending is added. 'Preferable', stressed at the beginning, keeps just one 'r'.

premier vs première
'Premier' can mean 'the most important', 'best', or 'head of state'. A 'première' is the first public performance of a show, film or piece of music.

prey is a victim, or food for a predator. To 'pray' is to communicate with a spiritual being, or god.

pries vs prise vs prize
'Pries' is part of the verb 'to pry' (meaning 'to intrude'): 'He pries on me.' To 'prise' is to force something open, or apart. A 'prize' is a reward for winning something.

primaeval/primeval
This word, which means 'from a very early time in the history of the world', can be spelt either of these ways.

principal vs principle
'Principal' can mean 'main', 'most important'. It can also mean the head-teacher of a school. A 'principle' is a moral standpoint, or belief: 'She has high principles.'

pricing	princesses	prized	productive
prick	principal	prizing	productively
pricked	principalities	probabilities	productivity
pricking	principality	probability	profession
prickle	principally	probable	professional
pricklier	principle	probably	professionalism
prickliest	principled	probation	professionally
prickly	print	probationary	professor
pride	printed	probe	proficiency
prided	printer	probed	proficient
priding	printing	probing	proficiently
pried	print-out	problem	profile
pries	prior	problematic	profit
priest	prioress	procedural	profitable
priesthood	priorities	procedure	profitably
priestly	priority	proceed	profited
prig	priory	proceeded	profiting
priggish	prise	proceeding	profound
priggishly	prised	process	profundity
prim	prising	processed	profuse
primarily	prison	processing	profusely
primary	prisoner	procession	profusion
prime	pristine	proclaim	program
primed	privacy	proclaimed	programme
primaeval/primeval	private	proclaiming	programmed
primitive	privately	proclamation	programming
primitively	privatisation/	prod	progress
primly	privatization	prodded	progressed
primmer	privatise/privatize	prodding	progression
primmest	privatised/privatized	prodigal	progressive
primness	privatising/	produce	progressively
primrose	privatizing	produced	prohibit
prince	privilege	producer	prohibited
princely	privileged	producing	prohibiting
princess	prize	production	prohibition

p

'pro-'
The word 'pro' is Latin for 'for'. When added to an English word with a hyphen (-), it implies 'in favour of', e.g. 'pro-hunting', 'pro-choice'.

proceed
Take care not to mix 'proceed', which means 'go forward': 'Let's proceed', with 'precede', meaning 'go before': 'the preceding week'.

production; profession; proficient
Note that the 'sh' sound is made by 'ti' in 'production', 'ssi' in 'profession', and 'ci' in 'proficient'.

productively; progressively
The letter 'v' is always followed by a vowel or 'y', so 'productive' and 'progressive' keep the silent '-e' when the ending '-ly' is added to make adverbs.

profit → profited; prohibit → prohibited
You don't double the 't' of these words when you add '-ed' because you emphasize the first part of the word when you say them. See 'benefited' and 'targeted', too.

program vs programme
The word 'program' is used about computers. A 'programme' is on television, or is a plan of events.

prohibitive
project
projected
projecting
projection
projectionist
projector
prologue
prolong
prolonged
prolonging
promenade
prominence
prominent
prominently
promise
promised
promising
promontories
promontory
promote
promoted

promoter
promoting
promotion
prompt
prompted
prompter
prompting
promptly
promptness
prone
prong
pronged
pronoun
pronounce
pronounced
pronouncement
pronouncing
pronunciation
proof
prop
propaganda
propagate

propagated
propagating
propagation
propel
propellant
propelled
propeller
propelling
propensities
propensity
proper
properly
properties
property
prophecies
prophecy
prophesies
prophesy
prophetic
proportion
proportional
proportionate
proportionately
proposal
propose
proposed
proposing
proposition
propped
propping
proprietor
propriety
propulsion
prose
prosecute

prosecuted
prosecuting
prosecution
prosecutor
prospect
prospected
prospecting
prospective
prosper
prospered
prospering
prosperity
prosperous
protect
protected
protecting
protection
protective
protectively
protector
protein
protest
protestation
protested
protester
protesting
prototype
protrude
protruded
protruding
protrusion
proud
prouder
proudest
proudly

---

projection; promotion; proportion; propulsion, etc.
Many nouns end with '-tion' or '-sion'. They sound exactly the same, so take care when you hear the 'shun' sound at the end of a word, and check your spelling.

promising
You drop the silent '-e' in 'promise' before you add '-ing'. Thousands of words follow this spelling pattern, so learn it if you can.

promontories; propensities; prophecies
Words ending in a consonant and a '-y' change to '-ies' in the plural.

propellant; pummelled, etc.
Always double the 'l' in words ending in a vowel and an '-l' before you add an ending that starts with a vowel. This applies to words ending with a vowel and '-p', too.

prophecy vs prophesy
Take care not to mix up 'prophecy' (noun): 'The prophecy was accurate', with 'prophesy' (verb): 'She likes to prophesy doom.'

protein does not stick to the spelling pattern: 'i' before 'e' except after 'c' when they make an 'ee' sound. 'Seize' is another exception, and you'll find more on page 4.

prove
proved
proverb
proverbial
proverbially
provide
provided
providing
province
provincial
proving
provision
provisionally
provocation
provocative
provoke
provoked
provoking
prow
prowess
prowl
prowled
prowler
prowling
proximity
proxy
prude
prudence
prudent
prudently
prudish
prune
pruned
pruning
pry

prying
psalm
pseudonym
psychiatric
psychiatrist
psychiatry
psychic
psychological
psychologically
psychology
pub
puberty
pubescent
pubic
public
publication
publicise/publicize
publicised/
publicized
publicising/
publicizing
publicity
publicly
publish
published
publisher
publishing
puck
pucker
puckered
puckering
pudding
puddle
puerile
puff

puffed
puffin
puffing
pull
pulled
pulley
pulling
pullover
pulp
pulped
pulping
pulpit
pulse
pulsed
pulsing
pulverise/pulverize
pulverised/
pulverized
pulverising/
pulverizing
puma

pummel
pummelled
pummelling
pump
pumped
pumping
pumpkin
pun
punch
punched
punching
punctual
punctuality
punctually
punctuate
punctuated
punctuating
punctuation
puncture
punctured
puncturing

p

punctuation is vital in written language, as it **helps a reader understand what the writer is saying**. Find out more on page 213, but here are the main punctuation marks you need to know:

Apostrophe (') That's my dog.
Comma (,) We ate bread, cheese, ham, olives and grapes for our picnic.
Full stop (.) I am sad.
Question mark (?) Where did he go?
Speech marks (" ") "Wait for me."
Exclamation mark (!) Stop it!
Hyphen (-) Shark-infested waters.

psalm; pseudonym; psychiatric, etc.
Look out for the silent 'p-' before the 's' in these examples, which are all from Latin and Greek words.
publicise/publicize; pulverise/pulverize, etc.
Most words can be spelt with an 's' or a 'z', but some, listed on page 4, can only have one or the other.
puerile, which means 'immature' or 'childish', comes from the Latin word for 'boy', 'puer'.
puma
Only words from other languages end in '-a'. 'Puma' is the Spanish name for a cougar, or mountain lion.

pungency
pungent
pungently
punier
puniest
punish
punishable
punished
punishing
punishment
punitive
punitively
punt
punted
punting
puny
pup
pupil
puppet
puppetry

puppies
puppy
purchase
purchased
purchaser
purchasing
pure
purée
purely
purer
purest
purgative
purgatorial
purgatory
purge
purged
purging
purification
purified
purifies

purify
purifying
purist
puritan
puritanical
purple
purpose
purposely
purr
purred
purring
purse
pursue
pursued
pursuing
pursuit
push
pushchair
pushed
pusher

pushier
pushiest
pushing
pushover
pushy
put
putt
putting
putty
puzzle
puzzled
puzzlement
puzzling
pygmies
pygmy
pyjamas
pylon
pyramid
pyre
python

punier; puniest
The '-y' of 'puny' changes to an 'i' before any endings are added to make the comparative form, 'punier', and the superlative, 'puniest'. This is a common pattern.

put *vs* putt
To 'put' means 'to place or position something somewhere': 'I put my hat onto my head.' A 'putt' is a short distance shot in golf.

pyjamas comes from the Indian name for baggy trousers tied at the waist, 'pai jamahs'. Europeans adapted them into a style of loose, cool nightwear.

Quick tip

Seeing the letters of a tricky word 'in your mind's eye' can help you spell it. A 'peninsula' is a piece of land that juts out, and is surrounded by sea on two sides, so try imagining an 'i' surrounded by two 'n's.

Some tricky words to spell that start with a 'p'

Here are some particularly tricky words starting with 'p':

pageant	pharaoh	privilege
pallor	playwright	pronunciation
pamphlet	plumb	psychiatrist
particular	prejudice	pyjamas
peninsula	prerogative	pyramid

Qq

quack
quacked
quacking
quad
quadrant
quadruped
quadruple
quadrupled
quadruplet
quadrupling
quail
quailed
quailing
quaint
quainter
quaintest
quaintly
quaintness
quake
quaked

quaking
qualification
qualifier
qualifies
qualify
qualifying
qualities
quality
quantities
quantity
quarantine
quarantined
quarantining
quarrel
quarrelled
quarrelling
quarrelsome
quarries
quarry
quart

quarter
quartered
quartering
quartet
quaver
quavered
quavering
quay
queasier
queasiest
queasy
queen
queer
queerer
queerest
quench
quenched
quenching
queries
query
querying
quest
question
questionable
questionably
questioned
questioner
questioning

questionnaire
queue
queued
queuing
quibble
quibbled
quibbling
quiche
quick
quicken
quickened
quickening
quicker
quickest
quickly
quiet
quieten
quietened
quietening
quieter
quietest
quietly
quill
quilt
quintet
quintuplet
quirkier
quirkiest

'quad-'; 'quin-'
Many words beginning with 'quad-' are to do with 'four' (such as quadruped and quadruple). Words beginning with 'quin-' (such as quintet and quintuplet) are to do with 'five'. The Latin for the number four is 'quattuor', and the number five is 'quinque'.

quadrupling; quaking; quarantining, etc.
Most words ending in a consonant and silent '-e' drop the '-e' when you add an ending that starts with a vowel.

qualities; quantities; quarries; queries
Notice that these words, ending in a consonant followed by a '-y', take the ending '-ies' in the plural.

quarantine is the time people or animals are kept separately, in case they are carrying an illness. 'Quaranta' is '40' in Italian, and 'quarantine' was first used in the 1600s, when ships had to wait outside Venice for 40 days before being allowed into port.

quarrelled; quarrelsome
When words end in a vowel and an '-l', you double it when you add an ending that begins with a vowel. If the ending starts with a consonant, you don't.

quay
A 'quay' is where boats tie up, but it sounds like 'key' (a tool which locks and unlocks things).

queue
A 'queue' is a line of people waiting, and is a really tricky word to spell. A 'cue' is a signal to do something, or the pole used in snooker.

q

quirky	quiver	quizzes	quotable
quit	quivered	quizzical	quotation
quite	quivering	quizzically	quote
quitter	quiz	quizzing	quoted
quitting	quizzed	quota	quoting

quit

This word is both the present and the past tense of the verb 'to quit'. "I quit!" is correct, as is 'She quit her job yesterday.' The future is 'She will quit.'

quite

This word, meaning 'a little' or 'not a great deal', is often confused with 'quiet', the opposite of 'noisy'. Take care when you need to use either of these words.

quota

Only words from other languages end in '-a'. 'Quota' is a Latin word, meaning 'how many' or 'how much'.

 Quick tip

Spelling sentences

Practise spellings by choosing, say, six words starting with the same letter and making up a sentence using them.

1. Choose six words, checking their spelling in a dictionary. Write them out carefully.
2. Make up a sentence that uses all six words.
3. Write the sentence out at least three times.
4. Now check your spellings. How did you do?

Your sentence need not make sense, but it's good to play about with words. For instance:

'The queue of quails quickly quietened when the quizzical queen quacked.'

Different meanings

Many thousands of words in English have **different meanings, but are spelt exactly the same. These are called 'homographs'.** Although the 'q' section of this dictionary is very short, there are no less than seven homographs in it:

- a **quack** can mean 'the sound a duck makes' or 'an amateur doctor'.

- to **quail** can mean 'to hesitate' or 'cower', but a 'quail' is also a small bird.

- a **quarry** can mean 'where stone is dug out of the ground', or 'something or someone that is being hunted'.

- a **quaver** is a musical note, but 'to quaver' means 'to wobble': 'His voice quavered slightly.'

- **queer** can mean 'peculiar' or 'unusual', but it is also an informal, rude word for a gay man.

- to **quiver** can mean 'to tremble' or 'shake', but it can also be the pouch in which an archer keeps arrows.

English has many thousands of homographs, but don't worry. You will get to know them as you use them.

Some tricky words to spell that start with a 'q'

Here are some tricky words that begin with the letter 'q':

quadrant	query	quiche
quadruple	questionnaire	quiet
quail	queue	quirky
quarrel	queued	quite
quay	queuing	quizzical

My sister's quite quiet.

My brother's quite quirky.

Rr

Rain reigned throughout their holiday.

rain *vs* **reign** *vs* **rein**
Take care with these words that sound the same. 'Rain' is drops of water falling from the sky; 'reign' means 'to rule' and a 'rein' helps control a horse (and is often in the plural: 'reins').

rabbit	radical	raindrop	ran
rabble	radicalism	rained	ranch
rabid	radically	rainfall	ranches
rabies	radio	rainforest	rancid
raccoon/racoon	radioactive	raining	rancorous
race	radioactivity	rainwater	rancour
racecourse	radish	raise	random
raced	radishes	raised	randomly
racehorse	raffle	raisin	rang
racial	raft	raising	range
racially	rafter	rake	ranged
racing	rafting	raked	ranger
racism	rag	raking	ranging
racist	rage	rallied	rank
rack	raged	rallies	ranked
racked	ragged	rally	ranking
racket	raging	ram	ransack
racking	raid	ramble	ransacked
racquet	raided	rambled	ransacking
radar	raider	rambler	ransom
radiance	raiding	rambling	rant
radiant	rail	rammed	ranted
radiantly	railed	ramming	ranting
radiate	railing	ramp	rap
radiated	railway	rampage	rape
radiating	rain	rampaged	raped
radiation	rainbow	rampaging	rapid
radiator	raincoat	rampart	rapidly

racing; raging; raking; rambling; rampaging, etc.
When you add an ending that starts with a vowel to a word that ends in a consonant and a silent '-e', remember you usually drop the '-e'.

racket *vs* **racquet**
A 'racket' is an informal word for a loud noise, but a 'racquet' is the piece of equipment used to hit the ball in games such as tennis. (You may see it spelt 'racket'.)

raisin *vs* **raising**
A 'raisin' is a dried grape. 'Raising' is part of the verb 'to raise': 'She was raising her arm to wave.'

ranches
Words that end in '-ch', '-ss', '-sh' or other hissing sounds usually take '-es' in the plural.

rancour → rancorous
When you add the ending '-ous' to a word that ends in '-our', you drop the 'u'. The words 'glamorous' and 'humorous' are other examples of this pattern.

rap
To 'rap' means to tap something hard. It is also a style of music. To 'wrap' is to cover something up (but you can't hear the 'w', so take care).

raping
rapist
rapped
rapping
rare
rarities
rarity
rascal
rash
rasher
rashest
rashly
raspberries
raspberry
rat
rate
rather
ratifies
ratify
ratifying
rating
ratio
ration
rational
rationale
rationally
rationed
rationing
rattle
rattled
rattlesnake
rattling
raucous
ravage
ravaged

ravaging
rave
raved
raven
ravenous
ravenously
ravine
raving
ravioli
ravish
ravished
ravishing
raw
ray
razor
reach
reached
reaching
react
reacted
reacting
reaction
reactor
read
reader
readier
readiest
readily
readiness
reading
readjust
readjusted
readjusting
readjustment
ready

ready-made
real
realisation/
realization
realise/realize
realised/realized
realising/realizing
realism
realist
realistic
realistically
realities
reality
really
realm
reap
reaped
reaper
reaping
reappear
reappearance
reappeared
reappearing
rear
reared
rearing
rearrange

rearranged
rearrangement
rearranging
reason
reasonable
reasonably
reasoned
reasoning
reassurance
reassure
reassured
reassuring
rebel
rebelled
rebelling
rebellion
rebellious
rebelliously
rebound
rebounded
rebounding
rebuild
rebuilding
rebuilt
rebuke
rebuked
rebuking

're-'

If you see 're-' at the beginning of a word, it often **gives the meaning of something being repeated, or done again**. To reappear means 'to appear again' for example. It may have a hyphen (-), especially if the word it comes before begins with an 'e', e.g. 're-evaulate'.

10 10

They rate that rat.

rat/rate
Adding an '-e' to 'rat' (a rodent) makes the vowel 'a' long, and a completely different word: 'rate' (to give a value to something). This is a common spelling pattern: see also 'rap/rape' and 'rip/ripe'.

rational vs rationale
'Rational' means 'sensible' or 'logical', but a 'rationale' is the logical basis of an idea or action.
ravioli
Only words from other languages end in an '-i'. 'Ravioli' is an Italian word for stuffed pasta parcels.
read
To 'read' (to rhyme with 'bleed') means 'to understand printed letters'. 'Read' (to rhyme with 'bled') is the past tense. A 'reed' is a plant, or a sliver of cane in the mouthpiece of a wind instrument.

Words beginning with an 'r' sound can have a silent 'w-' at the beginning. Check the 'w' pages if unsure.

recall — reduced

recall	recitation	reconcile	rectory
recalled	recite	reconciled	recuperate
recalling	recited	reconciliation	recuperated
recap	reciting	reconciling	recuperating
recapped	reckless	reconnaissance	recuperation
recapping	recklessly	reconsider	recur
recapture	recklessness	reconsideration	recurred
recaptured	reckon	reconsidered	recurrence
recapturing	reckoned	reconsidering	recurrent
recede	reckoning	reconstruct	recurrently
receded	reclaim	reconstructed	recurring
receding	reclaimable	reconstructing	recycle
receipt	reclaimed	reconstruction	recycled
receive	reclaiming	record	recycling
received	reclamation	recorded	red
receiver	recline	recorder	redcurrant
receiving	reclined	recording	redden
recent	reclining	recover	reddened
recently	recognisable/	recovered	reddening
receptacle	recognizable	recoveries	redder
reception	recognisably/	recovering	reddest
receptionist	recognizably	recovery	reddish
receptive	recognise/recognize	recreate	redeem
recess	recognised/	recreated	redeemed
recesses	recognized	recreation	redeeming
recharge	recognising/	recreational	redemption
recharged	recognizing	recruit	redemptive
recharging	recognition	recruited	red-handed
recipe	recoil	recruiting	redhead
reciprocal	recoiled	rectangle	red-hot
reciprocate	recoiling	rectangular	redress
reciprocated	recommend	rectifies	redressed
reciprocating	recommendation	rectify	redressing
reciprocation	recommended	rectifying	reduce
recital	recommending	rectories	reduced

r

real means 'genuine': 'It was a real snake.' A 'reel' can either mean 'a spool which thread is wound onto', 'a traditional sailor's dance', or 'to walk unsteadily'.

rebel → rebelled; recap → recapped, etc. Words of more than one syllable that end with a vowel and an '-l' or a '-p' double these letters before you add an ending that begins with a vowel.

receive follows the spelling pattern: 'i' before 'e' except after 'c' where the letters make an 'ee' sound.

recesses Words that end with '-ss' add '-es' in the plural.

reciprocation; reclamation; recognition; etc. You'll find '-tion' at the end of lots of nouns. As it sounds like '-sion', another common word ending, always take care when you hear the sound 'shun'.

recognise/recognize is from two Latin words, 're' (again) and 'cognere' (to know). To recognize someone really means 'to know them again'.

reconnaissance is a French word, and is used to mean 'finding out about a place in advance'.

reddish means 'like red', as the '-ish' ending means 'similar to'. Notice that the 'd' is doubled.

reducing	reflected	refurbish	regretful
reduction	reflecting	refurbished	regretfully
redundancies	reflection	refurbishing	regrettable
redundancy	reflective	refurbishment	regretted
redundant	reflectively	refusal	regretting
reed	reflex	refuse	regular
reef	reflexes	refused	regularity
reek	reflexive	refusing	regularly
reeked	reflexively	refute	regulate
reeking	reform	refuted	regulated
reel	reformation	regain	regulating
re-elect	reformative	regained	regulation
re-elected	reformed	regaining	regulator
re-electing	reformer	regal	rehabilitate
re-election	reforming	regally	rehabilitated
reeled	refrain	regard	rehabilitating
reeling	refrained	regarded	rehabilitation
re-evaluate	refraining	regarding	rehearsal
re-evaluated	refresh	regardless	rehearse
re-evaluating	refreshed	regenerate	rehearsed
re-evaluation	refreshing	regenerated	rehearsing
refer	refreshment	regeneration	reign
referee	refrigerate	reggae	reigned
reference	refrigerated	regime	reimburse
referendum	refrigerating	regiment	reimbursed
referendums	refrigeration	regimental	reimbursing
referred	refrigerator	region	rein
referring	refuel	regional	reincarnated
refine	refuelled	regionally	reincarnation
refined	refuelling	register	reindeer
refinement	refuge	registered	reined
refineries	refugee	registering	reinforce
refinery	refund	registrar	reinforced
refining	refunded	registration	reinforcement
reflect	refunding	regret	reinforcing

r

reed
A 'reed' is a plant, or a sliver of cane in the mouthpiece of a woodwind instrument. To 'read' means 'understand printed letters'.

reel
A 'reel' can mean 'a spool which thread is wound onto', 'a sailor's dance', or 'to walk unsteadily'. 'Real' means 'genuine'.

reflexes
Most words ending in '-x' or other hissing sounds add '-es' in the plural.

There's an igloo in my refrigerator!

refrigerate can be easy to misspell. Try thinking of an 'igloo' (Inuit house made of ice blocks), to help you remember the 'ig' in the middle of the word.

regretful; regretfully
When you add '-ful' to a word to mean 'full of', it only has one 'l': 'It is regretful.' When you add '-fully', to make an adverb, it has two: 'She regretfully declined.'

reinstate	relegate	relocated	reminiscence
reinstated	relegated	relocating	reminiscent
reinstatement	relegating	relocation	reminiscing
reinstating	relegation	reluctance	remission
reiterate	relent	reluctant	remit
reiterated	relented	reluctantly	remittance
reiterating	relenting	rely	remitted
reiteration	relentless	relying	remitting
reject	relentlessly	remain	remnant
rejected	relevance	remainder	remorse
rejecting	relevant	remained	remorseful
rejection	reliability	remaining	remote
rejoice	reliable	remand	remotely
rejoiced	reliably	remanded	remoter
rejoicing	reliant	remanding	remotest
relapse	relic	remark	removable
relapsed	relied	remarkable	removal
relapsing	relief	remarkably	remove
relate	relies	remarked	removed
related	relieve	remarking	remover
relating	relieved	remarried	removing
relation	relieving	remarry	rename
relationship	religion	remarrying	renamed
relative	religious	remedial	renaming
relatively	religiously	remedies	render
relax	relinquish	remedy	rendered
relaxation	relinquished	remember	rendering
relaxed	relinquishing	remembered	rendezvous
relaxes	relish	remembering	rendition
relaxing	relished	remembrance	renew
relay	relishing	remind	renewable
relayed	relive	reminded	renewed
release	relived	reminder	renewing
released	reliving	reminding	renounce
releasing	relocate	reminisce	renounced

regular; regularity; regulate; regulation, etc.
These words are all to do with rules and keeping things in order. They come from the Latin word 'regula', which means 'rule'.

rehabilitate
It can be useful to break long, tricky words down into parts. For example, breaking this word into 're-hab-il-i-tate' can help you remember each letter.

reign vs rein
To 'reign' means 'rule'. A 'rein' helps control a horse, and 'rain' means 'drops of water falling from the sky'.

reinforcement; reinstatement
Notice that you keep the '-e' at the end of 'reinforce' and 'reinstate' when you add the ending '-ment'. This is because the ending starts with a consonant.

relevance; reluctance; reminiscence, etc.
Take care not to mix up the spelling of nouns ending with '-ance' and those ending with '-ence', as they sound very similar.

relinquish
You'll find that the letter 'q' is always followed by a 'u' in English words.

renouncing	repelled	reporting	repulsive
renovate	repellent	repossess	repulsively
renovated	repelling	repossessed	reputable
renovating	repent	repossessing	reputably
renovation	repentance	repossession	reputation
renown	repentant	represent	reputed
renowned	repented	representation	reputedly
rent	repenting	representative	request
rental	repercussion	represented	requested
rented	repertoire	representing	requesting
renting	repertory	repress	require
renunciation	repetition	repressed	required
reorganisation/	repetitive	repressing	requirement
reorganization	replace	repression	requisite
reorganise/	replaced	reprieve	rescue
reorganize	replacement	reprimand	rescued
reorganised/	replacing	reprimanded	rescuer
reorganized	replay	reprimanding	rescuing
reorganising/	replayed	reprisal	research
reorganizing	replaying	reproach	researched
repaid	replenish	reproached	researcher
repair	replenished	reproaches	researching
repaired	replenishing	reproaching	resemblance
repairing	replenishment	reproduce	resemble
repay	replete	reproduced	resembled
repaying	replica	reproducing	resembling
repayment	replicate	reproduction	resent
repeal	replicated	reproductive	resented
repealed	replicating	reptile	resentful
repealing	replied	reptilian	resentfully
repeat	replies	republic	resentment
repeated	reply	republican	reservation
repeatedly	report	repulse	reserve
repeating	reported	repulsed	reserved
repel	reporter	repulsion	reserving

renovate; repetitive; reprieve, etc.
Remember that a 'v' always comes before a vowel (or a 'y').

'v' was always being followed by vowels.

renunciation is from 'renounce', which means 'reject' or 'give up': 'She renounced chocolate forever.' 'Pronounce → pronunciation' also follows this pattern.

repellent; repentant; resilient; resistant, etc.
It's easy to confuse the adjective endings '-ent' and '-ant'. Check spellings in a dictionary if you're unsure.

republic means 'a country that is ruled by a president, rather than a king or queen'. It comes from two Latin words, 'res publica' meaning 'public things'.

rescuing
Drop the '-e' at the end of 'rescue' before adding an ending that begins with a vowel, such as '-ing'.

reservoir means 'an artificial lake for storing water', and is a tricky word to spell.

reservoir
reset
reside
resided
residence
resident
residential
residing
residual
residue
resign
resignation
resigned
resigning
resilience
resilient
resist
resistance
resistant
resisted
resisting
resolute
resolutely
resolution
resolve
resolved
resolving
resonance
resonant
resonate
resonated
resonating
resort
resorted
resorting

resound
resounded
resounding
resource
resourceful
respect
respectability
respectably
respected
respectful
respectfully
respecting
respective
respectively
respiration
respiratory
respire
respiring
respond
responded
responding
response
responsive
rest
restaurant
rested
restful
resting
restless
restlessly
restlessness
restoration
restorative
restore
restored

restoring
restrain
restrained
restraining
restraint
restrict
restricted
restricting
restriction
restrictive
result
resultant
resulted
resulting
resume
résumé
resumed
resuming
resumption
resurgence
resurgent
resurrect
resurrected
resurrecting
resurrection
resuscitate
resuscitated
resuscitating
resuscitation
retail
retailer
retain
retained
retaining
retaliate

retaliated
retaliating
retaliation
retarded
retention
rethink
rethinking
rethought
reticence
reticent
retire
retired
retirement
retiring
retort
retorted
retorting
retract
retractable
retracted
retracting
retraction
retreat
retreated
retreating
retribution
retrieval
retrieve
retriever
retro
retrospect
retrospection
retrospective
retrospectively
return

r

resign
You'll usually find a silent 'g' before an 'n', as here in 'resign', or in 'gnat' and 'gnome'.

restrict; resurrect; retract, etc.
The harsh 'kt' sound is made with 'ct' in English words, never with 'kt' as in some languages.

resume vs résumé
'Resume' means 'start again', but a 'résumé' (which may also be spelt without the French accents) is a list of a person's qualifications and experience. In British English, it's often called a 'curriculum vitae', or 'c.v.'.

retirement keeps the silent '-e' of 'retire' because '-ment' begins with a consonant. If the ending you add starts with a vowel, drop the silent '-e': 'retiring'.

retractable
The ending '-able' means 'can be done'. Something 'rectractable' can be retracted: 'a retractable aerial'.

retro
Words beginning with 'retro-' refer to the past, as this Latin word means 'behind' or 'backwards': 'a retrospective look at the 1970s'. 'Retro' can also mean 'fashionably old-fashioned': 'decorated in a retro style'.

Look out for the silent 'h' after the 'r' at the beginning of some of the words on this page.

returned	revising	rhyme	ridge
returning	revision	rhymed	ridged
reunion	revival	rhyming	ridicule
reunite	revive	rhythm	ridiculed
reunited	revived	rhythmic	ridiculing
reuniting	reviving	rhythmically	ridiculous
revamp	revolt	rib	ridiculously
revamped	revolted	ribbed	riding
revamping	revolting	ribbon	rife
reveal	revolution	rice	rifle
revealed	revolutionaries	rich	rifled
revealing	revolutionary	richer	rifling
revel	revolve	riches	rift
revelled	revolved	richest	rig
revelling	revolver	richly	rigged
revelry	revolving	richness	rigging
revenge	revulsion	rickety	right
revenue	reward	ricochet	righteous
revere	rewarded	ricocheted	righteously
revered	rewarding	ricocheting	rightful
reverence	rewind	rid	rightfully
reversal	rewinding	ridden	right-handed
reverse	rewound	ridding	rightly
reversed	rhapsodies	riddle	right-wing
reversible	rhapsody	riddled	rigid
reversing	rhetoric	ride	rigidity
revert	rhetorical	rider	rigidly
reverted	rhetorically		
reverting	rheumatic		
review	rheumatism		
reviewed	rhino		
reviewer	rhinoceros		
reviewing	rhinoceroses		
revise	rhododendron		
revised	rhubarb		

rhetoric

'Rhetoric' is **writing or speaking persuasively**, and is often used in political speeches, or at formal occasions. A 'rhetorical question' is a question the speaker doesn't really expect to be answered, e.g. 'I wonder what he'll do?'.

revelled; revelling; rivalled; rivalling
Whenever you add an ending that starts with a vowel to a word that ends in a vowel and a single '-l', you need to double the 'l': 'revelled'. Try to learn this rule.

reversible
If you are unsure whether the word you need to spell ends in '-ible' or '-able', remember that words ending in an 's' sound usually take '-ible', as here, in 'reversible'.

revolutionaries; rhapsodies; rivalries, etc.
Words ending in a consonant and a '-y' take the ending '-ies' in the plural.

rid → ride; rip → ripe; rob → robe
Notice how adding a silent '-e' to a word, such as 'rid' or 'rip', makes the vowel sound long, as it is in 'ride' and 'ripe'. Many words follow this pattern.

right vs rite
The word 'right' can mean either 'the opposite of left', or 'correct'. A 'rite' is a ritual, or ceremony. 'Write' means 'to use letter-marks to compose words'. Make sure you use the right (as in 'correct') word.

A ring is a circular piece of jewellery for a finger, or the sound made by a bell. To 'wring' is to squeeze very hard.

rigorous	risking	robust	roosting
rigorously	risky	robustly	root
rigour	risotto	rock	rooted
rim	rite	rocked	rooting
rind	ritual	rocket	rope
ring	ritualistic	rocketed	roped
ringed	ritually	rocketing	roping
ringing	rival	rockier	rosaries
ringleader	rivalled	rockiest	rosary
rink	rivalling	rocking	rose
rinse	rivalries	rocky	rosemary
rinsed	rivalry	rod	rosette
rinsing	river	rode	rosier
riot	riveted	rodent	rosiest
rioted	riveting	rodeo	rostra
rioting	road	roe	rostrum
rip	roam	rogue	rosy
ripe	roamed	role	rot
ripen	roaming	roll	rota
ripened	roar	roll-call	rotate
ripening	roared	rolled	rotated
riper	roaring	roller coaster	rotating
ripest	roast	roller-skate	rotation
ripped	roasted	roller-skating	rotor
ripper	roasting	rolling	rotted
ripple	rob	romance	rotten
rippled	robbed	romantic	rotting
rippling	robber	romantically	rough
rise	robberies	roof	roughen
risen	robbery	roofing	rougher
riser	robbing	rooftop	roughly
risk	robe	rook	roughness
risked	robin	room	round
riskier	robot	roost	roundabout
riskiest	robotic	roosted	rounded

role *vs* roll
A 'role' is a part or character in a play, book or film. To 'roll' means 'to turn over repeatedly', and a 'roll' is a small, often round, loaf of bread.

In the film, the roll's role was to roll down the hill.

ACTION!

roof
Most words ending in '-f' add '-s' to make the plural, but some words change to '-ves' (see page 5).

root
A 'root' is a part of a growing thing that is below the ground. A 'route' is a journey plan.

rostra; rostrum
A 'rostrum' is a platform at the front of a theatre or lecture hall where the speaker stands. It's from the Latin 'rostrum', for 'ship's prow'. The correct Latin plural is 'rostra', but you may also see 'rostrums'.

rounder	rubber	rule	runway
roundest	rubbery	ruled	rupture
rounding	rubbing	ruler	ruptured
rouse	rubbish	ruling	rupturing
roused	rubble	rum	rural
rousing	rubies	rumble	rush
route	ruby	rumbled	rushed
routed	rucksack	rumbling	rushing
routine	rudder	rummage	rust
routinely	rude	rummaged	rusted
routing	rudely	rummaging	rustic
rove	rudeness	rumour	rustier
roved	ruder	rumoured	rustiest
roving	rudest	rumouring	rusting
row	rudimentary	rump	rustle
rowdier	rudiments	run	rustled
rowdiest	rug	runaway	rustler
rowdy	rugby	rung	rustling
rowed	rugged	runner	rusty
rowing	ruggedly	runner-up	rut
royal	ruin	runnier	ruthless
royalty	ruined	runniest	ruthlessly
rub	ruining	running	ruthlessness
rubbed	ruinous	runny	rye

route means 'a journey, or plan'. A 'root' is a part of a growing thing that is below the ground.

runaway; runner-up
Some compound words, such as 'runaway', join into a new word. Some, such as 'runner-up', are joined with a hyphen (-), while others stay as separate words.

rung
'Rung' can be part of the verb 'to ring', or a step on a ladder. 'Wrung' is the past tense of 'wring'.

rye is a brown grain, but if you have a 'wry' look on your face, it means you're amused by something.

Quick tip

The 'r' sound

Words that begin with the 'r' sound can hold hidden dangers for the speller, so always check them in this dictionary if you are unsure.

1. Some, such as 'write' and 'wren', **begin with a silent 'w-'**, to trip you up.

2. Others **begin with 'rh-'**, which is pronounced 'r', as in 'rhetoric' and 'rhyme'.

Some tricky words to spell that start with an 'r'

Here are some words that are tricky to spell that begin with the letter 'r':

recede	referred	religion	rhinoceros
receipt	refrigerator	reminisce	rhythm
recurrence	rehearsal	reservoir	ricochet

If you're looking for a word beginning with an 's' sound, remember to check words beginning with 'ce-', 'ci-', 'cy-' or 'ps-' if it isn't on the 's' pages.

sable — sap

Ss

sails on sale

ALL 50% OFF

sail vs sale
To 'sail' is to move in a boat powered by wind. A 'sale' happens when things are sold cheaply. Words that sound the same often have very different meanings.

sable	saddling	sake	sampling
sabotage	sadism	salad	sanctimonious
saboteur	sadist	salamander	sanction
sabre	sadistic	salami	sanctioned
sac	sadly	salaries	sanctioning
saccharin/	sadness	salary	sanctities
saccharine	safari	sale	sanctity
sachet	safe	salient	sanctuaries
sack	safeguard	saliva	sanctuary
sacked	safeguarded	salmon	sand
sacking	safeguarding	salon	sandal
sacrament	safekeeping	saloon	sanded
sacred	safely	salsa	sandier
sacrifice	safer	salt	sandiest
sacrificed	safest	saltier	sanding
sacrificial	safety	saltiest	sandpaper
sacrificing	sag	salty	sandwich
sacrilege	saga	salute	sandy
sacrilegious	sage	saluted	sane
sacrosanct	sagged	saluting	saner
sad	sagging	salvage	sanest
sadden	said	salvaged	sang
saddened	sail	salvaging	sanguine
saddening	sailed	salvation	sanitary
sadder	sailing	samba	sanitation
saddest	sailor	same	sanity
saddle	saint	sample	sank
saddled	saintly	sampled	sap

S

sac vs sack
A 'sac' is a fluid-filled bag, such as that surrounding an unborn baby or animal. A 'sack' is a large bag for storing things. To 'get the sack' means 'lose your job'.

A sachet is a small package. The ending '-chet' (say 'shay') is French. Also see 'bouquet', 'ricochet' and 'sorbet'. To 'sashay' means 'to glide elegantly, as if dancing'.

sacrifice; sacrificial
Notice that the second letter 'c' makes a soft, 's' sound in 'sacrifice' and a 'sh' sound in 'sacrificial'.

safari; saga; salami; saliva; salsa; samba
Only words from other languages end in an '-a' or an '-i'. 'Safari' means 'journey' in the African language Swahili; 'saga' is Old Norse for 'story'; 'salami' is an Italian spicy sausage; 'salsa' is Spanish for 'sauce' and 'samba' is a South American dance.

A salary is regular payment for a job. It's from the Latin word 'salarium', the money given to Roman soldiers to buy salt to season their food (which was regarded as very important, as a salary is today).

salmon has a silent 'l', so take care when you spell it.

sapling
sapped
sapphire
sapping
sarcasm
sarcastic
sarcastically
sardine
sardonic
sardonically
sari
sash
sashay
sashes
sat
satchel
satellite
satin
satire
satirical
satisfaction
satisfactorily
satisfactory
satisfied
satisfy
satisfying
satsuma
saturate
saturated
saturating
saturation
sauce
saucepan
saucer
saucier

sauciest
saucy
sauna
saunter
sauntered
sauntering
sausage
savage
savaged
savagely
savagery
save
saved
saving
saviour
savour
savoured
savouring
savoury
saw
sawdust
sawed
sawing
sawn
saxophone
say
saying
scab
scabbed
scabby
scaffolding
scald
scalded
scalding
scale

scaled
scaling
scallop
scalloped
scalp
scalped
scalpel
scalping
scaly
scamper
scampered
scampering
scampi
scan
scandal
scandalous
scanned
scanner
scanning
scant
scanty
scapegoat
scar
scarce
scarcely
scarcer
scarcest
scarcity
scare
scarecrow
scared
scarf
scarfs/scarves
scarier
scariest

scaring
scarlet
scarred
scarring
scary
scathing
scatter
scattered
scattering
scavenge
scavenged
scavenger
scavenging
scenario
scene
scenery
scent
scented
scenting
sceptic
sceptical
sceptically
scepticism
schedule
scheduled
scheme
scholar
scholarly
scholarship
school
schoolboy
schoolchild
schoolchildren
schooled
schoolgirl

saucy sauce

sarcasm means 'wounding someone with words'. It's from the Greek word, 'sarkazein', meaning 'tear someone's flesh'.

sashay means 'glide elegantly, as if you are dancing'. A 'sachet' is a small packet, often of sauce.

sauce is flavoured liquid served with food. 'Saucy' means 'cheeky'. The 'source' is the origin: 'We saw the source of the Nile.'

sausage; savage; scavenge; scrounge
The 'g' in these words makes a soft 'j' sound as it is followed by an '-e'. The letter 'j' and the letters 'dg' make the same sound, so take care.

saw
A 'saw' is a tool used for cutting wood, and the past tense of 'to see'. 'Soar' means 'glide effortlessly' and 'sore' means 'tender' or 'painful'.

saxophone
Adolphe Sax, a Belgian musician, invented the saxophone in the 1800s, and it was named after him.

S

schooling	scourge	screeches	scrupulous
schooner	scourged	screeching	scrupulously
science	scourging	screen	scrutinise/scrutinize
scientific	scouring	screened	scrutinised/
scientifically	scout	screening	scrutinized
scientist	scouted	screenplay	scrutinising/
scintillating	scouting	screw	scrutinizing
scissors	scowl	screwdriver	scuba
scoff	scowled	screwed	scuff
scoffed	scowling	screwing	scuffed
scoffing	scramble	scribble	scuffing
scold	scrambled	scribbled	scuffle
scolded	scrambling	scribbling	scuffled
scolding	scrap	scrimp	scuffling
scone	scrapbook	scrimped	sculleries
scoop	scrape	scrimping	scullery
scooped	scraped	script	sculpt
scooping	scraping	scripted	sculpted
scooter	scrapped	scripting	sculpting
scope	scrapping	scripture	sculptor
scorch	scratch	scroll	sculpture
scorched	scratched	scrounge	sculptured
scorching	scratches	scrounged	scum
score	scratching	scrounger	scummy
scored	scrawl	scrounging	scurried
scorer	scrawled	scrub	scurries
scoring	scrawling	scrubbed	scurrilous
scorn	scrawnier	scrubbing	scurry
scorned	scrawniest	scruff	scurrying
scornful	scrawny	scruffier	scurvy
scornfully	scream	scruffiest	scuttle
scorning	screamed	scruffy	scuttled
scorpion	screaming	scrum	scuttling
scour	screech	scrunchie	scythe
scoured	screeched	scruple	scythed

scale → scaling; scare → scaring, etc.
Notice that 'scale' and 'scare' drop the silent '-e' when the ending '-ing' is added. This is a very common spelling pattern, so learn it if you can.

scene
A 'scene' is a view, or vista: 'The scene was stunning.' 'Seen' is part of the verb 'to see': 'Have you seen her?'

scent
A 'scent' is a perfume, or smell. 'Sent' is part of the verb 'to send': 'I sent the letter.' Make sure you use the right word as they sound exactly the same.

scheme; scholar, etc.
Notice that 'sch' makes a hard, 'sk' sound here.

science; scoff; scythe
The letters 'sc' make a soft 's' sound when followed by an 'i', as in 'science', or a 'y', in 'scythe', but they make a hard 'sk' sound in 'scoff', 'scold' and 'scone'.

scuba is an acronym (made up of the first letters of the words in a phrase). 'Scuba' is an acronym of 'self-contained underwater breathing apparatus'.

scythe (a curved tool for cutting grass, which rhymes with 'lithe') has a silent 'c' after the 's'.

S

sea
seabed
seafarer
seafaring
seafood
seagull
seahorse
seal
sealed
sealing
seam
seaman
seamed
seaming
search
searched
searching
searchlight
seashore
seasick
seasickness
seaside
season
seasonal
seasoning
seat
seated
seating
seaweed
secateurs
secluded
seclusion
second
secondary
seconded

second-hand
seconding
secondly
secrecy
secret
secretaries
secretary
secrete
secretion
secretive
secretively
secretly
sect
section
sectional
sector
secular
secure
secured
securely
securing
securities
security
sedate
sedated
sedating
sedation
sedative
sediment
seduce
seduced
seducing
seduction
seductive
seductively

see
seed
seeded
seeding
seedling
seek
seeking
seem
seemed
seeming
seen
seep
seeped
seeping
seesaw
seethe
seethed
seething
segment
segmented
segregate
segregated
segregating

segregation
seize
seized
seizing
seizure
seldom
select
selected
selecting
selection
selective
selectively
self
self-confidence
self-confident
self-confidently
self-conscious
self-consciously
self-contained
selfish
selfishly
selfishness
selfless

'semi-'

Words beginning with 'semi-' mean 'half', as it is the Latin word for 'half' or 'partly'. You might see it in English words:

- joined to another word with a hyphen, as in semi-final (one of two competitions to see who is in a final); semi-skimmed (milk that has had half the fat removed), or semi-detached (a house attached to another on one side only).

- added to another word to make one word, as in semicircle (which is half a circle).

S

---

sea *vs* see

A 'sea' is a huge expanse of salty water. To 'see' is to use your eyes to look at or notice something or someone. This is the letter 'C'.

seam *vs* seem

A 'seam' is a line of stitches. To 'seem' is to appear to be: 'He may seem grumpy at first.'

secrecy

Here, the letter 'c' is soft, like an 's', as it comes before a 'y' (which makes an 'ee' sound, like a vowel). The letter 'y' behaves like a vowel in many English words.

secret *vs* secrete

A 'secret' is information not to be shared with everyone. To 'secrete' means 'to ooze': 'It secreted oil.'

secretively; seductively; selectively, etc.

These words keep the '-e' when you add '-ly'.

seed

A 'seed' is the part of a flower or tree that grows into a new one. To 'cede' a point or debate is to let someone else win it: 'He will cede the argument.'

seen is part of the verb 'to see': 'She has seen the film'. A 'scene' is a view, or vista.

selflessly
self-service
sell
seller
selling
selves
semaphore
semen
semicircle
semicircular
semicolon
semi-detached
semi-final
semi-finalist
semi-skimmed
semolina
senate
senator
send
sending
senile
senility
senior
seniority
sensation
sensational
sensationally
sense
sensed
sensibilities
sensibility
sensible
sensibly
sensing
sensitive

sensitively
sensor
sensory
sent
sentence
sentenced
sentencing
sentiment
sentimental
sentimentality
sentimentally
sentinel
sentries
sentry
separable
separate
separately
separating
separation
septic
sequel
sequence
sequin
serene
serenely
serenity
sergeant
serial
series
serious
seriously
seriousness
sermon
serpent
servant

semicolons

A 'semicolon' is the name for the punctuation mark (;). It can be used:

1. **To mark a pause in a sentence**, where it is stronger than a comma: 'He rarely ate fish; he preferred steak.'

2. **To separate the parts of a list**: 'We enjoyed the beaches; the mountains; the fresh air; the seafood, and swimming in the sea.'

serve
served
server
service
serviced
serviceman
servicewoman
servicing
serviette
session
set
setback
settee
setting
settle
settled
settlement
settler
settling
set-up
seven
seventeen
seventeenth
seventh
seventies

seventieth
seventy
sever
several
severally
severe
severed
severely
severing
severity
sew
sewage
sewed
sewer
sewing
sewn
sex
sexier
sexiest
sexiness
sexism
sexist
sextet
sexy
shabbier

S

seize breaks the spelling pattern: 'i' before 'e' except after 'c' when the sound made is 'ee'. There's a list of other words that do this on page 4.

sell means 'offer for money'. A 'cell' can be a room in a prison, or the smallest part of a living organism.

seller means 'a person who's selling something'. A 'cellar' is the basement of a house.

sensor

A 'sensor' is an instrument that senses movement, light, or sound. To 'censor' means 'to remove parts of a book, film or letter in case they are secret or rude'.

I'M FOR SALE

will this cell sell?

sent is the past tense of the verb 'to send', but a 'scent' is a perfume, or smell.

sew means 'join with thread', but 'so' is an adverb, with many meanings and uses. To 'sow' means 'plant seeds'.

sextet

A 'sextet' is a group of six musicians. It comes from the Latin word for 'six', 'sex'.

shabbiest	shamed	shave	sheltering
shabbily	shameful	shaved	shelved
shabbiness	shamefully	shaven	shelves
shabby	shameless	shaver	shelving
shack	shamelessly	shaving	shepherd
shade	shaming	shawl	sherbet
shaded	shampoo	she	sheriff
shadier	shampooed	sheaf	sherries
shadiest	shampooing	shear	sherry
shadiness	shamrock	sheared	shield
shading	shandies	shearer	shielded
shadow	shandy	shearing	shielding
shadowed	shanties	sheath	shift
shadowing	shanty	sheathed	shifted
shadowy	shape	sheathing	shifting
shady	shaped	sheaves	shifty
shaft	shapeless	shed	shilling
shaggier	shapelessly	shedding	shimmer
shaggiest	shapely	sheen	shimmered
shagginess	shaping	sheep	shimmering
shaggy	share	sheepdog	shin
shake	shared	sheepish	shine
shaken	sharing	sheepishly	shingle
shaker	shark	sheer	shinier
shakier	sharp	sheerer	shiniest
shakiest	sharpen	sheerest	shining
shaking	sharpened	sheet	ship
shall	sharpener	sheikh	shipment
shallow	sharper	shelf	shipped
shallower	sharpest	shell	shipping
shallowest	sharply	shelled	shipwreck
shallowly	sharpness	shellfish	shipwrecked
sham	shatter	shelling	shipyard
shamble	shattered	shelter	shire
shame	shattering	sheltered	shirk

S

shake vs sheikh
To 'shake' means 'to move up and down vigorously', or 'to shake hands', as in 'Let's shake on it'. It can also be a short version of 'milkshake'. A 'sheikh' is an Arab ruler.

The sheikhs shake over their shakes.

shading; shaking; shaming, etc.
Remember to drop the silent '-e' after a consonant before you add the ending '-ing'. This is a very common pattern.

shampoo comes from the Hindi word 'champna', which means 'to knead' or 'squeeze'. Its spelling doesn't change to make 'shampooed' or 'shampooing'.

shandies; shanties; sherries
Words ending in a consonant and a '-y' change to '-ies' in the plural.

shirked	shortening	showjumper	shrug
shirking	shorter	showjumping	shrugged
shirt	shortest	shown	shrugging
shiver	shorthand	showroom	shrunk
shivered	short-list	showy	shrunken
shivering	short-listed	shrank	shudder
shoal	short-listing	shrapnel	shuddered
shock	shortly	shred	shuddering
shocked	shortness	shredded	shuffle
shocking	short-sighted	shredding	shuffled
shoddier	short-term	shrew	shuffling
shoddiest	shot	shrewd	shun
shoddy	shotgun	shrewder	shunned
shoe	should	shrewdest	shunning
shoestring	shoulder	shrewdly	shunt
shone	shouldered	shrewdness	shunted
shook	shouldering	shriek	shunting
shoot	shout	shrieked	shut
shooting	shouted	shrieking	shutter
shop	shouting	shrill	shuttered
shopkeeper	shove	shriller	shuttering
shoplifter	shoved	shrillest	shuttle
shoplifting	shovel	shrillness	shuttlecock
shopped	shovelled	shrilly	shuttled
shopper	shoving	shrimp	shuttling
shopping	show	shrine	shy
shore	showdown	shrink	shyer
shorn	showed	shrinkage	shyest
short	shower	shrivel	shyly
shortage	showered	shrivelled	shyness
shortbread	showering	shrivelling	sibling
shortcake	showery	shroud	sick
shortcoming	showier	shrouded	sicken
shorten	showiest	shrouding	sickened
shortened	showing	shrub	sickening

S

shear vs sheer

To 'shear' a sheep is to cut its wool off. 'Sheer' is an adjective meaning 'complete', 'absolute' or 'very steep'.

sheaves; shelves

'Sheaves' is the plural of 'sheaf' (as in 'a sheaf of corn'), and 'shelves' of 'shelf'. Most words ending in '-f' just add an '-s' in the plural, but the ones that take '-ves' are listed on page 5.

shipwreck has a silent 'w', so beware.

shoot means 'to fire a gun, or another weapon'. A 'chute' is a tube people or things slide down.

shovelled; shrivelled; shrivelling

Words of more than one syllable that end with a vowel and a single '-l', double that 'l' before you add the endings '-ed' and '-ing'.

shriek follows the spelling pattern: 'i' before 'e' except after 'c' when the letters make an 'ee' sound.

shyly

Most words ending in a '-y' change it to an 'i' when you add an ending that starts with a consonant (e.g. 'nasty → nastiness'). Words with one syllable, such as 'shy', 'sly' and 'wry', usually keep the '-y', however.

sicker
sickest
sickly
side
sideboard
sidecar
sideline
sideshow
sideways
siding
siege
sieve
sieved
sieving
sift
sifted
sifting
sigh
sighed
sighing
sight
sighted
sighting
sightseeing
sightseer
sign
signal
signalled
signalling
signature
signed
significance
significant
significantly
signified

signifies
signify
signifying
signing
signpost
signposted
signposting
silence
silenced
silencing
silent
silently
silhouette
silhouetted
silhouetting
silk
silken
silkier
silkiest
silkworm
silky
sill
sillier
silliest
silly
silt
silted
silver
silvery
similar
similarities
similarity
similarly
simile
simmer

A **simile** is **a way of describing something by comparing it to something else.** It may include the word 'like', but doesn't always do so. Here are three examples:

'She was *as cold as ice*.'
'His hair was *like a flowing mane*.'
'It's *as plain as the nose on your face*.'

simmered
simmering
simple
simpler
simplest
simplicity
simplification
simplified
simplify
simplifying
simplistic
simply
simulate
simulated
simulating
simulation
simultaneous
simultaneously
sin
since
sincere
sincerely
sink
sinned
sinner
sinning

sip
siphon/syphon
siphoned
siphoning
sipped
sipping
sir
siren
sirloin
sister
sisterhood
sister-in-law
sit
site
sitting
situated
situation
six
sixes
sixteen
sixteenth
sixth
sixties
sixty
size
sizeable

---

sight *vs* site
'Sight' is the ability to see. It can also be a famous monument. A 'site' is a particular location, such as a 'building site' or 'campsite'.

sign has a silent 'g', so take care.

silhouette means 'a portrait without colour' or 'a black outline'. Silhouettes were named after the French finance minister Étienne de Silhouette, in the 1700s. The nobility commissioned artists to do silhouettes of them when Silhouette's cost-cutting policies made painted portraits extremely expensive.

silly → sillier → silliest
Notice how the '-y' of 'silly' changes to an 'i' to make the comparative ('I'm sillier than her') and the superlative ('He's the silliest of all'). Also see 'skinny'.

sinned; sipped; skidded; skimmed; skinned, etc.
Remember that words of one syllable, such as 'sin', 'sip', 'skid', 'skim' and 'skin', double their final consonant before you add an ending that begins with a vowel.

sixes
Words ending in an '-x', or sounds such as '-ch' or '-sh', take '-es' in the plural. 'Oxen' is an exception.

sized	skimmed	slanderous	sleep
sizing	skimming	slang	sleepier
sizzle	skin	slant	sleepiest
sizzled	skinned	slanted	sleepily
sizzling	skinnier	slanting	sleepiness
skate	skinniest	slap	sleeping
skateboard	skinning	slapped	sleepover
skated	skinny	slapping	sleepwalk
skater	skipper	slash	sleepwalked
skating	skirmish	slashed	sleepwalking
skeletal	skirt	slashing	sleepy
skeleton	skirted	slat	sleigh
sketch	skirting	slate	slender
sketched	skittle	slated	slenderer
sketchier	skull	slating	slenderest
sketchiest	skunk	slatted	slept
sketching	sky	slaughter	sleuth
sketchy	skylark	slaughtered	slew
skew	skylight	slaughtering	slice
skewed	skyline	slave	sliced
skewer	skyscraper	slaved	slicing
skewered	slab	slavery	slick
skewering	slack	slaving	slicker
ski	slacken	slay	slickest
skid	slackened	sleazier	slid
skidded	slacking	sleaziest	slide
skidding	slackness	sleazy	sliding
skied	slain	sled	slight
skies	slalom	sledge	slighter
skiing	slam	sledged	slightest
skilful	slammed	sledgehammer	slightly
skilfully	slamming	sledging	slim
skill	slander	sleek	slime
skilled	slandered	sleeker	slimier
skim	slandering	sleekest	slimiest

sizeable keeps the silent '-e' before '-able' is added, which can make it easy to misspell.

ski comes from an Old Norse word for 'snowshoes', 'skith'. Only foreign words end in an '-i' in English.

slalom is a race in which competitors swerve from side to side, zig-zagging to avoid markers. It comes from the Norwegian, 'sla lam', meaning 'sloping track', but is spelt differently in English, so take care.

slat → slate; slid → slide; slim → slime
Remember that adding a silent '-e' makes a vowel sound longer, as these words show.

slaughter; sleigh
Watch out for the silent 'gh' before the 't' in 'slaughter'. There's one at the end of 'sleigh', as well.

slay vs sleigh
To 'slay' is an old-fashioned word meaning 'to kill'. A 'sleigh' is a vehicle with two runners underneath it, which dogs or reindeer pull across snow.

sleuth
This word (pronounced 'slooth') is an old-fashioned word for a detective. 'Eu' is a rare letter combination, but you will find it in 'feud', 'neurosis' and 'queue'.

S

slimmer	sloppy	slur	smiling
slimmest	slosh	slurred	smirk
slimy	sloshed	slurring	smirked
sling	sloshing	slush	smirking
slinging	slot	slushy	smith
slink	sloth	sly	smitten
slinked	slotted	slyer	smock
slinking	slotting	slyly	smog
slinky	slouch	slyness	smoke
slip	slouched	smack	smoked
slipped	slouching	smacked	smokeless
slipper	slovenly	smacking	smoker
slippery	slow	small	smokier
slipping	slowcoach	smaller	smokiest
slipstream	slowcoaches	smallest	smoking
slit	slowed	smarmy	smoky
slither	slower	smart	smooth
slithered	slowly	smarten	smoothed
slithering	slowness	smarter	smoothing
slitting	sludge	smartest	smoothly
sliver	slug	smartly	smoothness
slob	sluggish	smartness	smother
slobber	sluggishly	smash	smothered
slog	sluice	smashed	smothering
slogan	sluiced	smashing	smoulder
slogged	sluicing	smattering	smouldered
slogging	slum	smear	smouldering
slop	slumber	smeared	smudge
slope	slumbered	smearing	smudged
slopped	slumbering	smell	smudging
sloppier	slump	smelled/smelt	smug
sloppiest	slumped	smelling	smugger
sloppily	slumping	smelly	smuggest
sloppiness	slung	smile	smuggled
slopping	slunk	smiled	smuggler

sluice
The letters 'ui' are only one of the six different ways of spelling the sound 'u' in English. The others are 'ew' ('chew'); 'o' ('do'); 'oo' ('choose'); 'ou' ('soup') and 'u' ('duty'). It's worth checking your spelling when you hear this sound in a word.

smog is a word that describes pollution in cities, and is a blend of the words 'smoke' and 'fog'. Nobody is quite sure when it was first used, or who invented it.

Is this smoke or fog?

Neither – it's smog.

sneak
The letters 'ea' are pronounced 'ee' in this word, but they can also make a shorter 'e' sound, as they do in 'bread' and 'dread', which can confuse spellers.

snorkel
A 'snorkel' is a pipe providing underwater swimmers with air. It's from the German 'Schnorchel' (the ventilation pipe for World War Two submarines).

snowball; snowdrop; snowflake; snowman, etc.
These compound words, made up of two words joined to form a new one, are all to do with snow.

smuggling	sneered	snout	soared
smugly	sneering	snow	soaring
smugness	sneeze	snowball	sob
smuttier	sneezed	snowballed	sobbed
smuttiest	sneezing	snowballing	sobbing
smutty	snide	snowdrop	sober
snack	sniff	snowed	sobered
snag	sniffed	snowflake	sobering
snagged	sniffing	snowier	soberly
snagging	snigger	snowiest	so-called
snail	sniggered	snowing	soccer
snake	sniggering	snowman	sociability
snaked	snip	snowmen	sociable
snaking	snipped	snowplough	social
snap	snippet	snowshoe	socialise/socialize
snapped	snipping	snowstorm	socialised/socialized
snapping	snob	snowy	socialising/
snapshot	snobbery	snub	socializing
snare	snobbish	snubbed	socialism
snared	snooker	snubbing	socialist
snaring	snoop	snuff	socially
snarl	snooped	snug	societies
snarled	snooping	snuggle	society
snarling	snooze	snuggled	sociological
snatch	snoozed	snuggling	sociologist
snatched	snoozing	snugly	sociology
snatching	snore	so	sock
sneak	snored	soak	socket
sneaked	snoring	soaked	soda
sneaker	snorkel	soaking	sodden
sneakier	snorkelled	soap	sofa
sneakiest	snorkelling	soapier	soft
sneaking	snort	soapiest	soften
sneaky	snorted	soapy	softened
sneer	snorting	soar	softening

snug
Words can change their meaning, and even their spelling, over time. 'Snug', meaning 'cosy', was once used as a verb: 'They snugged down.' Today, we often use 'snuggle' instead. The popular phrase 'snug as a bug in a rug' means 'very cosy indeed'.

so is an adverb, with many uses and meanings, including emphasis ('She danced so well'), and consequence ('I hate onions, so I left them'). To 'sew' means 'to pull thread through fabric with a needle'. To 'sow' means 'to plant seeds'.

soar means 'to glide effortlessly in the sky', but 'sore' means 'inflamed' or 'painful'. The word 'saw' is the past tense of 'to see': 'Josh saw the bus crash.'

sociable; socialism; society; sociology, etc.
These words are all to do with how people interact and live with each other. They are based on the Latin word 'societas', meaning 'fellowship', 'community'. 'Sociology' is the study of different human societies, for example, and a 'sociologist' studies them.

soften can be easily misspelt, as it is pronounced 'soff-un'. Don't forget about the 't' in the middle.

S

softer	solution	soppiest	soured
softest	solve	sopping	souring
softly	solved	soppy	sourly
software	solvency	sorbet	south
soggier	solvent	sorcerer	southward
soggiest	solving	sorceress	southwards
soggy	sombre	sorcery	souvenir
soil	some	sordid	sovereign
soiled	somebody	sore	sow
soiling	somehow	sorely	sowed
solace	someone	soreness	sower
solar	somersault	sorer	sown
sold	somersaulted	sorest	soya
solder	somersaulting	sorrier	spa
soldered	something	sorriest	space
soldering	sometime	sorrow	spacecraft
soldier	sometimes	sorry	spaced
sole	somewhat	sort	spaceman
soled	somewhere	sorted	spacemen
solely	son	sorting	spaceship
solemn	song	so-so	spacing
solemnity	songbird	sought	spacious
solemnly	son-in-law	soul	spaciousness
solicitor	sonnet	soulful	spade
solid	soon	soulfully	spaghetti
solidarity	sooner	sound	span
solidly	soonest	sounded	spangle
soliloquies	soot	sounding	spangled
soliloquy	soothe	soundly	spangling
solitary	soothed	soundtrack	spaniel
solitude	soothing	soup	spank
solo	sooty	sour	spanked
soloist	sophisticated	source	spanking
solstice	sophistication	sourced	spanned
soluble	soppier	sourcing	spanning

---

sold *vs* **soled; sole** *vs* **soul**
The word 'sold' is the past of the verb 'to sell': 'She sold her house.' Shoes are 'soled', as they have a flat bottom called a 'sole'. A 'soul', some people believe, is a person's spirit, which lives on after their death.

soliloquy; solitary; solitude; solo; soloist
These words are all from the Latin for 'alone', 'solus'. A 'soliloquy' is a speech an actor makes alone on stage; 'solitary' means 'one person on their own'; 'solitude' is being alone; a 'solo' means 'one person doing something', and a 'soloist' performs alone.

solving; soothing; sourcing; spacing, etc.
Remember to drop the final '-e' of 'solve', 'soothe', 'source' and 'space' before you add '-ing'.
some means 'not all', but a 'sum' is an amount of money, or a maths calculation.

son
A 'son' is a male child. The 'Sun' is a huge star that emits heat and light.

sophisticated
The 'f' sound can be spelt 'ph', as here, and can also be spelt with 'f' ('frog'), 'ff' ('giraffe'), and 'gh' ('laugh').

spare
spared
sparing
sparingly
spark
sparked
sparking
sparkle
sparkled
sparkler
sparkling
sparred
sparring
sparrow
sparse
sparsely
sparser
sparsest
spartan
spasm
spat
spate
spatial
spatter
spattered
spattering
spawn
spawned
spawning
speak
speaking
spear
speared
spearing
special

specialisation/
specialization
specialist
specialities
speciality
specially
species
specific
specifically
specification
specifies
specify
specifying
specimen
speck
speckled
spectacle
spectacular
spectator
spectral
spectre
spectrum
speculate
speculated
speculating
speculation
sped
speech
speeches
speechless
speed
speedboat
speedier
speediest
speedily

Quick tip — Spellcheckers

The **spellchecker** on a computer is designed **to check spellings and spot mistakes**. It can be useful, but is not infallible. It won't find anything wrong with how the words 'hare' (the animal, or 'to run') and 'hair' (on your head), are used here, for example:

- 'The girl's *hare* was long and blonde.'
- 'The *hair* had long, floppy ears.'
- 'The boys *haired* off in the other direction.'

a girl and her long blonde hare

Always check spellings in a dictionary as well.

speeding
speedometer
speedy
spell
spellchecker
spelled/spelt
speller
spelling
spend
spending
spent
sperm
spew

spewed
spewing
sphere
spherical
sphinx
sphinxes
spice
spiced
spicier
spiciest
spicy
spider
spied

S

---

sorceress has the ending '-ess', which is always female.

sore means 'tender' and 'painful', but a 'saw' is a tool used for cutting wood, and the past tense of 'to see'.

sort *vs* **sought**
To 'sort' is to organize, and a 'sort' is a type: 'That sort of person.' 'Sought' is the past tense of the verb 'to seek'.

source means 'starting point' or 'origin': 'We visited the source of the River Nile.' A 'sauce' is a flavoured liquid served with food, such as 'cheese sauce'.

souvenir is an Old French word for 'a memory or remembrance', so it follows a French spelling pattern.

sow means 'to plant seeds', and 'to sew' is to join with thread. 'So' is an adverb with a variety of meanings, such as emphasis ('It was so big') and consequence ('She lost her job, so she had no money.')

spartan means 'tough' or 'able to do without luxuries'. The word comes from the Greek city state of Sparta, whose people, the Spartans, were famous for their frugality and exceptional toughness.

species is both singular (for one species), and plural (for several species).

sphinx becomes **sphinxes** in the plural.

spies	spoiling	sported	spreadsheet
spike	spoilsport	sporting	spree
spiked	spoke	sportsman	sprig
spikier	spoken	sportsmanship	sprightlier
spikiest	spokesman	sportsmen	sprightliest
spiky	spokesmen	sportswoman	sprightly
spill	spokesperson	sportswomen	spring
spilled/spilt	spokeswoman	spot	springboard
spilling	spokeswomen	spotless	springing
spin	sponge	spotlessly	springtime
spinach	sponged	spotlight	sprinkle
spinal	sponger	spotlighted/spotlit	sprinkled
spindle	spongier	spotlighting	sprinkler
spine	spongiest	spotted	sprinkling
spinier	sponginess	spotter	sprint
spiniest	sponging	spottier	sprinted
spinning	spongy	spottiest	sprinter
spin-off	sponsor	spotting	sprinting
spinster	sponsored	spotty	sprite
spiny	sponsoring	spouse	sprout
spiral	sponsorship	spout	sprouted
spiralled	spontaneity	spouted	sprouting
spiralling	spontaneous	spouting	spruce
spire	spontaneously	sprain	sprung
spirit	spoof	sprained	spun
spirited	spookier	spraining	spur
spiriting	spookiest	sprang	spurious
spiritual	spooky	sprawl	spurn
spiritualism	spool	sprawling	spurned
spiritualist	spoon	spray	spurning
spiritually	spooned	sprayed	spurred
spit	spoonful	spraying	spurring
spitting	spooning	spread	spurt
spoil	spore	spread-eagled	spurted
spoiled/spoilt	sport	spreading	spurting

spies is the plural of 'spy'. Note that words ending in a consonant and '-y' change to '-ies' in the plural.

spilled/spilt; spoiled/spoilt
You will read both versions of these words, and both are correct. As a broad rule, however, British English tends to use 'spelt/spilt/spoilt', and American English, 'spelled/spilled/spoiled'.

sportsmen; sportswomen
To make compound words that end with '-man' and '-woman' plural, you change '-man' and '-woman' to '-men' and '-women'.

squabble; squad; squadron; squalid, etc.
A 'q' is always followed by a 'u' in English words.

squalor is easy to misspell, as it's not spelt like 'glamour' or 'honour', with '-our' at the end.

stabilise/stabilize
Most words can be correctly spelt with an 's' or a 'z'. There's a list of words which can only have one or the other on page 4.

stadia
You'll usually see 'stadiums' as the plural of 'stadium', but you may see 'stadia', the correct Latin spelling.

spy	squealing	stadia	stallion
spying	squeamish	stadium	stamina
squabble	squeeze	staff	stammer
squabbled	squeezed	staffed	stammered
squabbling	squeezing	staffing	stammering
squad	squelch	stag	stamp
squadron	squelched	stage	stamped
squalid	squelching	stagecoach	stampede
squall	squid	staged	stampeded
squalled	squiggle	stagger	stampeding
squalling	squiggled	staggered	stamping
squally	squiggling	staggering	stance
squalor	squint	staging	stand
squander	squinted	stagnant	stand-by
squandered	squinting	staid	stand-in
squandering	squire	stain	standing
square	squirm	stained	standpoint
squared	squirmed	staining	standstill
squarely	squirming	stainless	stank
squaring	squirrel	stair	staple
squash	squirt	staircase	stapled
squashed	squirted	stairway	stapling
squashing	squirting	stake	star
squat	stab	staked	starboard
squatted	stabbed	staking	starch
squatting	stabbing	stale	starched
squawk	stabilise/stabilize	stalemate	starching
squawked	stabilised/stabilized	staler	stare
squawking	stabilising/	stalest	stared
squeak	stabilizing	stalk	starfish
squeaked	stability	stalked	staring
squeaking	stable	stalking	stark
squeaky	stack	stall	starker
squeal	stacked	stalled	starkest
squealed	stacking	stalling	starkly

stake

A 'stake' is a wooden pole, often used for making fences. It can also mean 'a share of a business'. A 'steak' is a piece of lean meat.

There's a stake in my steak!

stair *vs* **stare**

A 'stair' is one of a series of steps leading upwards. To 'stare' is to look at someone for a long time, or rudely.

stampede

A 'stampede' is the word used to describe a large group of animals running out of control. It's from the Spanish word for 'a crash' or 'uproar', 'estampida'.

stank is the past tense of 'to stink'. English verbs don't all follow one pattern to make the past. Some add '-d' or '-ed' (e.g. 'sponged' and 'stacked') but many don't. You just have to learn which verbs do what.

S

starling	status	steering	stewardess
starred	statuses	stem	stewed
starring	statutory	stemmed	stewing
start	staunch	stemming	stick
started	staunchly	stench	sticker
starter	steadied	stencil	stickier
starting	steadier	stencilled	stickiest
startle	steadiest	stencilling	sticking
startled	steadily	step	sticky
startling	steady	stepbrother	sties
starvation	steadying	stepchild	stiff
starve	steak	stepchildren	stiffen
starved	steal	stepfather	stiffened
starving	stealing	stepmother	stiffening
stash	stealth	steppe	stiffer
stashed	stealthily	stepped	stiffest
stashing	stealthy	stepping	stiffly
state	steam	stepsister	stiffness
stated	steamed	stereo	stifle
stately	steam-engine	stereotype	stifled
statement	steamer	stereotypical	stifling
static	steaming	stereotypically	stigma
stating	steamy	sterile	stile
station	steel	sterilisation/	stiletto
stationary	steeled	sterilization	still
stationed	steeling	sterilise/sterilize	stillborn
stationery	steely	sterilised/sterilized	stiller
stationing	steep	sterilising/sterilizing	stillest
statistic	steeped	sterility	stillness
statistical	steeper	sterling	stilt
statistically	steepest	stern	stilted
statistician	steeping	sterner	stimulant
statue	steeple	sternest	stimulate
statuesque	steer	stew	stimulated
stature	steered	steward	stimulating

---

stationary vs stationery

'Stationary' means 'stopped', 'not moving', but 'stationery' means 'writing equipment', such as paper, envelopes and pens. Try thinking 'e' for 'envelopes', to help you remember which word you need.

steak is a piece of lean meat, but a 'stake' is a wooden fence-pole, or a share in a business venture.

steal vs steel

To 'steal' is to take something from its rightful owner. 'Steel' is a metal that never rusts. To 'steel yourself' means 'to prepare yourself to do something difficult'.

step vs steppe

A 'step' is made when you put one foot in front of the other. Before a noun, it means 'by a second marriage': e.g. 'stepmother'. A 'steppe' is an open, treeless plain.

stereotype

This word comes from the French name for a printing block used again and again. A 'stereotype' now means 'someone who conforms to a predictable image or type'.

sties is the plural of 'sty', which is a pig's home. Words ending in a consonant and '-y' become '-ies' in the plural.

S

stimulation	stole	stouter	strangled
stimuli	stolen	stoutest	stranglehold
stimulus	stomach	stove	strangling
sting	stone	stow	strangulation
stinging	stoned	stowaway	strap
stink	stonier	stowed	strapped
stinking	stoniest	straddle	strapping
stint	stony	straddled	strategic
stipulate	stood	straddling	strategically
stipulated	stool	straggle	strategies
stipulating	stoop	straggled	strategist
stipulation	stooped	straggler	strategy
stir	stooping	straggling	straw
stirred	stop	straggly	strawberries
stirring	stoppage	straight	strawberry
stirrup	stopped	straighten	stray
stitch	stopper	straighteners	strayed
stitched	stopping	straighter	straying
stitches	stopwatch	straightest	streak
stitching	storage	straightforward	streaked
stoat	store	straightforwardly	streakier
stock	stored	strain	streakiest
stockbroker	storeroom	strained	streaking
stocked	storey	strainer	streaky
stockier	stories	straining	stream
stockiest	storing	strait	streamed
stocking	stork	straitjacket	streaming
stockpile	storm	strait-laced	streamline
stocky	stormed	strand	streamlined
stodgier	stormier	stranded	streamlining
stodgiest	stormiest	strange	street
stodgy	storming	strangely	strength
stoke	stormy	strangeness	strengthen
stoked	story	stranger	strengthened
stoking	stout	strangle	strengthening

S

stigma

Only words from other languages end in an '-a'. A 'stigma' means 'a shameful thing'. It's the Latin word for the brand the Romans made on their slaves.

A stile is a step for climbing over a fence or wall. 'Style' is fashion, or a trend.

stimulus → stimuli

The plural of 'stimulus' is 'stimuli'. Most Latin words used in English no longer follow Latin plural patterns ('arena' becomes 'arenas' rather than 'arenae', for example), but a few words still do.

storey vs story

A 'storey' is a floor in a building: 'She lived on the third storey.' The plural is 'storeys'. A 'story' is a tale: 'The story was sad', and its plural is 'stories'.

straight vs strait

'Straight' means 'without a bend or curve'. A 'strait' is a strip of seawater between two pieces of land. 'To be in dire straits' is to be in deep trouble.

strangeness

The silent '-e' stays at the end of 'strange' when you add '-ness'. It keeps the 'g' sound in the word soft.

strenuous	stripped	strutting	stunning
strenuously	stripping	stub	stunt
stress	stripy	stubbed	stupendous
stressed	strive	stubbing	stupendously
stresses	striven	stubble	stupid
stressful	strode	stubborn	stupider
stressfully	stroke	stubbornly	stupidest
stretch	stroked	stubbornness	stupidity
stretched	stroking	stuck	sturdier
stretcher	stroll	stuck-up	sturdiest
stretching	strolled	stud	sturdy
strewn	strolling	studded	stutter
stricken	strong	student	stuttered
strict	stronger	studied	stuttering
stricter	strongest	studies	sty
strictest	stronghold	studio	style
strictly	strongly	studious	styled
stride	stroppiness	studiously	styling
strident	stroppy	study	stylish
stridently	strove	stuff	stylishly
striding	struck	stuffed	stylist
strife	structural	stuffier	suave
strike	structurally	stuffiest	subconscious
striker	structure	stuffing	subconsciously
striking	structured	stuffy	subcontinent
strikingly	structuring	stumble	subdivide
string	struggle	stumbled	subdivided
stringed	struggled	stumbling	subdividing
stringent	struggling	stump	subdivision
stringing	strum	stumped	subdue
stringy	strummed	stumping	subdued
strip	strumming	stun	subduing
stripe	strung	stung	subject
striped	strut	stunk	subjected
striping	strutted	stunned	subjecting

S

stressful is an adjective meaning 'full of stress', and has one 'l': 'It was a stressful day.' The ending '-fully' makes an adverb, and has two: 'It began stressfully.'

strict; subject; subtract; succinct
You'll never find a 'k' before a 't' to make the hard 'ct' sound, as these examples show.

strip; stripe; stripy
Notice how adding a silent '-e' at the end of 'stripe' makes the 'i' sound long, not short, as it is in 'strip'. The adjective 'stripy' ('She wore stripy socks') replaces the '-e' with a '-y', but the 'i' still stays long.

strip → stripping; stroll → strolling;
strum → strumming; strut → strutting
Notice that these one-syllable words all double their final consonant before an ending that starts with a vowel is added. You'll see this pattern a lot.

stubbornness; suddenness
Remember to keep the final '-n' of words ending with an '-n', such as these two, when you add '-ness'.

studious; stupendous; subconscious
Lots of words end with '-ous', which sounds like 'us'. They are usually adjectives: 'She was very studious.'

'sub-' is **the Latin word for 'under' or 'below'**, and words that begin with it usually have this meaning. A submarine moves underwater, and a subtitle is under the image on a screen, for instance. 'Sub-' is also used to divide big things into smaller parts, or subdivide them, as in 'subcommittee'.

a submerged submarine

subjective	subservient	subtitled
subjectively	subside	subtleties
sublime	subsided	subtlety
submarine	subsidence	subtly
submariner	subsidiaries	subtract
submerge	subsidiary	subtracted
submerged	subsidies	subtracting
submerging	subsiding	subtraction
submersion	subsidise/subsidize	suburb
submission	subsidised/	suburban
submissive	subsidized	suburbia
submissively	subsidising/	subversion
submit	subsidizing	subversive
submitted	subsidy	subway
submitting	substance	succeed
subordinate	substantial	succeeded
subscribe	substantially	succeeding
subscribed	substitute	success
subscriber	substituted	successful
subscribing	substituting	successfully
subscription	substitution	succession
subsequent	subterfuge	successive
subsequently	subtitle	successor
		succinct
		succinctly
		succulent
		succulently

succumb
succumbed
succumbing
such
suchlike
suck
sucked
sucker
sucking
suckle
suckled
suckling
suction
sudden
suddenly
suddenness
suds
sue
sued
suede
suffer
suffered
suffering
sufficiency
sufficient
sufficiently
suffix

suffix
A 'suffix' is the grammatical name for **an ending that's added to a word to alter its meaning**. These include '-able', '-less', '-ence' and '-ible'. Although the spelling of a suffix never changes, the word it's added to often does. See page 211 for more about suffixes.

S

style
A 'style' is fashion, or a trend. A 'stile' is an old-fashioned word for a step over a fence or wall.

subsidise/subsidize
You can spell many words like this with either an 's' or a 'z', but there's a list of those that can only have one or the other on page 4.

succeed; succinct; succulent; succumb
The letters 'cc' in 'succeed' and 'succint' have a hard 'ck' followed by an 's' sound: 'suck-seed', 'suck-sinct'. In 'succulent' and 'succumb' they make a 'ck' sound.

succumb has a silent '-b' after the 'm', but the end of it sounds like 'strum' (which has no '-b').

such can add emphasis: 'She was such a good singer.' It can pick something out: 'Many cities, such as London, are too busy.' The phrase 'such and such' means 'vague': 'Ask for such and such', and 'suchlike' means 'similar': 'Cake and suchlike delicacies.'

suede comes from a French phrase 'gants de Suède', which means 'gloves from Sweden' (from where suede, a soft, velvety leather, was first imported). Don't confuse it with the past of 'to sway', 'swayed'.

suffixes
suffocate
suffocated
suffocating
suffocation
sugar
suggest
suggested
suggesting
suggestion
suicidal
suicide
suing
suit
suitability
suitable
suitably
suitcase
suite
suited
suiting
suitor
sulk
sulked
sulking
sulky
sultan

sultana
sum
summaries
summarily
summarise/
summarize
summarised/
summarized
summarising/
summarizing
summary
summed
summing
summon
summoned
summoning
summons
sumptuous
sumptuously
sun
sunbathe
sunbathed
sunbathing
sunburn
sunburned/
sunburnt
sundae

sundial
sundries
sundry
sunflower
sung
sunglasses
sunk
sunken
sunlight
sunlit
sunned
sunnier
sunniest
sunning
sunny
sunrise
sunset
sunshine
sunstroke
suntan
suntanned
super
superb
superbly
supercilious
superciliously
superficial
superficially
superfluities
superfluity
superfluous
superhero
superheroes
superhuman
superimpose

superimposed
superimposing
superintendent
superior
superiority
superlative
supermarket
supernatural
supernaturally
superpower
supersede
superseded
superseding
supersonic
superstar
superstition
superstitious
superstitiously
supervise
supervised
supervising
supervision
supervisor
supper
supplant
supplanted
supplanting
supple
supplement
supplementary
suppleness
supplied
supplier
supplies
supply

'super-'
In Latin, this word means 'above' or 'over'. In English, it **can be joined to a word to add the meaning 'better and bigger'**. There are lots of examples of this in words on this page, including: **superhuman**, **supermarket**, **superpower** and **superstar**.

suite means 'a group of things', such as 'a suite of hotel rooms'. The word 'sweet' means 'the opposite of sour', or 'cute', 'kind': 'She was so sweet to help me.'

sum

A 'sum' is a mathematical calculation or a total. 'Some' means 'a few', 'not all of': 'Some children passed, but some failed.'

sun

The 'Sun' is the star giving heat and energy to sustain life on Earth. A 'son' is a male child.

sundae

A 'sundae' is a dessert made of ice cream, cream and fruit. 'Sunday' is a day of the week, and has a capital letter. (See page 202 for a list of all seven days.)

supplementary

The ending '-ary' means 'linked' or 'related to'. Take care not to mix it up with '-ery', as in 'bakery', which is more often found in nouns. Both endings sound identical.

I only eat sundaes on Sundays.

S

support	surgery	survey	swaggering
supported	surgical	surveyed	swallow
supporter	surgically	surveying	swallowed
supporting	surging	surveyor	swallowing
supportive	surlier	survival	swam
suppose	surliest	survive	swamp
supposed	surliness	survived	swampy
supposedly	surly	surviving	swan
supposing	surmise	survivor	swap/swop
supposition	surmised	susceptibility	swapped/swopped
suppress	surmising	susceptible	swapping/swopping
suppressed	surmount	suspect	swarm
suppressing	surmounted	suspected	swarmed
suppression	surmounting	suspecting	swarming
supremacy	surname	suspend	swashbuckling
supreme	surpass	suspended	swat
supremely	surpassed	suspender	swathe
surcharge	surpassing	suspending	swathed
sure	surplus	suspense	swathing
surely	surpluses	suspension	swatted
surer	surprise	suspicion	swatting
surest	surprised	suspicious	sway
surf	surprising	suspiciously	swayed
surface	surreal	sustain	swaying
surfaced	surrealism	sustainability	swear
surfacing	surrender	sustainable	swearing
surfboard	surrendered	sustained	swearword
surfed	surrendering	sustaining	sweat
surfeit	surreptitious	sustenance	sweated
surfer	surreptitiously	swab	sweater
surfing	surrogate	swabbed	sweatier
surge	surround	swabbing	sweatiest
surged	surrounded	swag	sweating
surgeon	surrounding	swagger	sweatshirt
surgeries	surveillance	swaggered	sweaty

S

surfeit sticks to the guideline: 'i' before 'e' except after 'c' when the letters make an 'ee' sound, as the letter 'ei' in this word make an 'i' sound, to rhyme with 'fit'.

surge; surgeon; surgical
The letter 'g' is soft when it's followed by an 'e' or an 'i', as in these words, or a 'y', as it is in 'gym'.

surmount; surpass; surplus, etc.
Words beginning with 'sur-' often mean 'over', 'more than'. It's the Old French word for 'in addition'.

surrogate is from the Latin 'surrogatus', 'in the place of another'. A surrogate is a stand-in, or substitute.

susceptible
Notice that the 'sc' makes a 'ss' sound in 'susceptible', not the 'sk' sound you might expect.

swab → swabbed; swap/swop → swapped/swopped; swat → swatted
Words of one syllable with a short vowel and a consonant, such as these, double the final consonant before you add an ending that starts with a vowel. It's a pattern you'll see a lot.

swayed is the past tense of 'to sway'. Don't confuse it with 'suede', the soft, velvety leather.

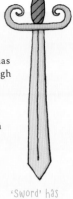

swede
sweep
sweeper
sweeping
sweet
sweetcorn
sweeten
sweetened
sweetener
sweetening
sweeter
sweetest
sweetheart
sweetly
sweetness
swell
swelled
swelling
swelter
sweltered
sweltering
swelteringly
swept
swerve
swerved
swerving
swift
swifter
swiftest
swiftly
swig
swigged
swigging
swill
swilled

swilling
swim
swimmer
swimming
swimmingly
swimsuit
swindle
swindled
swindler
swindling
swine
swing
swinging
swipe
swiped
swiping
swirl
swirled
swirling
swirly
swish
swished
swishing
switch
switchboard
switched
switching
swivel
swivelled
swivelling
swollen
swoon
swooned
swooning
swoop

syllable
A 'syllable' is **a single sound in a word**. The word 'syll-a-ble' itself has three syllables, for instance. A rough guide for working out how many syllables a word has is to see how many times your mouth moves, or your chin goes up and down, when you say it aloud. Try this with:

- **sword** (one syllable)
- **switchboard** (two syllables)
- **swimmingly** (three syllables)
- **sympathetic** (four syllables)

'Sword' has one syllable.

swooped
swooping
swop/swap
swopped/swapped
swopping/swapping
sword
swore
sworn
swum
swung
sycamore
syllabi/syllabuses
syllable
syllabus
symbol
symbolic
symbolically
symbolise/symbolize
symbolised/
symbolized
symbolising/

symbolizing
symbolism
symmetrical
symmetrically
symmetry
sympathetic
sympathetically
sympathies
sympathise/
sympathize
sympathised/
sympathized
sympathising/
sympathizing
sympathy
symphonies
symphony
symptom
symptomatic
synagogue
synchronisation/

The band decided to use a cymbal as their symbol.

swede
A 'swede' is a root vegetable, with a purply skin.
A 'Swede', with a capital letter, is a Swedish person.
sweet can mean either 'the opposite of sour', or 'cute' or 'kind': 'She was so sweet to Dad.' 'Suite' means 'a group of things', such as 'a suite of hotel rooms'.
swindle means 'to cheat' or 'use trickery'. It comes from the German word for 'a cheat', 'Schwindler'.
symbol
A 'symbol' is a sign that stands for something else. A 'cymbal' is a percussion instrument.

S

synchronization	syndicate	syntax	synthesiser/
synchronise/	syndicated	synthesis	synthesizer
synchronize	syndication	synthesise/	synthetic
synchronised/	syndrome	synthesize	synthetically
synchronized	synonym	synthesised/	syrup
synchronising/	synonymous	synthesized	system
synchronizing	synopses	synthesising/	systematic
syncopation	synopsis	synthesizing	systematically

'syn-'

Words that begin with 'syn-' are often to do with the idea of 'together' or 'at the same time'. If things are 'synchronized', they happen at the same time; a 'syndicate' is a group of companies working together. Sometimes, 'syn-' becomes 'sym-', as in 'sympathy'.

synopsis → synopses

Some words ending in '-is' become '-es' in the plural. 'Axis → axes' and 'oasis → oases' are among them. A 'synopsis' is a summary of a series of events, or a plot.

Quick tip

Starting with an 's'?

The sound 's' can be made in more than one way in English. This can make it very tricky to find a word that begins with this sound if you're not sure how the spelling of that word begins. If you can't find the word you need in this, the 's', section of the dictionary, try checking through the pages of words beginning with '**ce**' ('certain'); '**ci**' ('circuit'); '**cy**' ('cycle') and '**ps**' ('psychic'), to see if it's there instead.

synonym

A 'synonym' is **a word that means the same, or very nearly the same, as another word**. For example, the words 'cease', 'end' and 'terminate' are all synonyms of the word 'stop'.

synonymous

If something is said to be 'synonymous with' something else, it means that it's **always linked with that thing**, e.g. 'France is synonymous with fine food and wine.'

syntax

'Syntax' is **the written style of a sentence, or piece of language, and the way the words are arranged and used**. Different writing styles have different kinds of syntax. Some syntax might include compound sentences with lots of different parts to them (called phrases, clauses, and subordinate clauses). Simple syntax is more straightforward, and easier to read and understand.

S

Some tricky words to spell that start with an 's'

Here are some words beginning with 's' that are particularly tricky to spell. See how many of them you can get right. There are some tips to help you on page 7.

sacrifice	separate	sombre	success
satellite	sieve	soothe	sufficient
schedule	silhouette	souvenir	surfeit
science	similar	sovereign	surveillance
scythe	skilful	squalor	susceptible
seize	solemn	stomach	synonym

Tt

Mouse tells a tale
about his tail.

tail *vs* **tale**
A 'tail' is the part of an animal's body that starts at its bottom (and, in the case of some animals, wags to show happiness). A 'tale' is a story: 'A tale about the mountains.'

tab	tactless	talked	tangier
tabbies	tactlessly	talker	tangiest
tabby	tadpole	talking	tangle
table	tag	tall	tangled
tablecloth	tagged	taller	tangling
tablespoon	tagging	tallest	tango
tablespoonful	tail	tallied	tangy
tablet	tailback	tallies	tank
tabloid	tailed	tally	tankard
taboo	tailing	tallying	tanker
taciturn	tailor	talon	tanned
tack	tailored	tambourine	tanning
tacked	tailoring	tame	tantalise/tantalize
tackier	taint	tamed	tantalised/
tackiest	tainted	tameness	tantalized
tacking	take	tamer	tantalising/
tackle	takeaway	tamest	tantalizing
tackled	taken	taming	tantamount
tackling	takeover	tamper	tantrum
tacky	taking	tampered	tap
tact	takings	tampering	tape
tactful	talc/talcum powder	tampon	taped
tactfully	tale	tan	taper
tactic	talent	tandem	tapered
tactical	talented	tang	tapering
tactically	talisman	tangent	tapestries
tactics	talk	tangerine	tapestry
tactile	talkative	tangible	taping

tablecloth; tablespoon; tailback; takeaway
Some compounds (made up of two words) become one new word, like these.

tackling; taking; taming, etc.
Remember to drop the silent '-e' when you add '-ing' (or any ending that starts with a vowel).

tag → tagged; tan → tanned; tax → taxed, etc.
You need to double the final consonant of 'tag' and 'tap' before adding an ending that starts with a vowel. 'Tax' does not double its final consonant, however. You will never see a double 'x' in an English word.

talisman means 'an object people believe has special powers'. It comes from a Greek word, 'telesma', meaning 'holy thing'.

tantalise/tantalize; televise
Most words can be correctly spelt with either an 's' or a 'z'. 'Televise' is one of the few that cannot.

tartar *vs* **tarter**
The yellow coating 'tartar' can form on teeth. A 'tartar' is someone who is bad-tempered and difficult to deal with. 'Tarter' means 'more tart' (sour). Creamy 'tartare' sauce is often served with fish.

tapped
tapping
tar
tarantula
target
targeted
targeting
tariff
tarmac
tarnish
tarnished
tarnishing
tarot
tarpaulin
tarragon
tarred
tarring
tart
tartan
tartar
tarter
tartest
task
tassel
taste
tasted
tasteful
tastefully

tasteless
tastelessly
taster
tastier
tastiest
tasting
tasty
tattered
tatters
tattier
tattiest
tattoo
tattooed
tattooing
tatty
taught
taunt
taunted
taunting
taut
tauter
tautest
tautly
tautness
tavern
tawdrier
tawdriest
tawdry

tawny
tax
taxation
taxed
taxes
taxi
taxing
tea
teabag
teach
teacher
teaching
teak
team
teamed
teamwork
teapot
tear
tearaway
tearful
tearfully
tearing
tease
teased
teasing
teaspoon
teaspoonful
teat
technical
technicalities
technicality
technically
technician
technique
technology

teddies
teddy
tedious
tediously
tedium
tee
teem
teemed
teeming
teen
teenage
teenager
teepee/tepee
teeter
teetered
teetering
teeth
teethe
teething
teetotal
telecommunications
telegram
telegraph
telepathic
telepathy
telephone
telephoned
telephoning
telescope
telescopic
televise
televised
televising
television
tell

'tele-'
Words beginning with 'tele-', such as telegram, telephone, telescope and television, often have something **to do with distance, or something being far away**. 'Tele' is the Greek word for 'far'.

taught *vs* **taut**
'Taught' is the past of 'to teach': 'She taught me to play the piano.' 'Taut' means 'stretched tight'.
tawdry now means 'of poor quality' or 'showy'. This word comes from pieces of lace worn around ladies' necks, and sold each year at a fair in honour of St Audrey, who died in AD679. When fashion changed, this lace became known as 'tawdry lace'.

tea *vs* **tee**
'Tea' is a hot drink, made from the leaves of the tea plant. A 'tee' is the little stand for a golf ball.

team *vs* **teem**
A 'team' is a group of people playing or working together. 'Teem' can mean 'very busy and crowded', or 'to rain very heavily'.

technical; technique; technology, etc.
Notice that the letters 'ch' make a hard, 'ck' sound after the 'e' in these words, not the softer 'ch' sound they make in 'teach' and 'rich'.

tedious
You'll find the '-ous' ending on lots of adjectives. It sounds like 'us', so take care not to miss out the 'o'.

t

tellies
telling
telltale
telly
temerity
temper
temperament
temperamental
temperate
temperature
tempered
tempest
tempestuous
template
temple
temporarily
temporary
tempt
temptation
tempted
tempter
tempting
ten

tenacious
tenaciously
tenacity
tenancies
tenancy
tenant
tend
tended
tendencies
tendency
tender
tenderly
tenderness
tending
tendril
tenement
tennis
tenor
tense
tensed
tensely
tenser
tensest

tensing
tension
tent
tentacle
tentative
tentatively
tenterhooks
tenth
tenthly
tenuous
tenuously
tenure
tepee/teepee
tepid
term
terminal
terminally
terminate
terminated
terminating
termination
terminologies
terminology
terminus
terminuses
termite
terrace
terraced
terracotta
terrain
terrapin
terrestrial
terrible
terribly
terrier

terrific
terrifically
terrified
terrify
terrifying
territorial
territories
territory
terror
terrorise/terrorize
terrorised/
terrorized
terrorising/
terrorizing
terrorism
terrorist
terse
tersely
terser
tersest
tertiary
test
testament
tested
tester
testicle
testified
testify
testimonial
testimonies
testimony
testing
tether
tethered
tethering

---

tense

The 'tense' of a verb **shows when the action it describes takes place** - in the present, past or future. Different verbs follow different patterns, and many just have to be learnt. Here are three tenses of the verb 'to walk':

1. **Present tense:**
The dog *walks* twice a day.
2. **Past tense:**
The dog *walked* quickly.
3. **Future tense:**
The dog *will walk* all day.

---

tenor

A 'tenor' is a mid-range male voice, or a mood or atmosphere. A 'tenner' is a slang word for a ten pound note, so make sure you use the right word.

tense can mean 'stressed': 'I am tense', or, as a verb, 'to clench': 'He tensed his muscles.' It is also the grammatical name for the form a verb takes, e.g. past, present or future (as explained in the box above).

tenth is an ordinal number. These numbers tell you in what order something comes in a list: 'Jenny came tenth in the cake competition.'

terminus

A 'terminus' is the end of a journey or route. It is the Latin word for 'end'. You may see 'termini' as a plural, which follows the Latin grammar pattern, but 'terminuses' is more common.

text can mean 'a block of writing': 'The text was clear.' It can be an electronic message sent from a mobile phone, or a verb, as in 'I'll text you later.'

texture

The ending '-ture' can be found in many words, and it sounds like 'cher'. Take care when you spell it.

text
textbook
texted
textile
texting
textual
textural
texture
textured
than
thank
thanked
thankful
thankfully
thanking
thankless
thanksgiving
that
thatch
thatched
thatching
thaw
thawed
thawing
the
theatre
theatrical
theatrically
theft

their
them
theme
themed
themselves
then
theologian
theological
theology
theoretical
theoretically
theories
theory
therapeutic
therapies
therapy
there
therefore
thermal
thermometer
thermostat
thesaurus
thesauruses
these
theses
thesis
they
thick
thicken

their *vs* there *vs* they're
These three words are often confused, and misspelt, as they sound exactly the same:

- '**Their**' means '**belonging to them**': '*Their* home is big.' (Note the 'e' before the 'i', which breaks the usual spelling pattern).

- '**There**' means '**in that place**': 'The car is *there*.'

- '**They're**' is short for '**they are**': '*They're* coming to visit.'

> They're moving their suitcases over there.

thickened
thickening
thicker
thickest
thicket
thickness
thief
thieves
thieving
thigh
thimble
thin
thing
think
thinking
thinned
thinner
thinnest
thinning
third
thirdly
thirst

thirstily
thirsty
thirteen
thirteenth
thirties
thirtieth
thirty
this
thistle
thong
thorn
thornier
thorniest
thorny
thorough
thoroughbred
thoroughfare
thoroughly
thoroughness
those
though
thought

the
The grammatical name for 'the' is 'the definite article'. It **identifies or singles out a particular example of something in a sentence**, such as 'the king' or 'the singer'.

thankful; thankfully
When '-ful' is added to a word to mean 'full of', it only has one 'l'. If you add '-ly' to a word to make it into an adverb, it has a double 'l': 'thankfully'.

thesaurus
A 'thesaurus' is a book of lists of words with similar meanings, and examples of how to use them. It's from the Greek word for 'treasure', 'thesauros'.

thesis → theses
Several words ending in '-is' change to '-es' in the plural, including 'axis → axes' and 'crisis → crises'.

thief may rhyme with 'leaf', but it's spelt differently. Try thinking '**i**llegal **e**xploits' to help you remember the 'ie'. Note that the plural of 'thief' is 'thieves'. Many words ending in '-f' follow this pattern.

thigh; though
Look out for the silent '-gh' at the end of these words, as they are easy to leave out.

thirteenth; thirtieth
Ordinal numbers can also be used as adjectives, describing a noun: 'The thirteenth day of rain'; 'He succeeded with his thirtieth attempt.'

t

thoughtful	throb	thunderous	tile
thoughtfully	throbbed	thwart	tiled
thoughtfulness	throbbing	thwarted	tiling
thoughtless	throes	thwarting	till
thoughtlessly	throne	thyme	tilled
thoughtlessness	throng	tiara	tiller
thousand	thronged	tic	tilling
thousandth	thronging	tick	tilt
thrash	throttle	ticked	tilted
thrashed	throttled	ticket	tilting
thrashing	throttling	ticketed	timber
thread	through	ticketing	time
threadbare	throughout	ticking	timed
threaded	throw	tickle	timeless
threading	throwing	tickled	timely
threat	thrown	tickling	timer
threaten	thrush	tidal	timescale
threatened	thrushes	tide	timetable
threatening	thrust	tidied	timid
three	thrusted	tidies	timidity
thresh	thrusting	tidings	timidly
threshold	thud	tidy	timing
threw	thudded	tidying	tin
thrift	thudding	tie	tinder
thriftier	thug	tied	tinge
thriftiest	thumb	tier	tinged
thrifty	thumbed	ties	tingle
thrill	thumbing	tiger	tingled
thrilled	thump	tight	tingling
thriller	thumped	tighten	tinier
thrilling	thumping	tightening	tiniest
thrive	thunder	tighter	tinker
thrived	thunderbolt	tightest	tinkered
thriving	thundered	tightrope	tinkering
throat	thundering	tigress	tinkle

t

threw *vs* **through**
'Threw' is the past tense of 'throw'. 'Through' means 'going in one side and out the other'.

throb → throbbed; thud → thudded, etc.
Words with a short vowel and a consonant double that consonant before an ending that starts with a vowel, but 'h', 'j', 'k', 'q', 'v', 'w', 'x', and 'y' are never doubled.

throes; toiletries; tongs
These words are all plural nouns, so you'll never see them in the singular. Don't confuse 'throes' (pains or spasms) with 'throws' (as in 'She throws a ball.').

thumb; thumbed; thumbing
Silent 'b's, as here, often occur after an 'm'. For example: 'comb', 'lamb' and 'limb'.

thyme *vs* **time**
'Thyme' is a leafy herb. 'Time' is divided up into seconds, minutes, hours, days, weeks, months and years.

tic *vs* **tick**
A 'tic' is a nervous gesture, or movement, such as a twitch. A 'tick' is a parasite that lives on animals, and the positive symbol (✓). Make sure you use the right spelling for the word you need.

tinkled	toast	tolling	torches
tinkling	toasted	tomato	tore
tinned	toaster	tomatoes	torment
tinsel	toasting	tomb	tormented
tint	tobacco	tomboy	tormenting
tinted	tobacconist	tomorrow	tormentor
tinting	toboggan	ton	torn
tiny	tobogganing	tone	tornado
tip	today	toned	tornadoes
tipped	toddle	tongs	torpedo
tipping	toddled	tongue	torpedoed
tiptoe	toddler	tonic	torpedoes
tiptoed	toddling	tonight	torpedoing
tiptoeing	toe	toning	torrent
tirade	toenail	tonne	torrential
tire	toffee	too	torrid
tired	together	took	torso
tiredness	togetherness	tool	tortoise
tireless	toil	tooth	tortuous
tiring	toiled	toothache	torture
tissue	toilet	toothbrush	tortured
titanic	toiletries	toothbrushes	torturer
titbit	toiling	toothpaste	torturing
titillate	token	top	toss
titillated	told	topic	tossed
titillating	tolerable	topical	tossing
titillation	tolerance	topmost	tot
title	tolerant	topped	total
titled	tolerantly	topping	totalitarian
titter	tolerate	topple	totalitarianism
tittered	tolerated	toppled	totalled
tittering	tolerating	toppling	totalling
to	toleration	topsy-turvy	totally
toad	toll	top-up	totted
toadstool	tolled	torch	totter

t

tide vs tied
The 'tide' is the movement of the oceans each day. 'Tied' is the past tense of the verb 'to tie': 'He tied his shoelaces.'

tiptoeing
You usually keep the final '-e' when you add '-ing' to words which end with '-oe' (to make 'tiptoeing' and 'hoeing'); '-ee' ('agreeing'; 'seeing'), or '-ye' ('eyeing').

tire
To 'tire' is to become fatigued, or weary. A 'tyre' is a rubber covering for a wheel.

to vs too
The word 'to' is a preposition meaning 'in a certain direction': 'We went to China.' 'Too' means 'as well': 'Dad came too.' 'Two' is the number '2'.

A toe is one of the five digits on your foot. To 'tow' something is to pull it along behind you.

ton vs tonne
A 'tonne' is 1000 kilogrammes. In America, a 'ton' is 2000 pounds (around 907 kilogrammes), and a 'tonne' is called a 'metric ton'.

tornadoes and **torpedoes** end in '-oes' in the plural.

tottered	towing	tragically	transcript
tottering	town	trail	transfer
toucan	toxic	trailed	transferable
touch	toxin	trailer	transferred
touchdown	toy	trailing	transferring
touched	toyed	train	transfix
touchier	toying	trained	transfixed
touchiest	toyshop	trainee	transfixing
touching	trace	trainer	transform
touchy	traceable	training	transformation
tough	traced	trait	transformed
toughen	tracing	traitor	transforming
tougher	track	trajectories	transfusion
toughest	tracked	trajectory	transience
toughness	tracking	tram	transient
tour	tracksuit	tramp	transistor
toured	tract	tramped	transit
touring	traction	tramping	transition
tourism	tractor	trample	transitional
tourist	trade	trampled	transitory
tournament	traded	trampling	translate
tousle	trademark	trampoline	translated
tousled	trader	trance	translating
tousling	tradesman	tranquil	translation
tout	tradesmen	tranquillity	translator
touted	trading	transaction	translucent
touting	tradition	transatlantic	transmission
tow	traditional	transcend	transmit
towards	traditionally	transcended	transmitted
towed	traffic	transcendence	transmitter
towel	trafficked	transcendent	transmitting
towelling	trafficking	transcending	transparencies
tower	tragedies	transcribe	transparency
towered	tragedy	transcribed	transparent
towering	tragic	transcribing	transparently

touchy → touchier → touchiest
Notice how 'touchy' (an informal word for 'irritable', or 'sensitive') changes to 'touchier' in the comparative (meaning 'more touchy') and 'touchiest' in the superlative (meaning 'most touchy'). This is a common pattern.

tough
The letters 'gh' can make an 'f' sound, as here, a hard 'g' sound, as in 'ghost', or can be silent, as in 'tight'.

tow
To 'tow' something is to pull it along behind you. A 'toe' is one of the five digits on your foot.

The slaves had to tow the toe.

transpire	traversing	trembled	tricking
transpired	travesties	trembling	trickle
transpiring	travesty	tremendous	trickled
transplant	trawl	tremendously	trickling
transplanted	trawled	tremor	tricky
transplanting	trawler	trench	tricycle
transport	trawling	trenches	tried
transportation	tray	trend	tries
transported	treacherous	trendier	trifle
transporting	treacherously	trendiest	trifled
transvestite	treachery	trendy	trifling
trap	treacle	trepidation	trigger
trapeze	tread	trespass	triggered
trapped	treading	trespassed	triggering
trapping	treadmill	trespasser	trillion
trash	treason	trespasses	trilogies
trashed	treasure	trespassing	trilogy
trashier	treasured	trial	trim
trashiest	treasurer	triangle	trimmed
trashing	treasuring	triangular	trimming
trashy	treat	triathlon	trinity
trauma	treated	tribal	trinket
traumatic	treaties	tribe	trio
traumatise/	treating	tribesman	trip
traumatize	treatise	tribesmen	triple
traumatised/	treatment	tribulation	tripled
traumatized	treaty	tribunal	triplet
traumatising/	treble	tributaries	tripling
traumatizing	trebled	tributary	tripod
travel	trebling	tribute	tripped
travelled	tree	trick	tripper
traveller	trek	tricked	tripping
travelling	trekked	trickery	trite
traverse	trekking	trickier	triumph
traversed	tremble	trickiest	triumphal

t

triumphant
trivia
trivial
trivialise/trivialize
trivialised/trivialized
trivializing/
trivializing
trivialities
triviality
trod
trodden
troll
trolley
trombone
troop
trooped
trooper
trooping
trophies
trophy
tropic
tropical
trot
trotted
trotter
trotting
trouble
troubled
troublesome
troubling
trough
trounce
trounced
trouncing
troupe

trousers
trout
trowel
truancy
truant
truce
truck
truculence
truculent
trudge
trudged
trudging
true
truer
truest
truffle
truly
trump
trumped
trumpet
trumpeted
trumpeter
trumpeting
truncate
truncated
truncating
trundle
trundled
trundling
trunk
truss
trussed
trussing
trust
trusted

trustee
trustier
trustiest
trusting
trustworthiness
trustworthy
trusty
truth
truthful
truthfully
try
trying
tryst
t-shirt
tsunami
tub
tuba
tubbier
tubbiest
tubby
tube
tuber
tubing
tubular
tuck
tucked
tucking
tuft
tufted
tug
tugged
tugging
tuition
tulip
tumble

tumbled
tumbler
tumbling
tummies
tummy
tumour
tumult
tumultuous
tumultuously
tuna
tundra
tune
tuned
tuneful
tuneless
tunelessly
tunic
tuning
tunnel
tunnelled
tunnelling
turban
turbulence
turbulent
turbulently
turf
turkey
turmoil
turn
turned
turning
turnip
turnout
turnover
turnstile

troop *vs* **troupe**
To 'troop' means 'to go in a line': 'We trooped into class.' 'Troops' is a plural noun, meaning 'soldiers'. A 'troupe' is a group of entertainers or actors.

troubling; trouncing; trudging; truncating, etc.
If a word ends in a consonant and a silent '-e', you usually drop the '-e' when you add '-ing', as in these words.

This tuber plays the tuba.

truculence; truculent
'Truculent' means 'sulky'. Words ending with '-ent' are usually adjectives, and words ending with '-ence' are usually nouns.

trustworthy → trustworthiness
Notice how the '-y' changes to an 'i' before '-ness' is added. This happens in a lot of words.

tuba *vs* **tuber**
A 'tuba' is a brass musical instrument. A 'tuber' is the bulbous root of a plant such as a potato. Try not to get them mixed up.

turpentine	tweeted	twirl	tying
turquoise	tweeting	twirled	type
turret	tweezers	twirling	typecast
turtle	twelfth	twist	typed
tusk	twelve	twisted	typewriter
tussle	twentieth	twisting	typewritten
tutor	twenty	twitch	typhoid
tutored	twice	twitched	typhoon
tutorial	twiddle	twitching	typical
tutoring	twiddled	twitter	typically
tutu	twiddling	twittered	typifies
twang	twig	twittering	typify
twanged	twilight	two	typifying
twanging	twin	two-faced	typing
tweak	twine	twofold	typist
tweaked	twinge	twosome	tyrannical
tweaking	twinkle	two-time	tyrannosaurus
twee	twinkled	two-timed	tyranny
tweed	twinkling	two-timing	tyrant
tweet	twinned	tycoon	tyre

tunnelled; tunnelling
Words of more than one syllable that end in a vowel and a single '-l', double the 'l' before the ending '-ed' or '-ing' is added, wherever the stress of the word falls when you say it.

turquoise
The letter 'q' is always followed by a 'u'.

tweet
The sound small birds make is a called a 'tweet'. Messages put on the social network Twitter are also 'Tweets', and to post them is called 'tweeting'.

two means the number '2'. 'To' is a preposition showing direction: 'We went to Paris.' 'Too' means 'as well': 'He ate an apple, and I ate one too.'

typify → typifying
Notice that you keep the '-y' before you add '-ing'. This avoids having two 'i's in the middle of the word. All words ending in '-y' follow this pattern, e.g. 'study → studying'; 'verify → verifying'.

tyre
A 'tyre' is the rubber covering over the wheel of a car, bike or truck. To 'tire' means 'to become tired'.

t

Some tricky words to spell that start with a 't'

Here are some words that are tricky to spell that begin with 't':

tactic	their	through
tarpaulin	therapeutic	torrential
technical	thorough	tough
televise	thought	tranquillity
temperature	threw	tyranny

Uu

Her new dress was unbelievably uncomfortable.

'un-' at the beginning of a word **usually gives it a negative meaning**, e.g. unaffected means 'not affected'. A few words, however, such as 'unsung' (which means 'unrewarded') and 'untoward' (not expected), have a brand new meaning when 'un-' is added.

ubiquitous	unaided	uncertain	undemanding
udder	unambiguous	uncertainty	undeniable
uglier	unambiguously	unchallenged	undeniably
ugliest	unanimity	uncharacteristic	under
ugly	unanimous	uncharacteristically	underage
ulterior	unanimously	uncivilised/	underarm
ultimate	unannounced	uncivilized	undercarriage
ultimately	unappealing	uncle	underclass
ultimatum	unarmed	unclear	underclothes
ultrasonic	unashamed	unclean	undercover
ultrasound	unashamedly	uncomfortable	undercurrent
ultraviolet	unassuming	uncomfortably	undercut
umbrella	unattached	uncommon	undercutting
umpire	unattended	uncommonly	underdog
umpired	unauthorised/	unconditional	underdone
umpiring	unauthorized	unconditionally	underestimate
umpteen	unavoidable	unconscious	underestimated
unabashed	unavoidably	unconsciously	underestimating
unabated	unaware	unconsciousness	underfoot
unable	unawares	uncontrollable	undergo
unacceptable	unbalanced	uncontrollably	undergoes
unacceptably	unbearable	unconventional	undergoing
unaccompanied	unbearably	uncouth	undergone
unaccomplished	unbeatable	uncover	undergraduate
unaccountable	unbelievable	uncovered	underground
unaccountably	unbelievably	uncovering	undergrowth
unaccustomed	unborn	undaunted	underhand
unaffected	unbroken	undecided	underhanded

u

---

ubiquitous means 'everywhere', or 'always present': 'Mobile phones are ubiquitous these days.' It comes from the Latin word for 'everywhere', 'ubique'.

'ultra-'
At the beginning of words, 'ultra-' means 'exceptional' or 'extremely', e.g. 'ultra-fashionable'; 'ultra-popular'. It can also be added to scientific terms, as in 'ultrasound' (sound so high it's beyond human hearing) and 'ultraviolet' (light that can tan your skin, but cannot be seen by the human eye).

umbrella is from the Latin word for 'shade', 'umbra'.

unanimous
If a decision is 'unanimous', everybody who has a part in making that decision agrees. The word comes from the Latin 'unanimus', which means 'of one mind'.

unaware; unawares
The word 'unaware' is an adjective, often followed by 'of' or 'that': 'I was unaware of the problem.' 'Unawares' is an adverb: 'It caught me unawares.'

unbelievable; undesirable
You almost always drop the silent '-e' when you add '-able' to a word.

underlie
underline
underlined
underlining
underlying
undermine
undermined
undermining
underneath
underpants
underpass
underpasses
underpin
underpinned
underpinning
underprivileged
underrate
underrated
underrating
understand
understandable
understandably
understanding
understated
understatement
understood
understudies
understudy
undertake
undertaken
undertaking
undertone
undertook
undervalue
undervalued

undervaluing
underwater
underwear
underwent
undesirability
undesirable
undid
undivided
undo
undoes
undoing
undone
undoubted
undoubtedly
undress
undressed
undressing
undue
undulating
undulation
unduly
undying
unearthliness
unearthly
unease
uneasily
uneasiness
uneasy
unemployable
unemployed
unemployment
unending
unenviable
unenviably
unequal

unequally
uneven
unevenly
unevenness
uneventful
uneventfully
unexceptional
unexpected
unexpectedly
unfailing
unfailingly
unfair
unfairly
unfaithful
unfaithfully
unfamiliar
unfamiliarity
unfashionable
unfashionably
unfasten
unfastened
unfastening
unfavourable
unfavourably
unfeeling
unfit
unfold
unfolded
unfolding
unforeseen
unforgettable
unforgettably
unforgivable
unforgivably
unforgiving

unfortunate
unfortunately
unfounded
unfriendly
ungainly
ungrateful
ungratefully
unhappier
unhappiest
unhappiness
unhappy
unhealthily
unhealthy
unhinged
unhurried
unicorn
unicycle
unidentifiable
unidentifiably
unidentified
unification
unified
uniform
uniformity
unify
unifying
unilateral
unilaterally
uninhabitable
uninhabited
uninspired
uninspiring
unintentional
unintentionally
uninterested

u

uncontrollable
If you add an ending that starts with a vowel to a word ending in a vowel and an '-l', such as 'control', you double the final '-l'.

'under-'
'Under-' can be added to the beginning of a word, to mean 'beneath', or 'not quite adequate'. It may be followed by a hyphen (-), as in 'under-performing', or not, as in 'undercover'.

A unicorn
in uniform
on a
unicycle.

**underestimate → underestimating;
underline → underlining, etc.**
Drop the silent '-e' when you add '-ing'. This is a very common spelling rule, so learn it if you can.

'uni-'
Words beginning with 'uni-' are often to do with singleness. A 'unicorn' has a single horn, a 'unicycle' has one wheel and a 'uniform' is an outfit everyone in a certain group wears.

uninteresting	unlikely	unpaid	unruliness
union	unlimited	unpalatable	unruly
unique	unlit	unparalleled	unsatisfactorily
uniquely	unload	unpick	unsatisfactory
uniqueness	unloaded	unpleasant	unsaturated
unisex	unloading	unpleasantly	unsavoury
unison	unlock	unpleasantness	unscathed
unit	unlocked	unplug	unscientific
unite	unlocking	unplugged	unscrew
united	unloved	unplugging	unscrewed
uniting	unluckily	unpopular	unscrewing
unity	unlucky	unpopularity	unscrupulous
universal	unmarked	unprecedented	unscrupulously
universally	unmarried	unpredictable	unseemly
universe	unmistakable/	unpredictably	unseen
universities	unmistakeable	unprepared	unsettle
university	unmistakably	unprofessional	unsettled
unjust	unmitigated	unqualified	unsettling
unjustifiable	unmoved	unquestionable	unshakable/
unjustifiably	unnatural	unquestionably	unshakeable
unjustified	unnaturally	unravel	unsightly
unjustly	unnecessarily	unravelled	unskilled
unkempt	unnecessary	unravelling	unsolicited
unkind	unnerve	unreal	unsolved
unkindly	unnerved	unrealistic	unsound
unkindness	unnerving	unreasonable	unspeakable
unknown	unobtrusive	unreasonably	unspecified
unlawful	unobtrusively	unrelated	unspoilt
unlawfully	unoccupied	unreliable	unspoken
unleaded	unofficial	unreliably	unstable
unleash	unofficially	unrest	unsteadily
unleashed	unorthodox	unripe	unsteadiness
unleashing	unpack	unroll	unsteady
unless	unpacked	unrolled	unstuck
unlike	unpacking	unrolling	unsuccessful

u

unnatural; unnecessary; unnerve, etc.
Adding 'un-' to the front of these words
doesn't mean you drop their first 'n'.

unplugged; unravelled
If a word ends in a single vowel and a consonant,
you double the final consonant before adding '-ed'
or '-ing' if the stress falls at the end of the word
(as it does in 'unplug'). If the word ends with an '-l',
you double it wherever the stress falls: 'unravelled'.

unqualified; unquestionable
Remember that a 'q' is always followed by a 'u'.

unveil
The letters 'ei' are just one way of spelling the long
sound 'a'. The others are 'ai' ('unpaid'); 'ay' ('crayon');
'ea' ('steak'), 'ey' ('grey') and 'a' ('urbane').

unwrap → unwrapped
Words ending in a single '-p' always double it before
you add an ending that begins with a vowel, whatever
part of the word you emphasize when you say it.

up-and-coming; upbringing; up-to-date, etc.
Some compound words are joined with a hyphen (-).
Others, such as 'upbringing', are joined into one word.

unsuccessfully	unwelcome	up-market	urgently
unsuitable	unwell	upon	urging
unsuited	unwieldy	upper	urinate
unsung	unwilling	uppermost	urine
unsure	unwillingly	upright	urn
unsuspecting	unwind	uprising	us
untangle	unwinding	uproar	usable/useable
untangled	unwise	uproot	usage
untangling	unwitting	upset	use
unthinkable	unwittingly	upsetting	used
unthinkably	unworthy	upshot	useful
untidily	unwound	upstage	usefully
untidiness	unwrap	upstaged	useless
untidy	unwrapped	upstairs	uselessly
untie	unwrapping	upstream	user
untied	unwritten	upsurge	usher
until	up	uptake	using
untimely	up-and-coming	uptight	usual
untold	upbringing	up-to-date	usually
untouched	update	upturn	usurp
untoward	updated	upturned	usurped
untrained	updating	upward	usurping
untroubled	upgrade	upwardly	utensil
untrue	upgraded	upwards	utilities
untruthful	upgrading	urban	utility
untruthfully	upheaval	urbane	utmost
untying	upheld	urchin	utter
unused	uphill	urge	utterance
unusual	uphold	urged	uttered
unusually	upholding	urgency	uttering
unveil	upholstery	urgent	utterly
unveiled	upkeep		
unveiling	upland		
unwanted	uplifted		
unwarranted	uplifting		

urban; urbane
Adding a silent '-e' to a word changes its sound and meaning. 'Urban', meaning 'to do with towns and cities', rhymes with 'turban'. 'Urbane', with a long 'a', rhymes with 'mane', and means 'sophisticated'.

urn
An 'urn' is a container or pot. To 'earn' is to make money by doing a job.

use means 'to employ to do something': 'I used my key to open the door.' 'Ewes' is the plural of 'ewe', a female sheep.

Some tricky words starting with a 'u'

These 'u' words can be hard to spell:

unconscious	unusual
unenviable	unveil
unfortunate	unwieldy
unique	usual
unnatural	usurp

u

Vv

This vampire is vaulting.

verb
A 'verb' **describes an action, and is an active, 'doing' word**. Verbs can refer to something in the past, present or future, and may change their spelling in each case. Many verbs follow a set pattern, but lots don't.

vacancies	valet	vanity	veer
vacancy	valiant	vanquish	veered
vacant	valiantly	vanquished	veering
vacate	valid	vanquishing	vegan
vacated	validate	vapour	vegetable
vacating	validated	variability	vegetarian
vacation	validating	variable	vegetarianism
vaccinate	validity	variance	vegetation
vaccinated	valley	variant	vehemence
vaccinating	valour	variation	vehement
vaccination	valuable	varied	vehemently
vaccine	valuation	varieties	vehicle
vacuum	value	variety	vehicular
vacuumed	valued	various	veil
vacuuming	valuing	variously	vein
vagina	valve	varnish	velocity
vagrant	vampire	varnished	velvet
vague	van	varnishing	velvety
vaguely	vandal	vary	vender/vendor
vagueness	vandalise/vandalize	varying	vendetta
vaguer	vandalised/	vast	vending
vaguest	vandalized	vastly	veneer
vain	vandalism	vastness	venerable
vainer	vane	vat	venerate
vainest	vanilla	vault	venerated
vainly	vanish	vaulted	venerating
vale	vanished	vaulting	veneration
valentine	vanishing	veal	vengeance

V

vaccine
This word is based on the Latin for 'cow', 'vacca'. The first vaccine was created by giving people cowpox, which protected them from the much more deadly human version of the illness, smallpox.

vacuum is one of very few English words that contains a double 'u'.

vague
You don't pronounce the '-ue' at the end of 'vague'. The words 'catalogue', 'dialogue' and 'harangue' also follow this unusual spelling pattern.

vain *vs* **vane** *vs* **vein**
The word 'vain' means 'arrogant', but to do something 'in vain' means to do it pointlessly: 'He died in vain.' A 'vane' is a flat blade, which spins and shows which way the wind is blowing on a metal weather vane. A 'vein' is a thin tube in the body that carries blood around.

vale *vs* **veil**
A 'vale' is another word for a dip or valley. A 'veil' is a covering for a woman's face, head and/or hair.

validating; valuing; venerating, etc.
Most words drop the '-e' when you adding '-ing'.

Remember that the letter 'v' is always followed by a vowel or a 'y' in all English words.

venison — virtually

venison	versatility	vibrating	villager
venom	verse	vibration	villain
venomous	versed	vicar	villainous
vent	version	vicarage	villainy
vented	versus	vice	vindicate
ventilate	vertical	vicinity	vindicated
ventilated	vertically	vicious	vindicating
ventilating	verve	viciously	vindication
ventilation	very	viciousness	vindictive
ventilator	vessel	victim	vindictively
venting	vest	victor	vindictiveness
ventriloquist	vestige	victories	vine
venture	vestries	victorious	vinegar
ventured	vestry	victory	vinegary
venturing	vet	video	vineyard
venue	veteran	videoed	vintage
veranda/verandah	veterinary	videoing	vinyl
verb	veto	vie	viola
verbal	vetoed	vied	violate
verbally	vetoes	view	violated
verdict	vetoing	viewed	violating
verge	vetted	viewer	violence
verged	vetting	viewing	violent
verging	vex	viewpoint	violently
verifiable	vexed	vigil	violet
verifiably	vexing	vigilant	violin
verification	via	vigilante	violinist
verified	viability	vigorous	viper
verify	viable	vigorously	viral
verifying	viaduct	vigour	virgin
veritable	vibrancy	vile	virginity
veritably	vibrant	viler	virile
vermin	vibrantly	vilest	virility
vernacular	vibrate	villa	virtual
versatile	vibrated	village	virtually

vandal; vandalism
Tribesmen called Vandals attacked Rome in AD455. People who commit 'vandalism' (meaning 'wilful destruction of property') are still called 'vandals' today.
vanquish; ventriloquist
Remember that a 'q' is always followed by a 'u'.
variety → varieties; vestry → vestries
Words ending in a consonant and '-y', such as these two, become '-ies' in the plural.
vengeance keeps the silent '-e' after the 'g' when you add '-ance'. This keeps the 'g' sound soft.

versus means 'against': 'Liverpool versus Arsenal.' It's often shortened to 'vs'. Don't confuse it with 'verses', the plural of 'verse': 'The song has three verses.'
vice
The word 'vice' means a 'sin' or 'something morally wrong'. When joined to a word with a hyphen (-), 'vice-' means 'deputy': 'vice-president'.
violate vs violet
The word 'violate' means 'to rape' or 'attack'. It sounds a lot like 'violet', which is a purple colour or a wildflower. Take care to choose the right word.

V

191

virtue
virtuoso
virtuous
virtuously
virus
viruses
visa
visibility
visible
visibly
vision
visionaries
visionary
visit
visited
visiting
visitor
visor/vizor
visual
visualise/visualize
visualised/visualized
visualising/
visualizing
visually
vital
vitality
vitally
vitamin
vitriolic

vivacious
vivacity
vivid
vividly
vividness
vixen
vocabularies
vocabulary
vocal
vocalist
vocation
vocational
vociferous
vociferously
vodka
vogue
voice
voiced
voicemail
voicing
void
volatile
volatility
volcanic
volcano
volcanoes
vole
volition
volley

vowels

The five vowels in English are: **a, e, i, o, u.**
The other letters in the alphabet are
consonants. Some letters, such as 'v', are
always followed by a vowel or a 'y', and
'q' is always followed by 'u'. Vowels often
combine to make a different sound, such as:

- 'ai' in 'air'   - 'ea' in 'steak'
- 'ie' in 'field'   - 'ou' in 'vouch'

volleyball
volume
voluminous
voluntarily
voluntary
volunteer
volunteered
volunteering
voluptuous
voluptuousness
vomit
vomited
vomiting
voodoo
voracious
vote
voted
voter
voting

vouch
vouched
voucher
vouching
vow
vowed
vowel
vowing
voyage
voyager
vulgar
vulgarity
vulgarly
vulnerabilities
vulnerability
vulnerable
vulture
vuvuzela
vying

Quick tip Vowel or consonant?
**'Y' is a consonant, but often
behaves like a vowel.** For instance,
it makes a long 'ee' sound in 'velvety'; a short 'i'
sound in 'vinyl' and a long 'i' sound in 'vying'.

V

viruses
Remember that words ending with an '-s', '-x', '-ch'
or other hissing sounds take '-es' in the plural.
vocabulary; vocal; vocalist; vociferous, etc.
These words are to do with speaking, words and the
voice. They come from the Latin for 'voice', 'vox'.
volcano → volcanoes
Notice how 'volcano' changes to '-oes' in the plural.
There's a list of words that do this on page 5.
vomit does not double its '-t' when you add '-ed' or
'-ing', because you emphasize 'vom', the first syllable.

Some tricky words starting with a 'v'

Here are some tricky words that
start with the letter 'v':

vacuum
vegetable
vehicle
veil
vein

veterinary
vociferous
volcanoes
voluminous
volunteer

walkabout
Words often change their meaning over time. Today, 'walkabout' is mostly used to describe a famous person meeting and greeting fans. Originally, it was an Australian Aboriginal word for a long, exploratory walk into the bush.

wad	wail	wallaby	waning
wadding	wailed	walled	want
waddle	wailing	wallet	wanted
waddled	waist	wallop	wanting
waddling	waistcoat	walloped	war
wade	wait	walloping	warble
waded	waited	wallow	warbled
wader	waiter	wallowed	warbling
wading	waiting	wallowing	ward
wafer	waitress	wallpaper	warden
waffle	waitresses	walnut	warder
waffled	waive	walrus	wardrobe
waffling	waived	walruses	warehouse
waft	waiver	waltz	wares
wafted	waiving	waltzed	warfare
wafting	wake	waltzes	warhead
wag	wakeful	waltzing	warier
wage	waken	wan	wariest
waged	wakened	wand	warlock
wager	wakening	wander	warm
wagged	walk	wandered	warm-blooded
wagging	walkabout	wanderer	warmed
waggle	walked	wandering	warmer
waggled	walker	wane	warmest
waggling	walking	waned	warmly
waggon/wagon	walkway	wangle	warmth
waging	wall	wangled	warn
waif	wallabies	wangling	warned

wading; waggling; waging; waiving, etc.
Most words ending in a consonant and a silent '-e' drop the '-e' when you add '-ing'. This is a very common pattern, so try to learn it if you can.

wail
A 'wail' is a high-pitched cry of pain or distress. A 'whale' is a large sea mammal.

wait
To 'wait' is to pass time until something happens: 'We are waiting for Tom.' 'Weight' is how heavy something is: 'Her weight remained stable.'

waive
To 'waive' is to sacrfice: 'She waived her fee.' To 'wave' is to greet by moving your hand. A 'wave' is one of a series of water movements in the sea.

wander
To 'wander' is to walk around without a particular purpose. To 'wonder' is to want to know about something: 'I wonder who will pass the exam?'

war is an armed conflict, fought between opposing forces: 'The war was lost.' 'Wore' is the past of 'to wear': 'He always wore a pink waistcoat.'

W

warning
warp
warped
warping
warrant
warranted
warranties
warranting
warranty
warren
warring
warrior
warship
wart
wartime
wary
was
wash
washable
washbasin
washed
washer
washing
washing-up
wasp
wastage
waste
wasted
wasteful
wastefully
wasteland
wasting
watch
watchdog
watched

watches
watchful
watching
watchman
watchmen
water
watercolour
watercress
watered
waterfall
waterfront
watering
waterlogged
watermelon
waterproof
waterproofed
waterproofing
watershed
water-skiing
watertight
waterway
waterworks
watery
wattle
wave
waved
wavelength
waver
wavered
wavering
wavier
waviest
waving
wavy
wax

waxed
waxes
waxier
waxiest
waxy
way
wayside
wayward
we
weak
weaken
weakened
weakening
weaker
weakest
weakling
weakly
weakness
weaknesses
wealth
wealthier
wealthiest
wealthy
wean
weaned
weaning
weapon
weaponry
wear
wearier
weariest
wearily
weariness
wearing
weary

wearying
weasel
weather
weathered
weathering
weatherman
weathermen
weave
weaver
weaving
web
webbed
wed
wedding
wedge
wedged
wedging
weed
weeded
weeding
week
weekday
weekend
weekly
weep
weeping
weepy
weevil
weigh
weighed
weighing
weight
weighted
weighting
weightless

wave
To 'wave' is to greet by moving your hand. A 'wave' is one of a series of water movements in the sea. To 'waive' is to sacrfice: 'She waived her fee.'

way vs weigh
A 'way' is a route: 'the way forward'. To 'weigh' something is to see how heavy it is.

weak vs week
The word 'weak' means 'not very strong': 'She was a weak swimmer.' A 'week' is a period of seven days.

weakly vs weekly
'Weakly' means 'not strongly', but 'weekly' means 'every week' or 'once a week': 'Tom has a weekly swim.'

wear vs where
To 'wear' means 'to be dressed in': 'I always wear trousers.' 'Where' can be used in several ways, but is always to do with place, or position: 'Where are you?'

weather vs whether
'Weather' is how much sunshine, rain etc. there is. 'Whether' is a conjunction (linking word), often used between options: 'Whether to go, or stay.'

whereas; whereby; whereupon
These words all sound a little formal, but you may see them used to join parts of a sentence, or link ideas or choices. For example:

- She was nice, *whereas* he was nasty.

- The method *whereby* he won was suspect.

The school play ended, whereupon all the parents clapped.

weightlessness	welling	whaling	whether
weightlifter	wellingtons	wharfs/wharves	whetted
weightlifting	well-meaning	what	whetting
weighty	well-off	whatever	whey
weir	well-to-do	whatsoever	which
weird	well-worn	wheat	whichever
weirder	welt	wheel	whiff
weirdest	went	wheelbarrow	whiffy
weirdly	wept	wheelchair	while
welcome	were	wheeled	whilst
welcomed	werewolf	wheeling	whim
welcoming	werewolves	wheeze	whimper
weld	west	wheezed	whimpered
welded	westerly	wheezing	whimpering
welder	western	wheezy	whimsical
welding	westward	when	whimsically
welfare	westwards	whenever	whimsy
well	wet	where	whine
well-balanced	wetness	whereabouts	whined
wellbeing	wetted	whereafter	whinge
well-bred	wetter	whereas	whinged
well-done	wettest	whereby	whinging
well-earned	whack	whereupon	whining
welled	whacked	wherever	whinnied
well-heeled	whacking	wherewithal	whinnies
well-informed	whale	whet	whinny

weight means 'how heavy something is', but to 'wait' is to pass the time until something happens. Take care with 'waiting' and 'weighting', as well.

weir
A 'weir', pronounced 'wee-uh', is a low barrier built in a river to control its flow. Don't mix it up with 'we're', which is a shortened version of 'we are': 'We're free.'

weir; weird
These words are very often misspelt, as they break the spelling pattern: 'i' before 'e' except after 'c' when the letters make an 'ee' sound.

wellingtons
'Wellingtons' (shortened to 'wellies') are rubber boots named after the long leather boots worn by the 19th-century British soldier, the Duke of Wellington.

whale
A 'whale' is a large mammal that lives in the sea. A 'wail' is a high-pitched cry of pain or distress.

which
The word 'which' is an interrogative or relative pronoun (see page 214). A 'witch' is a woman who is believed to practise magic.

W

whinnying	whole	wield	wimp
whip	wholegrain	wielded	win
whiplash	wholehearted	wielding	wince
whipped	wholeheartedly	wife	winced
whipping	wholemeal	wig	winch
whir/whirr	wholeness	wiggle	winched
whirl	wholesale	wiggled	winches
whirled	wholesaler	wiggling	winching
whirling	wholesome	wigwam	wincing
whirlpool	wholly	wild	wind
whirlwind	whom	wilder	winded
whirred	whoop	wilderness	windfall
whirring	whooped	wildernesses	windier
whisk	whooping	wildest	windiest
whisked	whose	wildfire	winding
whisker	why	wildlife	windmill
whiskies	wick	wildly	window
whisking	wicked	wilful	windowsill
whisky	wickedly	wilfully	windscreen
whisper	wickedness	wilfulness	windsurf
whispered	wicker	wilier	windsurfed
whispering	wicket	wiliest	windsurfer
whistle	wide	wiliness	windsurfing
whistled	wide-awake	will	windswept
whistling	widely	willed	wine
whit	widen	willie/willy	wing
white	widened	willing	winged
whiteness	widening	willingly	winging
whiter	wider	willingness	wink
whitest	widespread	willow	winked
whiz/whizz	widest	willpower	winking
whizzed	widow	wilt	winner
whizzing	widowed	wilted	winning
who	widower	wilting	winter
whoever	width	wily	wintry

whit vs wit
'Whit' is an old-fashioned word for 'one bit': 'I don't care one whit.' 'Wit' is the display of clever humour.

who; whoever; whole, etc.
These words start with 'wh-', but begin with an 'h' sound. Take care when you spell them.
whole means 'all of': 'The whole thing.' A 'hole' is a pit in the ground or gap: 'I have a hole in my sock.'

whose
Don't confuse 'whose' ('Whose hat is this?') with 'who's' (short for 'who has' or 'who is': 'Who's he?').

wield follows the pattern: 'i' before 'e' except after 'c' when the letters make an 'ee' sound. It means 'to brandish' (a sword), or 'possess': 'He wields power.'

wigwam
A 'wigwam' is a circular tent, first built and used by Native American tribes, who called it a 'wikwam' (which means 'our house').

wily → wiliness; wiry → wiriness
Adjectives that end in a consonant and a '-y' change the 'y' to an 'i' before any endings are added: 'wily → wiliness'; 'wiry → wiriness'.

wipe	withheld	womanly	work
wiped	withhold	womb	workable
wiper	withholding	women	worked
wiping	within	won	worker
wire	without	wonder	workforce
wired	withstand	wondered	working
wiriness	withstanding	wonderful	workload
wiring	withstood	wonderfully	workman
wiry	witness	wondering	workmanship
wisdom	witnessed	wondrous	workmate
wise	witnesses	wondrously	workmen
wiser	witnessing	wonkier	workout
wisest	witticism	wonkiest	workshop
wish	wittier	wonky	world
wished	wittiest	woo	worldly
wishes	wittily	wood	worldwide
wishful	witty	wooded	worm
wishing	wives	wooden	wormed
wisp	wizard	woodland	worming
wispy	wizened	woodpecker	worn
wistful	wobble	woodwind	worried
wistfully	wobbled	woodwork	worrier
wit	wobblier	woodworm	worries
witch	wobbliest	woody	worry
witchcraft	wobbling	wooed	worrying
witches	wobbly	wooing	worse
with	woe	wool	worsen
withdraw	woeful	woollen	worsened
withdrawal	woefully	woollier	worsening
withdrawing	wok	woolliest	worship
withdrawn	woke	woolly	worshipped
withdrew	woken	word	worshipping
wither	wolf	worded	worst
withered	wolves	wording	worth
withering	woman	wore	worthier

win; wine
Notice that adding a silent '-e' to 'win' makes the vowel sound 'i' long (to rhyme with 'mine'), and changes the meaning of the word.

winches; wishes; witches; witnesses, etc.
Remember that words ending in '-ch', '-ss', '-x' or other hissing sounds add '-es' to become plural. 'Oxen' is an exception to this rule.

wine
'Wine' is an alcoholic drink made from grapes. To 'whine' is to make a high-pitched, mournful sound.

A witch is a woman who is believed to practise magic. The word 'which' is an interrogative or relative pronoun (see page 214).

won is the past tense of the verb 'to win': 'I won my race.' It is one of many irregular past forms in English. 'One' means 'the number 1'.

wonder means 'to want to know about something': 'I wonder who will win?' To 'wander' is to walk around without a particular purpose or destination.

wore is the past of 'to wear': 'He always wore a cravat.' A 'war' is an armed conflict.

worthiest	wrapper	wresting	wrist
worthiness	wrapping	wrestle	write
worthless	wrath	wrestled	writer
worthlessness	wreak	wrestler	writhe
worthwhile	wreaked	wrestling	writhed
worthy	wreaking	wretch	writhing
would	wreath	wretched	writing
would-be	wreathed	wretches	written
wound	wreck	wriggle	wrong
wounded	wreckage	wriggled	wrongdoing
wounding	wrecked	wriggling	wronged
wove	wrecking	wriggly	wrongful
woven	wren	wring	wrongfully
wrangle	wrench	wringing	wrongly
wrangled	wrenched	wrinkle	wrote
wrangling	wrenching	wrinkled	wrung
wrap	wrest	wrinkling	wry
wrapped	wrested	wrinkly	wryly

wrap
To 'wrap' is to cover, usually with paper. To 'rap' can mean 'to knock on something', such as a door, or a style of music which includes speech and rhyme.
wreak means 'to cause chaos or damage', e.g. 'Danny wreaked havoc in playgroup.' To 'reek' means 'to stink': 'This house reeks of dogs.'
wring
To 'wring' is to squeeze out water, usually from clothes. To 'ring' a bell is to make a sound with it. A 'ring' is also a piece of jewellery worn on a finger.

write means 'to use letters to put words on paper or a computer screen'. 'Right' can be the opposite of 'wrong', or the opposite of 'left' in 'left and right'.
wrung, the past of 'wring', means 'squeezed hard': 'Mum wrung the sheets.' 'Rung' can mean 'a step on a ladder', or be part of the past of 'to ring': 'She'd rung.'
wry means 'quizzical': 'She gave a wry smile.' 'Rye' is a grain which can be used to make bread.
wryly
Most short words ending in '-y' keep it when you add '-ly' to make an adverb, including 'shyly' and 'slyly'.

Quick tip

Don't write it wrong

Words beginning with a 'w' can cause spellers particular problems. For example, in 'write' and 'wrong', the 'r' is pronounced, but not the 'w'. In 'which' and 'what', you can hear the 'w' but not the 'h'.

Which witch is right and which is wrong?

Some tricky words starting with a 'w'

Here are some tricky words that start with the letter 'w':

wander	wrap
way	wreck
weather	wring
weigh	wrist
weird	write
wonder	wrong

W

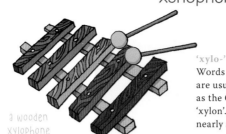

a wooden xylophone

'xylo-'
Words beginning with 'xylo-' are usually to do with wood, as the Greek for 'wood' is 'xylon'. Xylophones are nearly always wooden.

xenophobia   Xmas
xenophobic   **x-ray**
xerox   **x-rayed**
xeroxed   **x-raying**
xeroxing   xylophone

xenophobia is a strong dislike of foreigners. It's from the Greek word 'xenos', which means 'strange' or 'foreign'. (Also see the box on the right.)

xerox; xeroxed; xeroxing
Although this word is a trademark for Xerox, a company that makes printing and photocopying machines, it is often used as a verb: 'I xeroxed all the documents for the meeting.'

Xmas is often used as a shortened version of the word 'Christmas', the Christian festival celebrated on 25th December, to mark the birth of Jesus Christ.

Did you know?

'X' for Xhosa

Although few words begin with an 'x' in English, Xhosa, the southern African language, has lots of 'x's when it's written down. They often represent different clicking sounds the speaker makes.

'X' marks the phobia

All words ending in '-phobia' are **a particular fear or strong dislike of something**. They are based on the Greek word for 'fear', 'phobos'. Some, such as 'agoraphobia' (a fear or dislike of open spaces) and 'claustrophobia' (a fear of confined spaces), are well-known. Here are some much rarer phobias that all begin with the letter 'x':

- **xanthophobia**
a strong dislike, even fear of the colour yellow, or the word 'yellow'

- **xenoglossophobia**
a fear or strong dislike of hearing or learning foreign languages

- **xylophobia**
a fear or strong dislike of anything wooden, or to do with wood

- **xyrophobia**
a fear or a strong dislike of razor blades

'X' facts

The letter 'x' is rarely seen at the beginning of a word, but you'll come across it in many English words. Here are some facts about the letter 'x' that spellers need to know:

1. **You will never see a double 'x' in a word.** Even one-syllable words, such as 'tax' and 'fix', do not double the 'x' before you add '-ed' ('taxed') or '-ing' ('fixing').

2. **Nouns that end in an '-x'** (such as 'box' and 'fox') **add '-es' in the plural.** This may be because adding '-es' makes these plurals easier to pronounce.

3. **There are irregular plurals**, such as 'ox', which becomes 'oxen'. A few words ending with '-x' change to '-ces' in the plural, e.g. 'appendix/appendices' and 'vortex/vortices'.

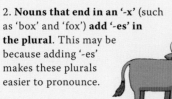

You'll just have to learn it's 'oxen' not 'oxes'.

~~oxes~~
oxen
for sale

x

Yy

a yodelling yak

yak; yodel; yoga
English includes lots of words from other languages. For instance, a 'yak' is a hairy ox from Tibet; 'yoga' is a system of movement and meditation from India, and 'yodelling' is a style of singing originally from the Alps.

yacht	year	yen	yoke
yachting	yearly	yes	yokel
yak	yearn	yesterday	yolk
yam	yearned	yet	yore
yank	yearning	yeti	you
yanked	yeast	yew	young
yanking	yeastier	yield	younger
yap	yeastiest	yielded	youngest
yapped	yeasty	yielding	youngster
yapping	yell	yob	your
yard	yelled	yobbish	yourself
yardstick	yelling	yodel	yourselves
yarn	yellow	yodelled	youth
yashmak	yellowing	yodeller	youthful
yawn	yelp	yodelling	youthfully
yawned	yelped	yoga	yo-yo
yawning	yelping	yoghurt/yogurt	yummy

yap → yapped; yob → yobbish
Words of one syllable with a short vowel and a consonant double the final consonant before adding an ending that starts with a vowel.
yashmak is from a Turkish word, 'yasmak', which is a veil some Muslim women wear over their faces. Only words which come from another language end with a '-k', such as 'trek' and 'flak'.
yen is the name for the currency (money) used in Japan. In English, to 'have a yen' to do something means 'have a longing': 'She had a yen to abseil.'

yew *vs* you
A 'yew' is an evergreen tree with red berries. 'You' means 'the person or group of people someone is talking to': 'You are kind.' A 'ewe' is a female sheep.

yoke *vs* yolk
A 'yoke' is a piece of wood joining two farm animals. The 'yolk' of an egg is the yellow part in the middle. The 'l' is silent, so both words sound the same.

yore *vs* your
'Yore' means 'in the past': 'He lived in days of yore.'
'Your' means 'belongs to you': 'Your car is scratched.'

Quick tip

All about 'y'
'Y' is an unusual letter, as it **can be a vowel, or a consonant**. At the beginning of a word, it's usually a consonant, as in 'yellow'. In the middle or end of words, as in 'rye' and 'shy', it sounds like a vowel. In many adverbs, such as 'gently', 'y' makes an 'ee' sound.

Some tricky words starting with a 'y'
Here are some tricky 'y' words:

yacht	yearn	yolk
yak	yield	your

Zz

'Zap', 'Zip' and 'Zoom'

zap; zip; zoom
Several informal words begin with a 'z'. You'll often see them in comics and cartoons. To 'zap' someone is to shoot them. To 'zip' is to move fast, and to 'zoom' is to move very fast indeed.

ZAP

ZIP

ZOOM

zanier	zigzagged
zaniest	zigzagging
zany	zinc
zap	zing
zapped	zingy
zapping	zip
zeal	zipped
zealot	zipping
zealous	zodiac
zealously	zombie
zebra	zone
zenith	zoo
zero	zoological
zeroed	zoologist
zeroes/zeros	zoology
zeroing	zoom
zest	zoomed
zigzag	zooming

Quick tip

'S' or 'Z'?
A lot of English words end with '-ise', or '-ize'. Examples include 'apologise/apologize'; 'emphasise/emphasize' and 'sympathise/sympathize'. **The '-ize' ending is becoming more commonly used, but both are still correct.** Just make sure you are consistent in your spelling, whichever version you choose to use.

Some words, including 'advertise', 'devise' and 'supervise', can only have an 's' in English. A few, such as 'capsize' and 'prize', can only have a 'z'.

You'll find a list of words that can be spelt with 's' or 'z', as well as those that can only have one or the other, on page 4 of this book.

zap → zapped; zip → zipped
Notice that you double the final consonant of 'zap' and 'zip' before you add an ending that begins with a vowel. This keeps the vowel sounds 'a' and 'i' short.
zebra is originally an Italian word for the black-and-white striped African animal.
zeroes/zeros
Some words ending in '-o' take '-es' in the plural: you'll find a list of them on page 5. The plural of 'zero' can be 'zeroes' or 'zeros', as both are correct. To 'zero in' on something means 'focus very closely' on it.

zip
A 'zip' is a toothed metal fastener, pulled up and down to open or close. In American English, it's 'zipper'. To 'zip' is an informal word for moving fast: 'I zipped to the shop.' To 'zip up' is to close, or be quiet.
zodiac is from the Greek 'zodiakos' (circle of small animals). Most of the signs of the zodiac are animals.
zoologist
The '-ist' ending often means 'a person doing something'. A 'zoologist' studies zoology (animals), which comes from the Greek for 'animals', 'zoa'.

Some tricky words to spell that start with a 'z'

See how many of these tricky words beginning with 'z' you can get right.

zany	zeroing	zinc	zoologist
zealous	zigzagged	zodiac	zoology

Z

Lists of specialist words

Here are some lists of words from more specific areas of English that you might find useful, including measurements, musical terms and some scientific vocabulary. These lists offer a starting point in each area, but can't include every relevant word. Specialist subject dictionaries will help you spell any words you can't find here.

Days of the week

Monday
Tuesday
Wednesday
Thursday
Friday
Saturday
Sunday

Months of the year

January
February
March
April
May
June
July
August
September
October
November
December

Musical words

adagio
allegro
alto
andante
baritone
bass
chromatic
con brio
concerto
contralto
crescendo (cres.)
crotchet
diminuendo (dim.)
forte (f)
fortissimo (ff)
harmonic
legato
mezzo-soprano
minim
octave
ostinato
overture
pianissimo (pp)
piano (p)
pizzicato (pizz.)
prelude
quaver
rallentando (rall.)
ritenuto (rit. / riten.)
semibreve
semiquaver
semitone
sonata
soprano
staccato
symphony
tempo
tenor
treble
virtuoso

Measuring words

acre (ac)
amp/ampere (A)
calorie (cal)
Celsius/centigrade (C)
centilitre (cl)
centimetre (cm)
degree (°)
Fahrenheit (F)
foot (feet) (ft / ')
gram/gramme (g)
hectare (ha)

hertz (Hz)
hour (h)
inch (in / ")
joule (J)
kilogram/kilogramme (kg)
kilohertz (kHz)
kilojoule (kJ)
kilometre (km)
kilowatt (kW)
knot (kn)
litre (l / L)

metre (m)
mile (mi)
milligram/milligramme (mg)
millilitre (ml)
millimetre (mm)
minute (min)
ohm (Ω)

ounce (oz)
pint (pt)
pound (lb)
second (s)
ton (t)
tonne (t)
volt (V)
watt (W)

> **Quick tip** Measurement words are often written in a short form, called an abbreviation, such as 'm' for 'metre'. The correct abbreviations are in brackets in this list.

Mathematical words (plurals in brackets)

acute
algebra
apex
(apexes/apices)
arc
axis (axes)
binary
bisect
calculus
circumference
concave
convex

cosine
cubic
diameter
ellipse
equilateral
geometry
heptagon
hexagon
hypotenuse
index
(indexes/indices)
isosceles

logarithm
mean
median
mode
octagon
parallel
parallelogram
pentagon
percentage
perpendicular
pi / π
polygon

protractor
quadratic
quadrilateral
radius (radii)
rhomboid
rhombus
scalene
sine
tangent
trapezium
trigonometry
vector

Scientific words (plurals in brackets)

aerodynamic
aerodynamics
aeronautical
aeronautics
alkali
alkaline
alkalinity
amoeba
(amoebae/amoebas)
amphibian
atom
bacterium
(bacteria)
carbon
cellular
celluloid
cellulose
centrifugal
centripetal
chloroform
chlorophyll
chromosome
chrysalis
(chrysalides/
chrysalises)
convection
crustacean
diffract
diffraction

dissect
dissection
ecosystem
electromagnetism
electron
euthanasia
fission
fluoride
forensic
fulcrum
fusion
gene
genealogy
genetic
genetically
genitals
genus
germinate
gravitational
gravity
gyroscope
hydraulic
hydrogen
inoculate
inoculation
invertebrate
ion
kinetic

kinetically
litmus
macrocosm
mammal
menstruate
menstruation
microcosm
molecular
molecule
mollusc
neutron
nitrate
nitrogen
nucleus (nuclei)
nutrient
oestrogen
osmosis
oxidation
oxide
oxidise/oxidize
oxygen
ozone
pasteurisation/
pasteurization
pasteurised/
pasteurized
phloem
photosynthesis

photosynthesise/
photosynthesize
phylum
pollinate
pollination
polyunsaturated
primate
prism
proton
pupa (pupae)
quotient
radioactive
radioactivity
refract
refraction
reptile
seismograph
silicon
sonar
species
testosterone
toxic
toxicity
toxin
unpasteurised/
unpasteurized
vertebrate
vivisection
xylem

Computing words

app	interface	server
attachment	internet	software
blog	intranet	spam
broadband	key-in	stream
byte (B)	kilobyte (KB)	tablet
chatroom	mainframe	torrent
cookie	megabyte (MB)	Trojan
cyber	megapixel	upgrade
database	microchip	upload
disc/disk	modem	username
dotcom	network	viral
download	offline	virus
email	online	voicemail
gigabyte (GB)	phishing	webcam
hacker	pixel	weblog ('blog')
hacking	podcast	website
hard-drive	pop-up	Wi-Fi
hardware	profile	wiki
hashtag (#)	program	wireless

Space words

asteroid	comet	meteor	solar
astronaut	constellation	meteorite	spacecraft
astronomy	crater	moon	star
atmosphere	eclipse	orbit	supergiant
black hole	galaxy	planet	supernova
celestial	gravity	rocket	telescope
cluster	lunar	satellite	universe

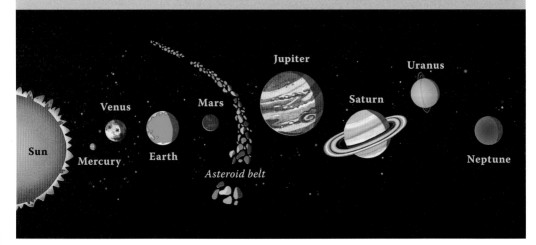

Map of the world

Arctic Ocean

North
West — East
South

The Arctic

Europe

Asia

North and
Central
America

Atlantic
Ocean

Africa

South
America

Indian
Ocean

Pacific
Ocean

Australasia
and Oceania

Southern
Ocean

Antarctica

Rivers

Amazon
Congo
Ganges
Indus
Mississippi
Nile
Rhine
Thames
Volga
Yangtze
Zambezi

Mountain ranges

Alaska Range
Alps
Andes
Appalachians
Atlas Mountains
Great Dividing Range
Himalayas
Pyrenees
Rocky Mountains
Sierra Nevada
Urals

Deserts

Arabian
Atacama
Gobi
Great Victoria
Kalahari
Namib
Negev
Patagonian
Sahara
Sonoran
Thar

Geographical words

archipelago	crevasse	global	map	reef
atlas	desert	grasslands	mountain	river
atoll	equator	hemisphere	oasis	swamp
canyon	fjord	island	ocean	tropical
cliff	forest	lake	plain	tundra
coastal	geyser	latitude	polar	valley
continent	glacier	longitude	rainforest	waterfall

Countries of the world

Afghanistan
Albania
Algeria
Andorra
Angola
Antigua and Barbuda
Argentina
Armenia
Australia
Austria
Azerbaijan
Bahamas
Bahrain
Bangladesh
Barbados
Belarus
Belgium
Belize
Benin
Bhutan
Bolivia, Plurinational State of
Bosnia and Herzegovina
Botswana
Brazil
Brunei Darussalam
Bulgaria
Burkina Faso
Burma (Myanmar)
Burundi
Cambodia
Cameroon
Canada
Cape Verde
Central African Republic
Chad
Chile
China
Colombia
Comoros
Congo

Congo, Democratic Republic of the
Costa Rica
Côte d'Ivoire (Ivory Coast)
Croatia
Cuba
Cyprus
Czech Republic
Denmark
Djibouti
Dominica
Dominican Republic
Ecuador
Egypt
El Salvador
Equatorial Guinea
Eritrea
Estonia
Ethiopia
Fiji
Finland
France
Gabon
Gambia
Georgia
Germany
Ghana
Greece
Grenada
Guatemala
Guinea
Guinea-Bissau
Guyana
Haiti
Honduras
Hungary
Iceland
India
Indonesia
Iran, Islamic Republic of
Iraq
Ireland
Israel

Italy
Jamaica
Japan
Jordan
Kazakhstan
Kenya
Kiribati
Korea, Democratic People's Republic of (North Korea)
Korea, Republic of (South Korea)
Kuwait
Kyrgyzstan
Lao People's Democratic Republic (Laos)
Latvia
Lebanon
Lesotho
Liberia
Libya
Liechtenstein
Lithuania
Luxembourg
Macedonia, The former Yugoslav Republic of
Madagascar
Malawi
Malaysia
Maldives
Mali
Malta
Marshall Islands
Mauritania
Mauritius
Mexico
Micronesia, Federated States of
Moldova, Republic of
Monaco
Mongolia

Montenegro
Morocco
Mozambique
Namibia
Nauru
Nepal
Netherlands
New Zealand
Nicaragua
Niger
Nigeria
Norway
Oman
Pakistan
Palau
*Palestine, State of
Panama
Papua New Guinea
Paraguay
Peru
Philippines
Poland
Portugal
Qatar
Romania
Russian Federation
Rwanda
Saint Kitts and Nevis
Saint Lucia
Saint Vincent and the Grenadines
Samoa
San Marino
Sao Tome and Principe
Saudi Arabia
Senegal
Serbia
Seychelles
Sierra Leone
Singapore
Slovakia
Slovenia

Solomon Islands
Somalia
South Africa
South Sudan
Spain
Sri Lanka
Sudan
Suriname
Swaziland
Sweden
Switzerland
Syrian Arab Republic
Tajikistan
Tanzania, United Republic of
Thailand
Timor-Leste
Togo
Tonga
Trinidad and Tobago
Tunisia
Turkey
Turkmenistan
Tuvalu
Uganda
Ukraine
United Arab Emirates
United Kingdom of Great Britain and Northern Ireland
United States of America
Uruguay
Uzbekistan
*Vatican City (Holy See)
Vanuatu
Venezuela, Bolivarian Republic of
Viet Nam
Yemen
Zambia
Zimbabwe

*These are 'non-member observer states' of the United Nations. Palestine is a disputed territory in Western Asia, and Vatican City is an independent city-state in Rome, Italy, where the Catholic Church is based.

Below is a selection of the languages spoken around the world. Most of the languages on this list are spoken by over six million people, but there are many more, some only used by a single tribe or community. The most widely-spoken language in the world today is Mandarin Chinese, followed by Spanish, with English taking third place.

Main languages of the world

Abkhaz
Afar
Afrikaans
Akan
Albanian
Amharic
Arabic
Aragonese
Armenian
Assamese
Avaric
Awadhi
Aymara
Azerbaijani
Bambara
Bashkir
Basque
Belarusian
Bengali/Bangla
Bhojpuri
Bihari
Bislama
Bosnian
Breton
Bulgarian
Burmese
Cantonese
  (Chinese)
Catalan
Cebuano
Chamorro
Chechen
Chhattisgarhi
Chichewa
Chuvash
Cornish
Corsican
Cree

Croatian
Czech
Danish
Divehi
Dutch
Dzongkha
English
Estonian
Ewe
Faroese
Farsi (Persian)
Fijian
Filipino
Finnish
French
Fula
Galician
Ganda
Georgian
German
Greek (modern)
Guaraní
Gujarati
Haitian Creole
Hausa
Hebrew
  (modern)
Herero
Hindi
Hiri Motu
Hungarian
Icelandic
Igbo
Indonesian
Inuktitut
Inupiaq
Irish Gaelic
Italian

Japanese
Javanese
Kalaallisut
  (Greenlandic)
Kannada/
  Kanarese
Kanuri
Kashmiri
Kazakh
Khmer
  (Cambodian)
Kikuyu
Kinyarwanda
Komi
Kongo
Korean
Kurdish
Kwanyama
Kyrgyz
Lanna
Lao
Latvian
Limburgish
Lingala
Lithuanian
Luba-Katanga
Luxembourgish
Macedonian
Magahi
Maithili
Malagasy
Malay
Malayalam
Maltese
Mandarin
  (Chinese)
Manx
Māori
Marathi

Marshallese
Marwari
Mongolian
Nauru
Navajo/Navaho
Ndebele
Ndonga
Nepali
Northern Sami
Norwegian
Nuosu
Occitan
Ojibwe/Ojibwa
Old Church
  Slavonic
Oriya
Oromo
Ossetian
Panjabi/Punjabi
Pashto/Pushto
Polish
Portuguese
Quechua
Romanian
Romansh
Russian
Rwandan
Samoan
Sango
Sanskrit
Sardinian
Scottish Gaelic
Serbian
Sesotho
Setswana/Tswana
Shona
Sindhi
Sinhalese

Slovak
Slovene
Somali
Spanish
Sundanese
Swahili
Swati
Swedish
Tagalog
Tahitian
Tajik
Tamil
Telugu
Thai
Tibetan
  Standard
Tigrinya
Tonga
Tsonga
Tswana/Setswana
Turkish
Turkmen
Twi
Uighur/Uyghur
Ukrainian
Urdu
Uzbek
Venda
Vietnamese
Walloon
Welsh
Western Frisian
Wolof
Xhosa
Yiddish
Yoruba
Zhuang/Chuang
Zulu

Religious words and festivals

Buddhism
Buddha
Buddhist
dharma
mandala
nirvana

Christianity
Ascension
Bible
Catholic
Christ
Christian
Christmas (Xmas)
Crucifixion
disciple
Easter
Epiphany
Eucharist
Good Friday
Gospel
Holy Communion
Holy Trinity
Jehovah
Jesus
Lent
Messiah
Nativity
Pentecost
Protestant
Resurrection
Testament

Hinduism
Bhagavad Gita
Brahma
Brahman
caste
dharma
Diwali
guru
Hindu
Holi
karma; samsara
Lakshmi
Om
Ramayana
Shiva
Trimurti
Upanishad
Veda
Vishnu

Islam
Allah
Ashura
burka
Eid-ul-Adha
Eid-ul-Fitr
Five Pillars of Islam:
shahadah, salah/salat,
zakat, sawm, hadj/hajj
halal
hijab
imam
jihad/jehad
Mohammed/
Muhammad
mosque
muezzin
Muslim/Moslem
niqab
Qur'an/Koran
Ramadan
sharia

Jainism
ahisma
Jain
karma
mahavrata
santhara/sallenkhana

Judaism
Bar Mitzvah
challah
Chanukah/
Hanukkah
Jew

Jewish
kosher
menorah
Passover/Pesach
Purim
rabbi
Rosh Hashanah
Sukkot
synagogue
Talmud
Torah
Yom Hashoah
Yom Kippur

Rastafari
dreadlocks
Rastafarian

Shinto
kami
makoto
matsuri
musubi

Sikhism
dharma
Diwali
gurdwara
Guru Gobind Singh
Guru Granth Sahib
Guru Nanek
karma
Khalsa
mukti
Sikh
The Five Ks: kara,
kanga, kaccha,
kesh, kirpan

Taoism
ch'i
chiao/jaio
Tao
Tao Te Ching
Yin and Yang

Human body words

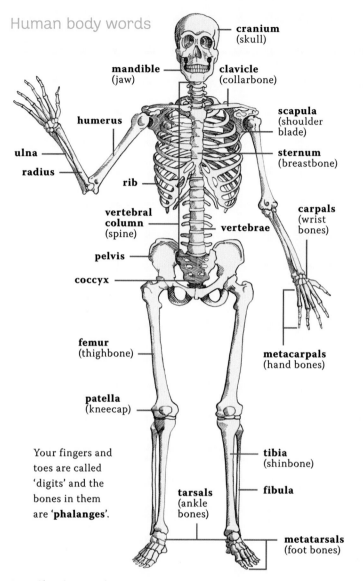

cranium
(skull)

mandible
(jaw)

clavicle
(collarbone)

scapula
(shoulder
blade)

humerus

sternum
(breastbone)

ulna

radius

rib

carpals
(wrist
bones)

**vertebral
column**
(spine)

vertebrae

pelvis

coccyx

femur
(thighbone)

metacarpals
(hand bones)

patella
(kneecap)

Your fingers and
toes are called
'digits' and the
bones in them
are **'phalanges'**.

tibia
(shinbone)

fibula

tarsals
(ankle
bones)

metatarsals
(foot bones)

anus
appendix
artery
bladder
bowel
brain
cartilage
cell
colon
cornea
diaphragm
heart
intestine
joint
kidney
larynx
ligament
liver
lung
muscle
nerve
oesophagus
pancreas
rectum
retina
stomach
tendon
vein

Medical words

adrenaline
asthma
bronchitis
caesarean
cardiac
cholesterol
coma
concussion
diabetes
diabetic

diarrhoea
eczema
epilepsy
gastric
haemorrhage
immunise/immunize
influenza ('flu')
insomnia
intravenous
leukaemia/leukemia

meningitis
metabolism
migraine
phlegm
placebo
respiration
resuscitate
stethoscope
syringe
vascular

A prefix is the grammatical name for a group of letters added to the beginning of a word to change its meaning. Most are never used on their own. Usually, a prefix doesn't change a word's spelling. For example, 'mal-' meaning 'bad', makes 'function' into 'malfunction'.

Prefix guidelines

1. Knowing what a prefix means can help you understand the word it's added to. 'Sub-' (meaning 'under') helps explain *submarine* (an underwater ship).

2. A few prefixes change their spelling to match the word they are joining. For example, the prefix 'in-' becomes 'im-' when it's added to a word beginning with 'p-': *implausible*.

3. Some prefixes change to make a word simpler to pronounce, e.g. *impossible* is easier to say than 'inpossible'. If you remember this, it may help you spell a word correctly.

4. When you add the prefix 'all-' to a word, it can drop an 'l', to make *almost* or *altogether*. However, if 'all' is joined to a word with a hyphen (-) it stays separate and its spelling does not change: *allout*'; *'all-inclusive'*. 'Post-' can also be added to a word, or joined with a hyphen: *postgraduate*'; *post-Revolutionary*'. 'Co-' and 'pro-' do the same.

5. Some prefixes, such as 'dis-', 'mis-', 'non-' and 'un-', give a word a negative meaning, e.g. *'disharmony'*; *'misunderstood'*; *'nondrip'*; *'unhappy'*.

Here are the main prefixes you'll come across:

ab-	*abduct*	**en-**	*endanger*	**over-**	*overweight*
ad-	*admit*	**epi-**	*epidemic*	**per-**	*permutation*
al-	*altogether* (but *all-inclusive*)	**ex-**	*expand* (but *ex-boss*)	**poly-**	*polygon*
				post-	*postmortem*
ante-	*antenatal*	**extra-**	*extraterrestrial*	**pre-**	*prehistory*
anti-	*antibacterial*	**hyper-**	*hyperactive*	**pro-**	*pro-choice*
auto-	*autobiography*	**hypo-**	*hypochondriac*		
bene-	*benefit*	**in-**	*inhuman* (see 2. above)	**quad-**	*quadruple*
bi-	*bicycle*			**quin-**	*quintet*
circum-	*circumference*	**inter-**	*international*	**re-**	*recycle*
co-	*co-star*	**intra-**	*intravenous*	**semi-**	*semi-detached*
col-	*collaborate*	**macro-**	*macrobiotic*	**sub-**	*submarine*
com-	*combat*	**mal-**	*malnutrition*	**super-**	*supermarket*
con-	*consolidate*	**maxi-**	*maximise/ maximize*	**sur-**	*surpass*
contra-	*contradiction*	**micro-**	*microscope*	**tele-**	*television*
de-	*defrost*	**mini-**	*minimum*	**trans-**	*transfer*
dia-	*diagonal*	**mis-**	*misfit*	**tri-**	*triplet*
dis-	*disrespect*	**non-**	*nonfiction*	**ultra-**	*ultrasound*
				uni-	*universal*

A suffix is the grammatical name for a group of letters added to the end of a word. A suffix is not a word on its own: it can only be added to an existing word, the spelling of which may change. In this dictionary, a suffix is called an 'ending'.

Suffix guidelines

1. Usually, if you add a suffix beginning with a vowel to a word ending with '-e', you drop the '-e': desire + ing = *desiring*.

2. If a word ends with '-ge' or '-ce' (e.g. 'change', or 'notice'), you keep the '-e' if you add a suffix that begins with 'a', 'o' or 'u'. This keeps the 'g' and the 'c' soft: *'changeable'*; *'noticeable'*.

3. If you are adding the suffix '-ful' to a word to mean 'full of', it only has one 'l': *'cheerful'*. When you add '-fully', to describe how something is done, it has two 'l's: *'She smiled cheerfully.'*

4. If you are adding the suffix '-ly' to a word that ends with '-le', such as 'gentle', you drop the '-e': *'gently'*.

5. When you add a suffix starting with a consonant, such as '-ness', to a word that ends with a '-y' (e.g. 'smelly') the 'y' becomes 'i': *'smelliness'*.

6. One-syllable words ending with a short vowel and a consonant usually double the consonant before a suffix that begins with a vowel: 'pat → *patting'*. Words with two vowels don't double the final consonant: 'feel → *feeling'*.

7. For words with more than one syllable, don't double the consonant if you stress the beginning of the word, as in 'offer': *'offering'*. However, if you stress the end of the word, as in 'forbid', you double the final '-d': *'forbidding'*.

8. Words ending with an '-l' or a '-p' always double these letters when you add an ending that begins with a vowel: 'cancel → *cancelled'*; 'wrap → *wrapped'*.

9. Words ending with '-our' (e.g. 'colour' or 'glamour') drop the 'u' before the suffixes '-ant', '-ary' or '-ous' are added: *'colorant'*; *'honorary'*; *'glamorous'*.

Here are the main suffixes you'll come across:

-able	*desirable*	**-ful**	*cheerful*	**-ling**	*duckling*
-ance	*admittance*	**-fully**	*wonderfully*	**-logy**	*biology*
-ant	*important*	**-hood**	*childhood*	**-ly**	*friendly*
-ary	*cautionary*	**-ible**	*edible*	**-ment**	*enjoyment*
-ation	*hibernation*	**-ic**	*iconic*	**-ness**	*kindness*
-ed	*baked*	**-ify**	*unify*	**-or**	*counsellor*
-ee	*employee*	**-ing**	*coming*	**-ory**	*advisory*
-en	*soften*	**-ise/-ize**	*categorise/ categorize*	**-ous**	*humorous*
-ence	*residence*			**-phobia**	*claustrophobia*
-ent	*efficient*	**-ish**	*childish*	**-ship**	*friendship*
-er	*diver*	**-ism**	*sexism*	**-sion**	*illusion*
-ery	*stationery*	**-less**	*homeless*	**-some**	*loathsome*
-escent	*adolescent*	**-let**	*piglet*	**-tion**	*creation*
-ette	*maisonette*	**-like**	*childlike*	**-y**	*icy*

How sentences work

A sentence can take many forms, but it must make sense on its own. This means that it needs a verb (a 'doing' word); must begin with a capital letter and must end with a full stop.

The main clause

Some sentences are very simple, and have one main part called a main clause, which has the verb in it:

> *'The house was beautiful.'*

Sentences like this can be very effective, adding clarity and impact.

Compound sentences

Other sentences, called compound sentences, are made up of several clauses, separated by a word called a conjunction. You'll find a list of these on page 214.

> *'The house was beautiful, but it was very dark.'*

In this sentence, the conjunction 'but' forms a link between the two clauses. Using compound sentences well takes practice, but it adds colour to your writing.

Subordinate clauses

Some sentences have even more elements to them, called subordinate clauses. In these, some parts of the sentence only make sense if you know the other parts, so they are 'less important' (which is what the word 'subordinate' actually means). For example, in the sentence:

> *'The house was beautiful, but it was very dark,*
> *so I always felt scared in it.'*

... you need to know that the writer is talking about a 'house', to make sense of the rest of the sentence (that it was 'dark' and therefore 'scared' the writer). The last two clauses are subordinate to that first, main, clause. Sentences like this add depth and variety to your writing, but be careful not to over-use them.

Phrases

You'll often find short groups of words, called phrases, in English sentences. They add more detail to a specific part of the sentence:

> *'The house was beautiful, but it was very dark,*
> *so, rather embarrassingly, I always felt scared in it.'*

The phrase 'rather embarrassingly' adds to what the reader learns about the writer.

Use with care

It's great to vary the kinds of sentences you use in your writing as much as you can. Try not to make your language more complicated than it needs to be, however. Your main aim is always to be understood by your reader.

If every sentence has a subordinate clause, or is made up of several elements, it can make reading what you have written feel like hard work. The main thing is to vary both the type of sentence and the words and language you use, so that you express yourself clearly and well.

Punctuation is very important, as it can help a reader make sense of what you have written. Just one comma shows the difference between: 'Let's eat, Granny' and 'Let's eat Granny'. Here are the main punctuation marks you need to know:

apostrophe (')
This shows that a letter has been left out: *'It's my dog'* instead of 'It is my dog'. It also shows possession: *'Kate's hair'* and *'the girls' skirts'* (where it comes after the 's' of a plural noun, 'girls').

colon (:)
This often comes before a list, or a quotation. It can also be used before an explanation:

> *'I can't drink milk: it makes me ill.'*

comma (,)
This marks a pause in a sentence, between each part or idea:

> *'Her hair was long, brown and curly.'*

exclamation mark (!)
This comes after an exclamation, and is often used after an interjection (an expression of surprise) in written English:

> *'Hooray!'*

full stop (.)
This shows where a sentence ends:

> *'I am very good at spelling.'*

"You're not going to eat that out-of-date sandwich, are you?"

"Yes, I am! I'm tired, lazy and hungry. You needn't worry: I've done it before."

question mark (?)
This always follows a question:

> *'Did he really do that?'*

hyphen (-)
This links two words:

> *'The hotel was all-inclusive.'*

semi-colon (;)
This comes between the elements of a list, or the related clauses in a sentence, and is a stronger break in a sentence than a comma:

> *'The family enjoyed their holiday; it ticked all the boxes.'*

speech marks (" ")
These go at either end of something that's spoken in written English:

> *"I am so tired," she murmured.*

Pronouns are used in a sentence instead of naming a person or thing. Here are examples of the different pronouns you may see:

Subjective
I, you, he, she, it, we, they, what, who

Objective
me, him, her, it, us, you, them, whom

Possessive
mine, yours, his, hers, ours, theirs

Demonstrative
this, that, these, those

Interrogative
who, whom, which,
what, whose, whoever,
whatever, whichever

Relative
who, whom, whose, which,
that, what, whatever, whoever,
whatever, whichever

Reflexive
myself, yourself, himself, herself,
itself, ourselves, themselves

Intensive
myself, yourself, himself, herself,
itself, ourselves, themselves

Reciprocal
each other, one another

Indefinite
anything, everybody, another,
each, few, many, none, some, all,
any, anybody, anyone, everyone,
everything, no-one, nobody, nothing,
none, other, others, several, somebody,
someone, something, most, enough,
little, more, both, either, neither,
one, much, such.

Conjunctions

Conjunctions link the parts of a sentence together, so are often known as 'linking words'. You'll see them in most sentences as it's hard to make sense without them. Here are the main ones you will come across:

after	even if	since	You often see these conjunctions together in a sentence, as they relate to each other in some way:
although	even though	so	
and	for	so that	
as	however	than	
as if	if	though	
as long as	in case	till	either/or
as much as	in order that	unless	neither/nor
as soon as	nevertheless	until	
as though	nor	when	whether/or
because	once	where	
before	only if	wherever	both/and
but	or	while	
by the time	provided that	yet	not only/but also

'The princess knew that, *as soon as* she got engaged, the king would order her prince to live in the palace *until* the wedding, *in case* he *as much as* thought about changing his mind.'

Prepositions and phrasal verbs

Prepositions come before or after nouns or pronouns in a sentence, and connect them in some way. Many are to do with time and place. Here are some of the main prepositions you'll see:

aboard	beside	inside	since
about	besides	into	than
above	between	like	through
across	beyond	minus	till
after	but	near	to
against	by	of	toward
along	concerning	off	towards
alongside	considering	on	under
amid	despite	onto	underneath
among	down	opposite	unlike
amongst	during	outside	until
around	except	over	up
as	excepting	past	upon
at	excluding	per	versus
before	following	plus	via
behind	for	regarding	with
below	from	round	within
beneath	in	save	without

Phrasal verbs

A 'phrasal verb' is a verb which has a new meaning when it's followed by a preposition or an adverb. They're often used in everyday speech or writing. You might see or hear 'make fun of' instead of 'mock', or 'put off' instead of 'postpone'. Here are some more examples:

This sentence uses the phrasal verb 'break down' (which means 'to cry'):

'When her wig flew off, she *broke down*.'

This one uses the phrasal verb 'put up with' (which means 'to tolerate'):

'Miss Boon won't *put up with* all this noise.'

You may also see some phrasal verbs separated into two parts:

'We will *pick* you *up* at six o'clock.'

'Please *keep* the children *from* swimming today.'

'He's *messed* all the arrangements *up* again.'

Becoming a good speller is mainly about practice, and there are lots of useful websites that can help you to improve. We have selected some great sites with all kinds of online activities that let you practise spelling in fun ways, and at different levels. There are spelling challenges, games, quizzes, puzzles, an online 'spelling bee' and plenty more.

For links to useful spelling websites go to:

www.usborne.com/quicklinks

and enter the keywords

"spelling dictionary"

When using the internet, please follow the internet safety guidelines shown on the Usborne Quicklinks Website. The links at Usborne Quicklinks are regularly reviewed and updated, but Usborne Publishing is not responsible and does not accept liability for the content on any website other than its own. We recommend that all children are supervised while using the internet.

Edited by Felicity Brooks

Editorial assistants:
Hannah Wood and Rachel Wilkie

Cover and additional design: Matthew Durber

Additional illustrations: Nathalie Ragondet,
Ian McNee, Benedetta Giaufret and Enrica Rusiná